ANDROSCOGGIN HEAD START
AND CHILD CARE

CHILDREN
OF THE
DOME

BY

Rosemary Smith

Pathfinder Publishing of California
3600 Harbor Blvd., # 82
Oxnard, CA 93035

CHILDREN OF THE DOME

Pathfinder Publishing of California
3600 Harbor Boulevard, # 82
Oxnard, CA 93035
805-984-7756

"Link by Link" and "Butter" reprinted with permission from *After Goodbye,* by Ted Menten copywrite 1994, published by Running Press, Philadelphia and London

Library of Congress Cataloging-in Publication Data

Smith, Rosemary 1999
        Children of the Dome/ by Rosemary Smith
        p. cm

ISBN 0-934793-69-7 : $27.00

1. Bereavement - Psychological aspects. 2. Grief, I. Title

Dedication Page

For the angels who continue
to inspire me—
Drew and Jeremiah Smith

Acknowledgments

So many angels have inspired this book. Although I was only able to include twenty-eight families, so many others have encouraged this project.

My heartfelt thanks to Jim Taylor, Peggy O'Connor, Denis O'Connor, Myra Stamper, Brian Penkalski, Roger Herndon, Scott Shannon, Gretchen Geier, Kellie Carpenter, Christopher Freundorfer, Shelby Warner, Michael Price, Frannie Smith, Kristie Kauffmann, Mitch Warren, George Diebold, AnnaBeth Burnett, Brandon Holbrook, Taiann Wilson, Don V. Drye, Andrew Gutgsell, John Donan, John Foss, Ralph Coomer, Ryan Young, Heather Perdue, Merri Kathryn Prater, Buzzy Greer, Stephen Greer, Todd Greer, and Kami Greer.

Although I never knew most of you on this earth, your lives have inspired me beyond words.

To the parents of these amazing young men and women I thank you for sharing your families and baring your souls. Your loss has not gone unnoticed. Your children have made a tremendous impact on many lives.

My deep gratitude goes to Margaret Foley for her invaluable input in the editing of this book and more importantly for her friendship and encouragement.

Finally, my love and devotion goes to my husband, Luther, and to our son, Jordan. Without your love, patience, and support this book would have never been written.

Foreword

By Terence L. Gutgsell, M.D.

On rounds today at the Hospice Care Center, an in-patient hospice unit at Saint Joseph Hospital in Lexington, Kentucky, I saw one of my favorite patients whose name is Flora. Flora is an eighty-eight year old lady with advanced malignant lymphoma now being treated for pain due to a recent outbreak of shingles. Despite a thirty pound weight loss over the past six months and pain that has been difficult to control, her mood and spirit have been remarkably upbeat in the weeks that I've cared for her. She greets me daily with a smile on her face and a sparkle in her eye. She is mentally clear but physically very fragile.

Flora loves music and often has a tape or a CD on when I enter her room. My wife, Kathy Jo, a nurse/musician, weekly brings her harp to the Hospice Care Center and sings to and with patients. Flora eagerly awaits these visits and gladly takes part in the singing…usually Christian hymns. Today, I asked Flora where she learned to love music so much. She responded that her mother loved music and had her sing for family and friends from the age of four on. It was at that moment that a different look came over Flora's beautifully aged face. It was a look that spoke of pain and sadness. I quietly sat at the bedside, giving Flora time. Eventually, she told me that when she was eight years old, her mother died because of heart failure at the age of forty-nine. Several tears flowed down the cheeks of that aged woman…tears that spoke of sorrow born eighty years ago…tears of pain that had not completely healed. I was reminded by the tears on Flora's face that the pain of death, especially a death out of sequence, is a pain that never completely goes away. It is a rent in the fabric of the soul that eventually becomes integrated and blended into one's life. I can imagine that little girl of eight being at first confused at the time of her mother's death and then gradually coming to understand the finality of her loss. In my mind's eye I saw that over the years she perhaps vacillated between intermittent acceptance of her loss and at other times feeling lost and out of balance with the world, perhaps even coming close to despair.

As I now look at this beautiful woman of eighty-eight years, I see a human being that in some mysterious way has made peace with a terrible event that changed her life completely eight decades ago. As I look on this woman I come to some sense of hope that my own journey may end in the same way. I hope that at the end of my life I will see myself as having been a happy and productive person. Remembering my losses, I will shed tears, but I will live in hope that the world is a safe and wonderful place. I will believe that in some mysterious way we will meet those who have passed before us. Flora said that she knows her own death is coming soon and that its sting is softened by the knowledge that she'll once again be with her dear mother.

I tell this story as a parent who has lost a child to death. I marvel at the complexity and paradox of life, finding at times the most amazing joy in the midst of agonizing pain and despair. The death of our son, Andrew, has completely changed our family life and structure. It has changed our relationship with our children, our extended families, and our life's work. Of all the experiences of my life, that event has had the most profound effect. We survived Andrew's death in large part because of the friendship of those so similarly affected. We had a marvelous group of parents who continuously raised each other up. We have shared innumerable letters, phone calls, meetings, book recommendations, and retreats. Although I cannot say enough about the tremendous support that we received from family, friends, and our church, the sharing of our grief with other bereaved parents has been the critical ingredient in our survival and continued hopefulness.

To you who have lost a child to death, I offer you this wonderful book of personal stories to let you know you are not alone. Hopefully, you'll discover some similar themes or experiences that will resonate with your own story. My true desire is that this book will, for you so affected parents, stimulate a search for others who have walked this hard path before you. You'll find people who can, in the flesh, offer what no one else can: true understanding of the depth of your sorrow. From that depth of understanding and sharing somehow healing can gradually take place. With healing comes a sense of hope for the future. My wish for you is that if you reach the grand age of eighty-eight, you'll possess the countenance of my patient Flora: an old heart full of love, grace and hope, tinged and tempered with the sorrow of loss. I also wish for you that in some way the hope comes of one day being reunited with your child.

For those of you who have not lost a child but are reading this book, my hope is that the love and courage shown in each story will speak to your heart.
God bless you all.

Terence L. Gutgsell, M.D.
Medical Director
Hospice of the Bluegrass
Lexington, Kentucky

CHILDREN OF THE DOME

TABLE OF CONTENTS

TABLE OF CONTENTS

TABLE OF CONTENTS

12

CHILDREN OF THE DOME

BY

Rosemary Smith

Chapter One
Drew and Jeremiah Smith

DREW AND JEREMIAH SMITH

By Rosemary Smith

I have been married twenty-seven years, more than half my life. At times the years before my marriage seem like a distant dream. The person I am now has formed slowly, sometimes painfully over the years.

My husband, Luther, and I met when we were in the same pharmacy class at the University of Kentucky in Lexington, Kentucky. Although my family lived in New Albany, Indiana, I was always expected to go to U.K. like my father had. Being the oldest child of a family that included two younger brothers, I did as expected and eventually met my husband Luther in the fall of 1967 as we entered our first year of pharmacy school.

After a whirlwind courtship, Luther and I married on February 18, 1971, in Shepherdsville, Kentucky. We had both taken jobs after graduation in Louisville, Kentucky, with different chain drug companies. The next three years were idyllic. We loved the big city life of Louisville but often traveled to southern Indiana across the river where we boarded our horses. Those years were wonderful, but we were anxious to begin the family we both wanted.

The year 1974 brought many changes to our family. We were expecting our first child, and we were on top of the world. Since they didn't use ultrasound like they do today, we had no idea what sex our child would be. Secretly, we both wanted a son, but we were so thrilled with the prospect of the miracle of a child that we didn't really care. Our first son, Andrew Siler Smith (Drew), was born on April 27, 1974. That day was the happiest day of my life without doubt. Drew came into this world looking like a dried-up, slightly yellow old man, but Luther and I thought he was beautiful!! Both Luther and I often reminisce about the morning we took Drew home.

I can clearly recall walking up the steps to our small house and looking at Luther and nervously asking him what we were going to do with this baby. Neither of us had any experience with children, and frankly we were scared to death. My mother, Almara, came to our rescue, and we survived those first few weeks and months. At that point, my mother was dying of breast cancer. At age forty-seven, she had a double mastectomy and lymph node involvement which indicated that the cancer had spread. She had survived for six years, mainly on sheer willpower of wanting to see her first grandchild. Having seen Drew born, she blossomed. After I returned to work, she was able to baby sit for Drew until her health deteriorated. She died in November of 1975 when Drew was seventeen months old.

In January of 1975, we made a move that undoubtedly set the course for how our lives were to evolve. Luther's brother, a local physician in the small community of Beattyville, had offered Luther a position in Beattyville to work in a clinic pharmacy. We both saw this as a wonderful chance to work for ourselves and not be tied to chain pharmacies. Twenty years ago, many independent pharmacies were thriving in the rural areas, so we quit our jobs and headed back to the mountains of eastern Kentucky with Drew in tow. The only reservation we had was taking our son to an area where the school systems were not up to our expectations.

The next two years passed so quickly that it seemed to be a wonderful dream. Luther worked full-time, but I only did relief pharmacy work which allowed me to spend much more time with Drew. He was such a warm, loving child. Beginning his first Christmas, we sent out picture Christmas cards to all our family and friends. The first card was of a smiling, plump Drew in his green walker! He was always on the move.

I discovered that I was expecting again in November of 1976 with our second child due sometime in early July of 1977. We were thrilled that Drew would have a sibling and now more openly wished for a daughter. My second pregnancy went well, and after attending a pre-July 4th picnic at the home of friends, Luther rushed me to the hospital in Lexington. We got stuck in the middle of a parade but finally arrived at the hospital on the afternoon of July 3rd. After experiencing the birth of your first child, you feel you can never love a second child as much as you do the first one. As our second son was born at 12:01 A.M. on the 4th of July, this notion was swept aside in an instant. Jeremiah Cottle Smith was absolutely the most beautiful dark-headed baby ever born. His brother Drew had dark brown hair and brown eyes, but Jeremiah had black hair and huge blue eyes. Those eyes blazed with the intelligence of an old soul from birth. Jeremiah was remarkably perceptive and seemed to always know what mood we were in. He never slept through the night until he was over a year old, but when we would come to care for him during the night, he would comfort us by his personality. It was as if he were calming us down rather than the other way around. Drew welcomed this intrusion to his life after a few shaky experiences. He loved his younger brother after he realized we still loved him as much as before. These brothers were close as we moved through their younger years in this small, rural town where everyone knew everyone else.

The next four years again passed as if we were in a dream. Professionally, we had gone from working at one clinic pharmacy owned by Luther's brother to now owning our own pharmacy in Beattyville and starting the first unit-dose pharmacy in eastern Kentucky that serviced nursing home patients. We had plans for adding a second retail location in Booneville, Kentucky, in the adjoining county. After a hair-raising first day in which Drew screamed he absolutely wasn't going to go to school, he did start kindergarten in Lee County. From the beginning, it was evident how bright Drew was. He made friends very easily and really enjoyed his time in grade school.

Luther and I decided to try one more time to have a

daughter. The boys were really almost all we could handle, but I desperately wanted a little girl. Our third child was also going to be born in July like Jeremiah. On July 15, 1981, a little over four years after the birth of Jeremiah, we had our third son! Luther said he remembers that I seemed disappointed at first when my doctor said that we had another boy, but I only remember being thrilled the baby was healthy. Jordan Cox Smith entered the world with two big brothers and many days and nights of rough-housing ahead of him. Jordan, like his brothers before him, had a family name for his middle name. Both Drew and Jeremiah welcomed Jordan into their lives wholeheartedly. We have their Christmas picture that year; Jordan is looking up at these two big boys with the most puzzled expression on his face. I'm sure he was wondering what in the world he had been born into.

Jeremiah entered kindergarten at age five and again we realized that he too was a very intelligent child. As it turned out after testing in the third grade, Jeremiah had a genius IQ to go along with his keen perception of the feelings of others. Both Drew and Jeremiah enjoyed school and progressed very well through elementary school in Lee County. Our family was always in a state of constant motion. The boys played baseball, basketball, and were on the academic teams in their schools. Several parents arranged for a gymnastic teacher to come from Lexington to conduct classes in our rural town. It was a very successful program, and both Drew and Jeremiah took classes for several years. During one class when he was seven, Jeremiah started choking on a Lifesaver. The only thing that saved his life that day was that he was able to get some air through the hole in the Lifesaver. Several people tried unsuccessfully that afternoon to dislodge the candy by using the Heimlich maneuver. In a total panic, I finally grabbed Jeremiah in my arms and started to run to my car to hopefully get him to the doctor (his uncle) before he choked to death. Suddenly, he was able to swallow the Lifesaver and finally begin breathing.

He had turned blue and, as I noticed, had petechial hemor-rhages around both of his eyes, something they teach you in pharmacy school that means he had been without oxygen. I rushed both boys home, and both Luther and I sat and held Jeremiah for hours thanking God that he had not died. I will never forget the fear on his face as his eyes begged me to help him as he was choking. I'm positive he never forgot this inci-dent. None of us mentioned it, but the memory never left any of us.

Our family traveled constantly both on business and vacation as the boys were growing. Each summer we would go to the beach on Hilton Head Island, South Carolina, one of our favorite vacation spots. One memory of Jeremiah and the beach stands out particularly vividly in my mind. As soon as we would arrive at our rental house, the boys would literally race each other to get that first glimpse of the ocean. Jeremiah was three on this memorable day. I can still see him in his white shirt with green sleeves, blue jean shorts, and most im-portantly the red baseball hat he always wore. As everyone rushed into the water, he stopped at the edge of the ocean and stood surveying what was in front of him. He had his little hands crossed behind his back, not moving at all. He looked like a general looking over his troops. He remained that way for several minutes, so in awe of the power before him. Luck-ily, I had my camera that day to record that scene, but even if I hadn't, it still would be emblazoned on my mind.

Snow skiing and water skiing were among the many sports that our family enjoyed. We took many ski trips to Breckenridge, Colorado, where all three boys enjoyed skiing and snowmobiling. Both Drew and Jeremiah were expert ski-ers long before Jordan was old enough to join us on our fam-ily trips. When Jeremiah was nine, he entered a NASTAR time trial on the slopes of Breckenridge and placed in the top five of all skiers from Kentucky. He was invited to a pre-Olympic ski camp which he declined so he could attend an overall sports camp. Drew's first love was the water. We boated as a family from his first summer. He learned to swim at age three and was constantly in the water doing either tubing, knee boarding, or water skiing every summer thereafter. He and I would have a contest each year over who had the best sun tan. Drew usually won.

As Drew entered middle school, we discussed where he would be attending high school. His older cousin from Beattyville was going to The McCallie School, a college preparatory high school in Chattanooga, Tennessee. Drew was very familiar with McCallie since he had attended a summer sports camp program there every summer since he was eleven. Jeremiah also attended the McCallie Sports Camp from the summer when he was seven. Drew applied and was admitted to The McCallie School for the fall of 1988 for his ninth grade year. This was a difficult decision for both Drew and for us as his parents. We knew we wanted our sons to have every opportunity when it came to being educationally prepared for college, but to not have them at home with us made the decision very difficult. Drew wavered back and forth from going to McCallie to wanting to stay home. He was the first of the boys to strike out on his own. Although he was very intelligent, he suffered through a period of low self-esteem due in part to our position in the community. At this point, our company had grown from the one retail location to six retail locations and a seventh location that was an institutional pharmacy. This last pharmacy is a closed-door operation that services patients in long-term care facilities, residential psychiatric treatment centers, and prisons. Our sons felt the pressure of a successful family business in a small town environment.

Drew Smith did enter McCallie in the fall of 1988 as a freshman from a very rural eastern Kentucky educational background. Overnight, he moved into a dorm with a strange roommate, had to budget his time to study and to do his laundry, and had to cope with homesickness. More importantly, he was entering a very academically oriented school where each student was going to college and much was expected of each student in other areas. To say Drew and each of us didn't have a hard first semester would be a lie! Nightly phone calls and at least monthly visits to Chattanooga made each month easier but a struggle nevertheless. By his second semester, Drew had joined the band, the McCallie Chorus, the baseball team and was maintaining an A average. We were so proud of him, but he somehow failed to see his accomplishments. Back at home, Jeremiah had assumed the role of the older brother, and Jordan was adjusting as we were to Drew being away at school. Drew's freshman year ended well, but he still had some reservations as he headed back to McCallie for his sophomore year. This year was much easier as we all watched Drew mature into a wonderful young man. On each visit to McCallie, Jeremiah would say how much he was looking forward to joining his brother there when he would be a freshman. Drew was a conscientious student and a caring young man who developed many social skills while at boarding school. The friends he made there were ones he would have had for a lifetime.

Right before the Christmas break during Drew's sophomore year at McCallie, we received a call from the school asking if we would agree to let a student from China spend the Christmas holiday at our home in Kentucky. As the dorms at McCallie were closed for the holidays, each boarding student had to have a place to go. Little did we know how that phone call would affect our lives. My husband and I were going to China that next February and thought this would be a wonderful opportunity for us and for our sons to meet someone from that country. Drew knew that there was an exchange student from China at McCallie but had never met him. Immediately we accepted their invitation to host Fong Zhu, a nineteen year old student from Nanjing, China.

Drew introduced himself to Fong on campus before final exams that year. Fong had been in the United States since

August, the same summer the Chinese students were massacred in Tiananmen Square. The McCallie School had given him a full scholarship to study his senior year in this country. He was one of the top students in China, having attended the prestigious English Language school in his home city.

Fong arrived at our home in Beattyville after he and Drew had survived a harrowing drive in a blinding snow storm. I can still see his face as he stepped into our kitchen that first night. Jeremiah and Jordan ran to greet their brother and his friend from school. We were all somewhat nervous. Our fears were allayed as we realized that Fong's English was very good, and he seemed comfortable in our home. Many years later, Fong would say that he thought we all were a little crazy that first night. I guess we were after all. We had an early flight the following morning for a skiing trip to Colorado in which we had been able to include Fong at the last minute. Everyone ran around in a flurry packing, so excited about Drew being home and our holiday trip.

Fong Zhu skied that first Christmas in our country. What a joy to see him participating in a sport he had never tried. Really, this trip was an eye-opening experience for all of us. Fong and I had a three hour "last run" in which he gamely fell almost every three feet all the way down the mountain. This was the beginning of a long and treasured relationship with this remarkable young man.

By the time Drew and Fong returned to McCallie, they were friends. Drew had exhibited some jealousy at an older boy joining our family for the holidays just because he was the first born and the one home from school. That feeling seemed to dissipate as we all grew to know Fong. When we would visit Drew that next semester, we would naturally see Fong as well. As the year progressed and we made our trip to China, we saw the conditions that Fong must have suffered living under Communist rule. His parents had longed to have him out of China, even for a year, to experience freedom. That to me was the supreme sacrifice.

In April of that year as Drew and Fong were home for Drew's birthday, we offered to sponsor Fong so that he could stay in the United States for college if he so chose. He declined our offer but with great regret. His family and girlfriend, Xinyu, remained in China, and his chances of ever seeing them again would be slim if he did not return as planned in June. At that point, I remember feeling relieved. What could we have been thinking…offering to take on the responsibility of a teenager who would become a dissident if he remained with us?

Drew's sophomore year, also Fong's senior year, went very well. Both boys excelled academically and continued to be involved in various activities. As graduation approached, we knew we would all attend since we were Fong's only family in this country. Two weeks before graduation, Fong called our home deeply upset and spoke to me. It appeared that the Chinese government would not allow him to study at Fudan University in Shanghai as planned. His future was uncertain if he returned to China because the government was dispersing the intellectuals to quell any future democratic uprisings. After much prayer and discussion with his parents, Fong made the heartbreaking decision to not return to China. He remained in this country where he lives to this day as an integral part of our family. God sent him half way around the world to our family, we realized later. Fong entered the University of Kentucky that summer and graduated Phi Beta Kappa four years later.

In the Fall of 1991, Jeremiah joined his brother at McCallie when he entered as a freshman. Drew was a senior, so the boys had one year together in Chattanooga. On his sixteenth birthday the year before, we had given Drew a red Mazda Miata convertible. Being an A student, he was allowed to take his car to school for his senior year. I can clearly recall loading up our truck and following the two boys in the Miata down to Chattanooga. There was a downpour the day we traveled, so they started their shared adventure at McCallie in bad weather.

For the three of us left at home, this semester was very hard. We had become used to Drew being away, but to now have Jeremiah gone too was a blow. Looking back, I now feel this year was practice for us to be able to exist without Drew and Jeremiah. Each of the boys called us every night. Some nights, I would be on the phone with Drew and the call waiting would beep and Jeremiah would be on the other line. Although they lived in separate dorms, Drew and Jeremiah spent most of their time together that year. We all noticed how much closer they had become. While at home, they would often fight and disagree but always had love underneath any disagreement. Now, the boys never fought. They both were maturing in their own ways, and in this environment they found that indeed their best friends were each other.

Jordan had our house to himself that year and seemed to blossom without two older brothers vying for our attention. Jordan is our most extroverted child. At the age of nine, he had started modeling for an agency in Lexington, Kentucky. There he took acting and modeling classes, landing several local television commercials. He attended the IMTA convention in New York one summer and won an Honorable Mention for one of his commercials. Drew and Jeremiah were proud of Jordan but sometimes would cringe when he would get up in the middle of a restaurant and start break dancing. Secretly, they loved their talented little brother who was never self conscious.

In March of Drew's senior year at McCallie, he auditioned for the cast of *Camelot*, a joint production of McCallie and GPS. GPS is a girls' school in Chattanooga that conducts several joint programs with the all-boys McCallie School. One night after rehearsal, Drew called home and flatly stated that he had met the girl of his dreams. At this point, Drew had only dated a few girls and always said the perfect girl did not exist.

With this one phone call, Drew Smith was a changed young man. Although his self-esteem problems had subsided in the three years he had attended McCallie, they were still somewhat evident. Drew told us about Erin Grist, a junior at GPS who was also in the cast of *Camelot*. He wanted us to meet her when we came to Chattanooga for the performance. He described Erin in such glowing terms that I doubted any girl could be that perfect. I was wrong!! Jeremiah called home several days later and said he also loved this girl Erin that we had never met. Well, weeks later we met Erin after the performance of *Camelot*. She was a beautiful, blue-eyed blonde, but despite her beauty, her presence was almost angelic. I have often said that Erin is an angel on this earth, and many who know her agree with me.

Drew's last semester at McCallie was a whirlwind of activity that revolved around school and of course Erin. They attended both proms at McCallie and GPS and were rarely seen without each other. Drew and his best friend and roommate, Ted Webster, were on the yearbook staff that year and stayed busy compiling photos and text. In the yearbook, Drew's senior quote was very revealing. It was as follows: "<u>People been telling me to forget my dreams but these dreams keep me going. The dream of rock n' roll, pleasing my parents and a life with Erin will never cease.</u>" Drew dreamed of being in a band. That seemed very unusual for a student who had been admitted to Rhodes College in Memphis, Tennessee, with a pre-med major. Who knows what he might have done?

Jeremiah had an amazing freshman year at McCallie. He had a 3.81 GPA that year which was extraordinary for a student away at boarding school at age fourteen from a rural Kentucky background. When we went to Boarding Parents weekend his first semester, his Honors English professor asked if we were mad at him. He was the only professor who had given Jeremiah less that an A. He laughed and said that he had never seen a student more aggressive than Jeremiah. He had a lot to live up to following Drew, but Jeremiah accepted the challenge with a vengeance. Jeremiah was an accomplished drummer and piano player, so he also joined the McCallie band and orchestra. Both boys had excellent voices so they were in the chorus and in every musical performance together that year. Jeremiah stayed in the shadow of his older brother his freshman year. His time was to come the next year when he would be alone at McCallie.

Drew's graduated from McCallie in May of 1992, one of only eleven four-year boarders. He graduated cum laude which surprised many of his friends. I thought it was interesting that so many boys came up after graduation and commented that they didn't know that Drew was so smart. He worked so hard to be accepted and liked by everyone. All of our family traveled to Chattanooga for the graduation. Erin and her parents were our guests for the ceremony and for lunch afterwards. Again, Jeremiah seemed to be standing in the background, waiting for his turn in the limelight to come.

The summer of 1992 was in retrospect the finest of our lives. Luther and I had a wonderful marriage in which we shared the lives of our three exceptional children. We looked forward to having both Drew and Jeremiah home for the summer, although we realized how hectic our house would be. After graduation we loaded up all their possessions and headed back north to Kentucky. On the way home we stopped in Williamsburg, Kentucky, to visit Glenos and Nancy Cox, the great-grandparents of the boys. Neither was able to attend Drew's graduation because they were in their late eighties, so we all wanted to share our joy with them that day. That was to be the last time either of my grandparents saw Drew or Jeremiah. Pictures we took that day show beaming parents with all three of their sons beside their aging grandparents. We arrived back in Beattyville late that day and unloaded a car full of dirty clothes, computers, and books for the summer.

Chapter 1

How vividly I recall the early part of that summer. We left for Hilton Head Island and the beach two weeks after graduation. Drew invited Erin down, so she flew for the first time, and we picked her up at the local airport. Fong was with us. Everyone loved Hilton Head. We had been going there every summer since Drew was born and had rented houses all over the south end of the island. That summer, we rented our favorite home only three houses from the ocean. We had a wonderful vacation enjoying the beach, parasailing, bicycling, and eating at the great restaurants on the island. I took a picture of Erin and Drew that week in Harbour Town that has become my favorite photo of that summer.

Jeremiah went to McCallie Sports Camp again that June. This was his eighth summer at this camp, and he loved it. He had attended McCallie Sports Camp West the prior December when the camp went snow skiing in Breckenridge, Colorado. That would prove to be Jeremiah's final ski trip. At the closing ceremony that June, Jeremiah was chosen the MVP of his team and received an award as the camper who had attended the most years. The camp photographer caught Jeremiah in his favorite red Boogie hat, and that picture has become my fondest memory of how happy Jeremiah was that summer. Red hats…memories of a little boy at the beach and now a tall boy on the brink of manhood.

June passed quickly with vacation, camp, work, and family outings. Drew and Erin were inseparable, always together either in Beattyville or in Chattanooga. July promised more wonderful times. The weather that summer was beautiful both in Kentucky and in Hilton Head. Everyone was looking forward to Jeremiah's fifteenth birthday and our annual July 4th company picnic. Jeremiah, already a bit impatient being the second son in the family, always felt cheated that his birthday had to be celebrated with a party for our employees and their families. Drew and Jeremiah went to Lexington together to pick out Jeremiah's present, a stereo that he had been longing for. I remember their call to me at my drugstore to tell me what they had chosen. To their surprise, we agreed to let them buy it even though it was more expensive than we had expected. Our picnic and the first Smith family reunion two days later were happy occasions, but we all noticed that Jeremiah was rather withdrawn on his birthday and especially during the reunion. He would not come out of his room without coercion and absolutely would not allow anyone to take his picture.

A week prior to his birthday, I had asked Jeremiah if he had thought about what kind of car he wanted for his sixteenth birthday the next summer. His answer sent cold chills over my body. He said that he would never get a car and not to worry, it was okay. I brushed this off but months later would recall that conversation combined with other things he did that summer. I believe Jeremiah indeed knew he was going to die soon.

Drew and Erin left our house on July 5th that summer just after the reunion. Weeks later, we learned that Drew had asked Erin to marry him on July 8th, and she had accepted. They both knew it would be several years before they could marry because they had college first. Drew thought we would be upset, but we were ecstatic. Erin would be the perfect daughter-in-law, and we had seen the transformation she made in Drew's life. Life was perfect at that moment. Drew was eighteen and leaving later that month for Rhodes College in Memphis. Jeremiah had just turned fifteen, still had his braces, was looking forward to driving and going to McCallie by himself. Jordan was eleven and was delighted to have his two big brothers at home for the summer. Both Drew and Jeremiah seemed to have a higher tolerance for their younger brother that summer. All three boys made home movies with our camera and seemed the closest without fussing that they had ever been.

Drew was an avid Guns n' Roses fan and had found out earlier in the year that they were going on tour that summer with Faith No More and Metallica, the "concert of the decade." After calling for the tour locations, we decided the closest concert would be on July 22, 1992, in Indianapolis, Indiana. Both boys had been avid concertgoers both at home and while at McCallie, so this concert was not out of the ordinary. As parents, we always wanted our children to go places they would enjoy. The previous spring break, Drew had gone on a cruise to the Bahamas, and Jeremiah had gone on a McCallie Spanish trip to Costa Rica. With wild anticipation, both boys looked forward to their trip to Indianapolis. Jeremiah had evolved into a heavy metal fan, especially Guns n' Roses, and would have it no other way than to go with Drew on this trip. The distance to Indianapolis posed no problem for Drew since both he and Jeremiah had traveled many times by themselves back and forth from school in Chattanooga.

Erin and Drew had returned from a visit to Chattanooga the week before the big concert. On Friday, July 17th, we got a call that one of Luther's dear aunts had died in a nearby town. She was very close to each of us and had never had any children. Her husband was our beloved Uncle Luther after whom my husband had been named. He had passed away several years before, so we were the only ones to make the arrangements for her funeral. We buried Aunt Levadas that following Sunday, and Drew served as one of her pallbearers. Jeremiah had been asked to be a pallbearer too, but he refused. He was still acting oddly and was very withdrawn during the funeral.

Luther had experienced peculiar feelings the week prior to his aunt's death. On an unusual trip with his brother to Lexington, they had ended up in the historic Lexington Cemetery trying to decide on a location for a family plot. When Luther told me of this later, I shuddered and said I didn't want to discuss cemetery plots. Well, after Aunt Levadas died, we both felt like this was what had been bothering Luther. Her death was sudden and very sad, but at her age death was not unexpected. Erin went to this funeral as a part of our family and everyone there remarked at how wonderful she was and how much all three of our sons had grown. Many had been at our house earlier in the month for the Smith reunion, but some had not.

Wednesday, July 22nd, was the week after the death of our aunt. Luther and I both went to work at our drugstores and left the three boys and Erin asleep. Drew called me about noon to see if I had gotten them money for their concert trip. He was anxious to leave and said that both he and Jeremiah were ready. About thirty minutes later, both boys came in to my store in a rush. I will never forget how they were dressed. The McCallie boys who always wore dress shirts, ties and dress pants now looked like heavy metal band members. Drew had on jeans that a McCallie student had painted "Guns n' Roses" on and a weird shirt. He wore orange sneakers and was as excited as I have ever seen him. Jeremiah was much more subdued but looked the part nevertheless. Both boys said hello to each of my employees, and everyone seemed glad to see them so excited. I gave Drew and Jeremiah their money and followed them out to their car. It was a beautiful, sunny July day. They had the top down on the Miata, and both boys put on sunglasses and baseball hats. I gave them a portable phone for safety and the directions I had written down for them to the hotel where I had made their reservations. For their safety, we had decided that they should spend the night in Indianapolis, a block from the concert. They were to check in to the hotel then walk to the concert. As the boys started to leave, I noticed that they had forgotten to put on their seat belts. We always insisted that everyone wear their seat belts. The last words I ever said to my two oldest sons were to put on their seat belts. I told them to be careful as every mother and father says to each of their children each time they leave. We fully expect them to return safely, but we always tell them to be careful. About four hours later Jeremiah called me from the car, and I had to guide them by phone to their hotel. They were already in Indianapolis and within blocks of the hotel but had gotten turned around. Minutes later, they called back that they had checked in and had already seen the lead singer for Metallica in the lobby of their hotel. Jeremiah was so excited as he talked of getting the singer's autograph. That autograph is a vivid reminder of that fateful day. They told me that they were walking over early to the concert and would call back after it was over.

The four of us spent a restful evening at home in Beattyville. Erin felt at home with us and was excited for Drew about the concert. This concert was not the type for a girl, so there was never a question that she go with Drew instead of Jeremiah. How different things might have been. At about 2 A.M. our phone rang, and I immediately answered it. Drew was talking so fast that it was hard to understand him at first. He asked me to listen to him before I said "no", so I did. He wanted to come home that night. They had just gotten out of the concert, and it was "awesome". Jeremiah tried to say something to me in the background, but Drew cut him off saying he could tell me all about the concert when they got home. Well, I didn't even think twice before I said that they could not come home that late. They had a long drive; they were tired, and it was not safe to drive in the dark. I told them to go to sleep, and I would call them and wake them up in the morning. Drew called Erin in his room on his number, and they talked for awhile. Those two conversations were the last any of us had with the boys. How I would have loved to have been able to talk to Jeremiah. Both boys were as exuberant as I have ever heard them. What a way to spend their last night.

Thursday, July 23, 1992, dawned as did every other day. Luther and I went to work and left Jordan and Erin asleep that morning. At 9 A.M. I called the Canterbury Hotel in Indianapolis and asked for Drew and Jeremiah's room. The woman who answered the phone said that the boys had not checked out, so she rang the room. The phone rang and rang. I was not worried at this point because both boys always were heavy sleepers and often did not hear the phone. I was on the phone again at about 9:15 A.M. when a friend came into my store and asked where the boys were. I said that they were in Indianapolis, and that I was on the phone while security was going to their room to wake them up. The hotel still insisted that they had not checked out (which later proved to be untrue). Luther just happened to be in my drugstore and came up by me as I was on the phone. He normally would have been at his drugstore in the same small town, but we were opening a new drugstore in an adjoining county, and he was on his way there that morning.

Never in our lives did Luther or I ever expect to hear the next words. Our police chief came up to us and said, "Drew is dead!" What? The boys were safely asleep in a hotel in Indianapolis, so how could Drew possibly be dead? Well, we learned that the boys had been in a single car accident on the Mountain Parkway, a four lane highway only thirty minutes from our house.

There are no words to describe the terror of hearing your child is dead. It doesn't even register. Thank God you are numbed to the prospect of living the rest of your lives without that child at that moment of truth. Luther and I both reacted the same to the death of our son. We cried and reached out to our wonderful employees who had to live through the terror of that moment with us. For an instant, we did not even mention Jeremiah. In my mind, I visualized that he was all right and at worst, being taken to the hospital. We looked at the policeman and finally voiced our concern for our second son. Luther and I have discussed that, at that moment, we put aside Drew's death and prayed against hope that at least Jeremiah was alive. We suffered through about twenty minutes in which calls were made back and forth to the funeral home that had responded to the accident call. Finally, the policeman turned to us and had to confirm our worst fears: Jeremiah too had died in the accident.

Many people have asked us how we survived the loss of two children. I ask them how anyone survives the loss of one child. In our case, we had lost two of the most precious children in the world. Both Drew and Jeremiah had been the light of our lives. They were exceptional boys who were very intelligent and had a love for other people that few teenagers possess. Only eight days before their deaths, they had helped me for two days with a benefit I had coordinated for a local teenager with cancer. We had all worked long hours helping others; that was a vital part of our lives.

Luther and I left our store that day in a daze. Many offered to drive us, but we just wanted to go home alone. We knew Jordan and Erin had to hear the news from us. The world seemed so different on that short drive through our small town. People were still going to the post office and coming into our drugstores. Didn't they know that the world had ceased to exist? Even though the sun was shining that day, a darkness like none I had ever known settled over my whole body. Was this a dream? The car seemed real as we drove up our driveway, but nothing else did.

As we entered our house for the first time, neither of us knew how we could tell Jordan and Erin. Could we actually vocalize what had happened? Luther went to wake up Jordan, and I went in to wake up Erin. I will never forget the look on her face. She faced this crisis with the courage and faith she has shown all her life. Jordan cried, but for an eleven year old who has just lost his only two siblings, he handled it remarkably well. He told us much later that he thought when he saw our faces that one of our dogs had died. That should be the worst news any eleven year old should have to endure, not the loss of his two older brothers.

Within minutes of our arrival at home, our families, friends and customers began arriving with food and condolences. Small Kentucky towns rally around the family of the deceased, and the loss of these two brothers touched the lives of everyone. Many families say they don't remember much about these first days, but both Luther and I do. We were completely enveloped by loving people who literally held us up. These six years later, I can still recall certain friends arriving that first day. Did their faces mirror what I was feeling? I believe so. The looks of total sorrow and disbelief seemed surreal. Our dear friends, Margaret and Tom Hickey, flew in immediately from their home in Longview, Washington. Their love and support has never wavered. After the funeral Margaret stayed with us for two weeks, sensing we feared being alone. During that time she and I went through the rooms of both boys, crying over each lost treasure, a task I could never have done alone.

Erin's parents, Carol and Al Grist, turned from acquaintances to close friends that fateful Thursday afternoon. They loved Drew as we do Erin. Both he and Jeremiah had stayed at their home in Chattanooga, so they too felt our double loss. Moreover, they had to console their only daughter who had just seemingly found the love of her young life. I continue to grieve the loss of Drew and Erin's love. As I have said, she is an angel on this earth.

Our Episcopal church members were there for us in every way. As each new person came to our house, we felt the love and prayers of each of them. Our faith was severely tested during this time. I personally screamed at God. How could he let these two wonderful boys die? How could neither boy go to college, never have a wife or a child, never give us a grandchild? As for Jeremiah, this next year was finally to be his year out from under the shadow of his brother. We asked "Why?" over and over again. Then, we started with the tormenting question every bereaved parent asks, "What if…?" What if I had let the boys come on home early that morning after the concert? What if we had not bought Drew a red convertible sports car? The what ifs go on and on, day after day and night after sleepless night. Time gives us the only answer to these questions which is that there is no answer at all. God did not choose our sons to die that morning. It was simply their time to pass on.

We both wanted to know what had happened in the accident. We knew that no other car had been involved and that there had been a woman who witnessed the accident. My brothers, Gary and Bill, talked to her that day, but it was over a year before I could call her and ask her about the final moments in the lives of our precious sons.

We were allowed to see our sons in the local funeral home late that afternoon. Each time I pass this place even now six years later, I cringe at what we had to face that day. Both Drew and Jeremiah had died instantly, their necks broken. Thankfully, they did not suffer. The woman who witnessed the accident reached each of them within seconds and assured us that they died instantly. Being a mother of teenagers herself, she held each boy knowing they were someone's children, never knowing they were brothers.

Our sons looked beautiful the afternoon of their deaths. Jeremiah had only a few scratches on his face and otherwise looked like he was sleeping. Drew had an abrasion on his right cheek but otherwise looked as handsome as ever. Who could believe that you would have to go into a room and see two of your sons lying side by side beneath white sheets, heads together so that we could touch both at the same time? This picture never leaves me. They were so peaceful, so beautiful. I wish I could go back to that day and spend more time by their sides. Luther and I were not left alone with them, probably because we didn't know to ask. Looking back, I should have savored my last time to touch them and to brush back their still-wet hair.

Flashes of memories never change…Jeremiah still had his braces on! I remember contemplating asking to have them taken off before the funeral. Such an odd thought in the midst of such a tragedy, but nevertheless one that bothered me. As I have reviewed my journals over the years, I have noted many entries where I still fretted that Jeremiah never got his braces off. Jeremiah was wearing the gold chain he had been so proud of. We decided to let them bury him with it. Luckily, my brother removed the necklace and gave it to me several days after the funeral. I had lamented not keeping the necklace when Gary quietly told me that he had it. What joy! That necklace comforts me each day as I faithfully wear it in memory of Jeremiah. Luther has never taken off Drew's bracelet, so we each have a part of them with us at all times. I am glad we saw the boys that afternoon because the next night at their wake, they looked so puffy and unlike themselves that we probably should not have opened their caskets. Erin's comment that she could let Drew go only because "he doesn't even look like himself" gave me comfort that night.

The morning following the accident, we agonized over where to bury the boys. How odd that Luther and his brother had just been to the Lexington Cemetery two weeks before. Since then we had lost Aunt Levadas and six days later our two sons. At first I wanted to bury the boys in Beattyville. I had Luther and my brothers walking all over our farm to find an area to start a family cemetery. In reality, I would have put them in our living room to keep them near me if that had been possible. What crazy thoughts you have as you try to make some sense of this kind of tragedy. Luther finally convinced me to drive the seventy-five miles to Lexington and at least look at the Lexington Cemetery. Truthfully, I only considered this after Jordan voiced his opinion that the boys' graves would always be maintained in Lexington. Who knew if we would always own this farm in Beattyville? That at least made sense to me for some reason. My brother, Gary, drove us to Lexington, and we instantly felt that this was the place we wanted to bury our sons. After looking at various plots, we chose a family plot in the historic section of the cemetery and made plans for the funeral to be held the next day. Weeks later, we realized that Luther and his brother had stood by the exact lots we chose for the boys only weeks earlier during their unplanned trip to the Lexington Cemetery. Fate? Who can say.

At the wake the night before the funeral, there were over five hundred people and more flowers than anyone had ever seen in our town. Luther and I stood and greeted each person, their hugs literally giving us the strength to stand. As the line progressed, faces appeared that we had not seen in years along with family members, friends, fellow students and our customers. A dear friend, Avis Thompson, softly played the piano for hours that night. One poignant memory is of a man suddenly being the next in line and raising his arms to embrace us. We realized that this man knew what we were going through; he too had lost a teenage son. His eyes haunted me. Would I always look as he did that night? One valuable lesson I have carried from the wake is how important it is to the family that people come to pay their respects.

Over eighty students and faculty members came from The McCallie School, including Headmaster Spencer McCallie. Friends from McCallie and from Beattyville served as pallbearers for our sons. Young men who had only days before talked and joked with Drew and Jeremiah now had the responsibility to carry them to their final resting place. "This should not have happened!" I raged inwardly. Young men in their prime are not supposed to die.

The funeral for Drew and Jeremiah was held on Saturday, July 25, 1992, in our small historic St. Thomas Episcopal Church. Each detail of that day is so clear to me, just as if it happened yesterday. As we followed the two hearses up the hill to the church, I heard the church bells tolling thirty-three times. Was that for the total of thirty-three years that our sons lived? No, it was for the age of Jesus. It didn't seem unusual that both totaled thirty-three. When we arrived at the church, it was filled to capacity. Many had to stand on the porch and in the basement, but that did not stop them from attending.

Since that day, I still visualize two coffins draped in colored cloths at the front of our church when I sit in our customary pew. The music still rings in my ears from the beautiful service. The prayers of the people that day still support me. How did we manage to walk out of that church following the coffins of Drew, our oldest son, then Jeremiah, our second son? God was walking with us that day.

Jordan did not attend the funeral for his brothers. A few hours after we told him the tragic news, he left our home to stay with the family of his best friend, Jonathan Charles. He could not bear to be in our house with all the grief and sorrow. No words can ever express to the Charles family how much they helped all of us those first few weeks. They brought Jordan to the wake the night before the funeral. The three of us went in alone so that he could see his brothers. He dissolved in tears and left a few minutes later. His memories of his brothers have always been wonderful ones, not those of their funeral and wake.

As we left Beattyville to drive the seventy-five miles to Lexington for the burial, there was a caravan of over one hundred cars following the two hearses. I can remember being on the four lane interstate and not being able to see the end of the line of cars. The boys were laid to rest that afternoon among their family and friends and amid much sadness. As the pallbearers stood valiantly trying to hold back tears, I hugged each one of them and thanked them for being such good friends to our sons. Many had been friends of both Drew and Jeremiah. They stood there so young and healthy in the shade of the stately trees towering over the graves. My mind still could not sort out that these wonderful boys were alive and that my sons were now buried there, never to be their friends again. As I was forced to leave, I still couldn't believe they were dead. Four close friends, Dave and Judy Lauer and

Mike and Maureen Patrick, stayed until everyone had gone and the graves were covered. Their act of friendship in staying with our sons when we could not always brings tears to my eyes as it has as I am writing this today. Thus began the longest road imaginable, one that the three of us still travel day to day to survive.

Yellow butterflies have always been very special to me. The connection began as I stood at my mother's grave over ten years ago, four years before the boys died. My visits were infrequent because my mother is buried about seventy miles away from our home at a small country church yard in Wolf Creek, Kentucky. My emotions had spilled over with tears of sorrow that day. My mother was only fifty-three when she succumbed to the breast cancer she had fought for six years. Her death was so devastating to me because we had always been very close. As her only daughter, I considered her my best friend and confidante. I felt her death was the most sorrow I could bear. That proved not to be the case. Anyway, that one particular day, as I stood at her grave, I felt so alone. Suddenly, a huge yellow butterfly started circling around my head. It would not go away, lazily circling. I realized that the spirit of my Mom was with me. I felt more comfort than I ever had in the years since her death.

I never told anyone about this experience with the yellow butterfly. Many other times over the years, I would see a yellow butterfly in times of trouble. Still, I told no one. The afternoon of July 23, 1992, the day of the boys' accident, I managed to walk out our front door to try and grab a few moments to myself. As I walked down our walk, THREE yellow butterflies surrounded me. The joy I felt is indescribable. The significance of three butterflies was not lost on me even though I was in such horrible shape mentally. Well, again I did not mention this to anyone. Later, as we walked the farm looking for a burial site, three yellow butterflies kept circling around me. Finally, one of my brothers commented on it, and I told my story. I don't know what everyone, including Luther, thought that day, but I knew that this was a powerful message from our sons who had joined my mother. The story continued as we drove behind the hearses the day of the funeral. Everyone in the car knew the story by then, so we began counting the butterflies. When we passed one hundred, we stopped counting. Many times, two yellow butterflies would come from each side of the hearse in front of us and merge side by side to come directly at our car. Their presence made that most difficult ride of my life bearable.

Pain, despair, hopelessness, anger...just a few of the emotions of the beginning of our life "after the boys' accident". This is how we divide time in our family. The years before the accident seem so idyllic; long forgotten are the trials of raising three sons and building our pharmacy business. Now, the days seemed interminable, filled with such despair that at times I didn't recognize myself in the bathroom mirror. Those were not my eyes. My eyes had always sparkled with the promise of each new day with Luther and our boys. I prayed that I would not wake in the morning. I wasn't suicidal, but neither was I able to imagine a lifetime ahead of me without Drew and Jeremiah.

Two of Jeremiah's closest friends, Michael Patrick and Leah Bush, came to our home the week after the funeral to spend time in Jeremiah's room. I can vividly recall sitting with them on his bed, surrounded by his posters and drums, listening to them talk about Jeremiah. It seems that Jeremiah had been having a recurring nightmare in which he and another person had been killed in a car accident. He saw the accident and then found himself suspended above two coffins. The driver of the car, the occupant of the second coffin, was never visible. This dream bothered Jeremiah to the extent he discussed it with his friends but not us. Could we have changed what was to come if he had told us? I doubt it. As I have said, it was their time to pass over. Looking back, I believe Jeremiah knew he was going to die that summer. As he sat at a desk in my office that summer, I can vividly recall how he answered me when I asked if he would like to go look at cars that weekend. His sixteenth birthday would be the next summer, and we were deciding what car he would get. With an unfamiliar sadness in his voice, he said, "Don't worry Mom, it's okay. I'll never have a car." And he didn't!

About two weeks after the boys died, I received a grief workbook from a woman I did not know. Her name was Dinah Taylor. She and her husband lived close to us in a small town in southeastern Kentucky and were bereaved parents. Their only child, a son, Jim, had been killed one year before on the night before he was to graduate from high school. She had included her phone number, so I desperately called her to see how she had survived the past year. Several days later, Luther and I drove to meet this wonderful woman. She welcomed us into her home and shared her grief with us. From that first meeting we realized that maybe we could make it. After all, this couple had and were willing to share our loss with us. Dinah Taylor became a life preserver to me that day.

After that meeting and two other conversations with mothers who had recently lost children, I began what I now feel is my mission on earth. I had read about two teenage girls who died on August 14th in a single car accident just like Drew and Jeremiah. I called Judy Carpenter, the mother of one of the girls, Kellie, the driver of the car. Not knowing what to say, I just told Judy that she didn't know me, but that I knew what she was going through because of the loss of our sons. We instantly became friends, and Luther and I had another couple who understood our loss. From that first call to Judy and Dennis Carpenter, I have called over seven hundred families that have lost children. Most deaths I have learned about from the newspaper, but often people call me with families they would like me to contact. As I would contact each new family, I would then call Dinah. She would send them her workbook. The group that we finally named Fellow Travelers grew from these first few calls. As our numbers increased, Dinah decided to write a newsletter for these bereaved parents and the first issue of *Lamentations* appeared in September of 1992.

Many activities helped me get through the first months after our loss. I read every single book I could find about the loss of a child, grief, and near-death experiences. Reading these books let me know that I wasn't alone. Others had survived the loss of a child. After a suggestion from Dinah, I started writing a daily journal to Drew and Jeremiah. Just expressing what I was feeling was therapy in itself. Those journals have been a useful chronicle of my grief progression. During one of the periods when I felt like I was never going to be any better, I would read my entries from those first few weeks. The darkness was lifting bit by bit.

It became a passion for us, like many parents who lose a child, that Drew and Jeremiah not be forgotten. Luther and I established a Drew and Jeremiah Smith Scholarship Fund at The McCallie School shortly after their death. Many friends and relatives contributed then and continue to do so in their memory. Both of our sons would be so proud that other students are being helped in their memory. We also decided to give two scholarships in our hometown of Beattyville, Kentucky, to the Lee County High School valedictorian and salutatorian in each graduating class. The notes that we have received from these students over the years are treasured keepsakes. Certainly, something positive has come from the tragedy.

Since The McCallie School had been so influential in the lives of our sons, we wanted to donate something to the school in their memory. We chose a bust by Glenna Goodacre called *The Athlete* to be placed in the new Student Activity Center at McCallie. The dedication was held in conjunction with a memorial service for Drew and Jeremiah for the school's over six hundred students. Friends of both boys spoke eloquently that day as we choked back tears. The voices of their fellow choral students filled the chapel where we had such wonderful memories of many McCallie performances. At the end of the service, Headmaster Spencer McCallie presented us with a collage of pictures of both boys from their days as boarding students. Truly, this was a gift from heaven because many of the pictures were ones we had never seen.

Time stood still for us that first fall. Our lives could simply not go on as before, two integral parts were missing. It was as if both of my arms were missing. Many tears were shed then and still are now. In my journal entry dated August 2, 1992, I wrote, "When I cry, my right eye cries tears for my beloved Jeremiah Cottle Smith. My left eye cries tears for my beloved Andrew Siler Smith. I love you boys." Incredibly I would often shed tears from only one eye depending on my focus of grief being Drew or Jeremiah that day.

Jordan had to return to school less than three weeks after the death of his brothers. To make matters worse (if that is possible), he was going into the sixth grade at a new middle school. The courage it took to walk into school that first day had to come from an inner strength few eleven year olds possess. Jordan had that strength. As I left him that day, I literally sobbed for what he had to face and for those two missing boys that would never enter another school building.

On September 1st of that first year, Jordan asked me if he could write something in my journal. The following is his entry: "Drew and Jeremiah, I miss you so much. I had no idea what happened. I thought that the dog had got killed but it wasn't. I died. I wish I was with you but I'll see you soon. You know when they say the person or people you love, they walk you up into the light of heaven? Well, you're the only people that I would ever want. I love you brothers."

Love…do any of us really know how much we love someone until they are gone? We all think we do, but most of us do not live day to day. We plan the futures of our children with a false sense of security when we should be living every day as if it were our last. Bereaved parents know this reality too well. Drew and Jeremiah were vibrantly alive one day and lost from us the next. Our memories never die. They become sweeter with each passing day. If you try to look too far in the future after the loss of a child, you will be overwhelmed by the sense that there are too many days left in your life before you are reunited with your child. Both Luther and I know that we have to take our lives one day at a time. It is possible to manage the grief of one day, but when we start thinking of all the "tomorrows" it becomes unbearable.

While reading a comforting grief book by John Bramlett, I was touched by his description of the compassionate man, Al Fantoni, who had designed the monument for his son. Something told me that I must contact this man. We had agonized over an appropriate memorial for our sons, so maybe this was our answer. After contacting Al by phone, Luther and I flew to Barre, Vermont, to meet with him to discuss the design for an obelisk that Luther had envisioned. Al Fantoni is an exceptional man, a spiritual man. He and his lovely wife, Silvana, had come to this country over twenty years before from their native Italy, where he had studied the art of sculpture in his hometown of Carrera. The marble of Carrera was used by Michangelo for his *David*.

Al Fantoni took us into his arms that weekend in Vermont. After hearing about our boys and looking at what Luther had drawn, he began sketching his vision of our memorial. Naturally, it was perfect. I asked if my favorite poem, one that had comforted me on many sympathy cards, could be inscribed on the sides of the obelisk, and he said that it could. This is the poem that I chose:

> *A rose once grew where all could see,*
> *sheltered beside a garden wall,*

And, as the days passed swiftly by,
it spread its branches, straight and tall.

One day, a beam of light shone through
a crevice that had opened wide—
The rose bent gently toward its warmth
then passed beyond to the other side.

Now, you who deeply feel its loss,
be comforted—the rose blooms there,
Its beauty even greater now,
nurtured by God's own loving care.

Years after our obelisk was in place, we had Al Fantoni design a bench for our plot. Luther and I had spent countless hours standing, kneeling, or just sitting on the ground by our boys. This bench would allow us some comfort as we grieved. As seasons changed, we would sit or walk around the cemetery visiting the graves of the children in our group, always returning to our bench. The inscription that Al carved into this bench is one that is carved into my soul:

And could not one suffice
Once, twice the arrow flies

Holidays were always such happy times for our family. I can mentally picture Drew and Jeremiah pulling up in our driveway from school, the car so loaded that Jeremiah had his feet resting on luggage on the floor. How I would anticipate their arrival! Each sound would have me running to the window so that I would not miss greeting them before they could get out of the car. All three of us waited through Halloween, Thanksgiving, and Christmas in 1992 for them to come home. How could they not be coming? My head knew they were dead, but my heart did not.

Our family did not follow the same traditions those first holidays nor do we to this day. Halloween had been a fun holiday for the Smith boys as they grew through the years. We would always have parties where they could wear the masks they had collected. Silence now greeted us on that previously joyous day.

Thanksgiving was always that family holiday when our house would be crammed from top to bottom with as many as seventeen relatives at a time. Now, Thanksgivings are spent at the beach with my brother, Gary, and his wife, Karen, with whom we share a special closeness. Being with Gary is like having Drew in the room. Not only were they alike physically, but were remarkably alike in their personalities. They shared a special bond, much closer than just uncle and nephew.

The days and months moved very slowly that fall of 1992. One incident clearly lifted our spirits right before Christmas. On the morning of December 21st, Jordan and I had dressed and gone downstairs preparing for work and school. Luther had kissed me goodbye and turned over to go back to sleep. All of a sudden, I heard him cry out my name. I could tell he was crying, so I ran up the stairs as fast as I could. Tears of joy were streaming down his face, not the usual tears of sorrow.

Just as I had left the bedroom only minutes earlier, Luther had turned over to face away from my side of the bed. As he was drifting back to sleep, he felt me get back into bed. He turned over and there was Drew! No spoken words passed between them, but they communicated through an awareness from one brain to another. Luther reached for Drew and held him in his arms. The feeling was one he could not describe. Drew said, "Dad, don't worry. We can't get hurt here." Luther then asked where Jeremiah was. Drew replied, "Oh, you know him. He's around here somewhere." That is exactly what Drew would have said.

A noise from the opposite side of the room shifted

Luther's attention, and he saw Jeremiah! Jeremiah moved at an unnatural speed toward the bed and slid under him, coming up between him and Drew. The feeling of Jeremiah passing under him was hard to explain. I had no problem understanding. All of a sudden, Luther consciously realized what he had lost, and both boys disappeared in an instant. Both of us had been given a rare gift that morning. Our sons were in heaven, happy, at peace, and together. What a load off two weary parents. Was this a dream? Was it a vision? It really does not matter.

We could not bear to celebrate Christmas in our home, so we took Jordan, Erin, Fong, Leah, and our friend and business manager, Greg Mays, to Paris, France, during the holidays. The experience comforted us greatly, but we soon realized that holidays and birthdays were never going to be the same. The structure of our family had changed forever, but the family had survived. Jordan often lamented, "Why can't things be like they used to be?" If only that could happen. His childhood lack of fear had been shattered by the accident.

Out of the ashes, a new Smith family evolved, severely broken, but determined to live our lives as best we could. Each of us understood that to survive we must live day to day, pray for strength and guidance, strive to help others, grieve individually, and work to keep the memory of Drew and Jeremiah alive. My solace came from calling newly bereaved families and sending them my grief packet. Each new family and child became an integral part of my life. Sharing lessens grief in some unexplainable way. Sharing relieves the depression that leaves us with twenty pound arms and legs that cannot support us. After receiving my packet, so many wonderful mothers have written me expressing their sympathy and commenting about our boys. Music to my ears…Drew and Jeremiah are not forgotten!

Erin's parents, Al and Carol Grist, have never forgotten our sons, especially Drew. As you will see from the following incident that happened only months after his death, they have a special connection.

Carol writes: *In the fall of 1992, I wanted to smock my grandson, A.C., an outfit for Thanksgiving. After I had smocked the inset for the little suit, I was going to use it in a pattern called "David" from the Martha Pullen Company. I started working on the pattern and everything was going fine until I came to the back of the outfit. No matter what I tried, I could not get the instructions on the pattern to work. I thought I might be reading the instructions wrong, so I took the whole mess over to a friend who sewed and did smocking. She was able to help, but I finally had to call the company that made the pattern. I spoke to Kathy McMakin who went through the pattern step-by-step with me. With her helpful advice, I was able to finish the outfit. It turned out just great.*

At the end of our telephone conversation, Kathy apologized for the problem I had encountered with the pattern and said she would like to send me some things from her company. I told her she did not have to do that, I had just wanted help with the pattern.

A few days later I received a package that had a box of Victorian paper dolls (which I loved), a package of Heirloom Sewing Needles (which I had been wanting), and some patterns. The last pattern I took out of the package was a Martha Pullen pattern for a baby's playsuit called, "DREW AND ERIN'S BUBBLE"... To this day I am still astounded!

That night I told Al about this when he came home from work. As I showed him the pattern, his mouth literally dropped open. Everyone I have told about this has reacted in a similar manner.

The next fall we went to a craft fair in Danville, Kentucky, (any excuse to visit Erin at college), and I came upon a rack of smocked children's outfits. I was drawn to them, and as I started looking through the outfits I came upon one made from the "Drew and Erin's Bubble" pattern. I pulled it out and showed it to Al. It seemed so strange that this is the only outfit I have ever seen from this pattern and that it should be in Kentucky.

I do not know why I received this particular pattern, but I have to believe it was a personal link with Drew and not just a coincidence.

When Carol told me this story and showed me the pattern, I too was amazed. This was no coincidence. What are the chances of a pattern having the two uncommon names of Drew and Erin being sent to Carol only months after Drew's death? What was the significance of the name of the pattern? My belief is that it represented the "bubble" of Drew and Erin's future being burst with his untimely death. After looking in many stores, Carol was able to find only one other "Drew and Erin's Bubble" pattern which she presented to me. Seriously, I have to look at it from time to time to really believe this entire incident happened. It was music to my ears.

Speaking of music, it can evoke so many special memories, and it certainly does for us. For our family, the song *Every Breath You Take* by the Police was a special song. As the background music for an early McCallie Sports Camp video, this song became a favorite of all five of us. At first, it amazed us that we would invariably hear the song on the radio every summer while driving from Kentucky to Chattanooga for sports camp. After the third year we actually began joking, "When do each of you think our song will be played?" *Every Breath You Take* became "The McCallie Song" to us over the years. No one else knew the importance and significance of this song until after the deaths of our sons.

Two days after the burial of Drew and Jeremiah, Luther and Jordan drove the seventy-five miles to Lexington to try to escape the oppressive cloud over our home for a little while. Margaret Hickey, my dear friend, and I were spending the day cleaning out the boys' rooms. Luckily, no one was there to witness our tears. Each trip to Lexington involved passing the accident site twice, a daunting proposition. On the return trip, just as Luther and Jordan were approaching the scene, *Every Breath You Take* came on the radio. Remember, this song was popular in 1984 and was rarely played eight years later. Jordan said, "Dad, the boys are playing the McCallie song." This was the first of many occasions when at our most vulnerable times, we were comforted by this song. Each time I hear it now, the words seem to be speaking directly to our loss.

Our family limped through the end of 1992 and the beginning of 1993. On many occasions, our spirits were lifted when we would hear our "McCallie song". It seemed that when we would hit rock bottom, the song would drift to our ears in the grocery store or on an unfamiliar station as we were traveling. It continues to this day to bring us comfort.

Many loving family members and friends literally held us up those first few years. Their prayers and kindness supported us when we were not able to support ourselves. I could never mention everyone, but three women stand out in my mind: Sister Mary Kay Drouin, Mary Ann Combs, and Kimberly Smith. Sister Mary Kay has always been a friend of our family. She arrived at our home within an hour after Drew and Jeremiah had their accident. Over the course of the next months, she would arrive unannounced to just sit with us and try to make some sense of our loss. We asked her tough questions that she really could not answer, but her presence always had a spiritual calming effect on all of us. To this day, she continues to support us in every way she can. She is truly doing God's work with Resurrection House, her shelter for abused women in Beattyville. Thank you Sister Mary Kay.

Mary Ann Combs had been a customer of mine at my drugstore for years. My description of her is that she too is an angel on this earth like Drew's Erin. In the years prior to our loss, I had watched as Mary Ann helped so many as a Hospice volunteer or by caring for an elderly person in the community. After the boys died, she never missed sending me a card on a weekly basis for over two years. Months after all the cards and calls stopped from others, Mary Ann never forgot. Each card would move me to tears that someone had not forgotten Drew and Jeremiah. To this day, she supports all three of us in so many ways. Thank you Mary Ann.

Kimberly Smith, the former wife of our nephew, has so many talents. One of these is flower arranging, and her loving gift to our family for almost two years was to decorate Drew and Jeremiah's graves on a weekly basis. No one ever asked Kimberly to do this. She did it in memory of our sons. I clearly remember that first Christmas when Kimberly decorated our obelisk and lot at the Lexington Cemetery. The touch of her loving hand will never be forgotten. Thank you Kimberly.

As April of 1993 came upon us, we had to face the first of our sons' birthdays. Drew would have been nineteen on April 27th of that year. On that day that had been the happiest day of my life nineteen years before, I cried all day. Many friends called, but I could not answer the phone. Luther and I drove to Lexington, past the accident site, and spent most of the day at the cemetery. Spending Drew's birthday like this would have been utterly unimaginable only nine months before. Parents should be having a party for their nineteen year old, not standing at his grave. The following quote by Thomas Mann was part of my journal entry from that day: "A man's dying is more the survivor's affair than his own."

Erin graduated from high school a month later from G.P.S. in Chattanooga, Tennessee. Naturally, all three of us went. With mixed emotions, we watched as she and her friends made that transition into adulthood. Flashes of Drew's graduation a year before flooded my eyes with tears. It still was not possible that he and Jeremiah were gone. I would never see Jeremiah cross the stage at McCallie as his brother had. Erin chose to come to Kentucky to attend Centre College that fall. We were thrilled that we would be close to her. Over the next four years, we enjoyed many times with Erin and her college friends. She is like a daughter to us. Luther and I were there in June of 1997 as she crossed the stage again on her graduation day at Centre College. How proud Drew must have been for her that day.

Summer came, and it was not like the joyous arrival of all the other summers. Drew and Jeremiah did not return from school with their car loaded with dirty clothes, stereos, and books. That part of our life was gone forever. As July approached, a dread settled over all of us. Jeremiah's sixteenth birthday would have been on July 4th of that year. How we had planned for that day. Don't all parents look forward to their child's sixteenth birthday? I always did because I knew how important a milestone it was for the boys. Somehow we got through Jeremiah's birthday, and I can say that their birthdays after that year have gotten easier. That has been true as well for Mother's Day, Father's Day, and the other holidays. Time <u>does</u> help. Your child is never out of your mind, but time allows us to look back less painfully and treasure the glorious memories so much more with each passing year.

July 23rd of 1993 brought us to the first anniversary of the deaths of Drew and Jeremiah. As with many other days, the anticipation of this day was much worse than the actual day. I relived each day prior to the accident saying, "This time last year Drew and Jeremiah were…" July 23rd came and we spent it at the beach with my brother, Gary, and my sister-in-law, Karen. Their support has been unstinting. Part of my journal entry for that day includes, "I know we suffer when we go home and face that empty house and especially those empty bedrooms." Time spent away has always seemed to get us through the most difficult situations. Crossing that time line between the accident and the year after seemed to lift a ten ton load off my shoulders. I still cannot explain the relief I felt in making it one year, a seemingly impossible task only months before.

Fong and I spend the last half of 1993 working diligently so that his girlfriend, Xinyu, could come from China to the United States. Two obstacles stood in her way: the Chinese government and the American government. Surprisingly, it turned out that Xinyu got her Chinese exit visa with little trouble, but months of effort failed to secure a student visa from our government. She was, unfortunately, trying to enter the country when most Americans were putting pressure on the government to limit the number of immigrants. With the help of several Kentucky Senators and Congressmen, Xinyu did get a call from the American Embassy in China on December 2, 1993, notifying her that she must come immediately to pick up her visa. She was advised to leave the country as soon as possible in case the Chinese government decided to cancel her exit visa. Thirteen days later, Xinyu boarded a plane in Shanghai and flew alone to the United States. Imagine a young Chinese girl, never having flown before, leaving her native country to fly over twenty hours to be reunited with her boyfriend. Xinyu and her parents knew that they might never see each other again. Once again, we marveled at the supreme sacrifice made by Chinese parents who want their children to be free. Finally there would be a joyous occasion for the Smith family. The look on Fong's face as he first saw Xinyu that night is beyond description. They had not seen each other in over five years, but that time seemed trivial as they raced into each other's arms. Even the passengers waiting to board planes later that night were in tears. They had seen this quiet young man clutching a dozen roses nervously pacing back and forth for over an hour. The object of his excited pacing had finally arrived!

Fong and Xinyu are an integral part of our family. They were married on April 22, 1994, in our Episcopal church in Beattyville. Fong graduated from the University of Kentucky and went on to complete his MBA degree at the Owens School of Business at Vanderbilt University. Xinyu graduated from David Lipscomb University in Nashville and is sitting for her CPA exam this year. Neither has ever returned to China; maybe they never will. Presently, they live in Nashville and had our first "grandchild", Andrew Robert Zhu, on November 22, 1997! Although their son was named for Drew, he will be called Andy ("Drew Zhu" seemed to rhyme a little too well). As I have said before, we believe Fong and Xinyu were sent to us by God from half way around the world.

Luther and I continued to explore ways to memorialize our sons. Our parental duty had not stopped with their deaths. True, the physical responsibilities of care had stopped but not the emotional ones. These two young men had lived…they <u>had</u> made a difference. Their lives were short, but we could not allow their memory to just fade away like a ship in the fog. Our love was stronger than death.

Our good friends, Dinah and Jim Taylor, presented us with a wonderful opportunity to memorialize our sons. Dr. Taylor is the president of Cumberland College in Williamsburg, Kentucky. Their only child, Young Jim, was killed in a car accident a year before Drew and Jeremiah. Cumberland College was building an inn which would contain a dome in the lobby. Luther and I commissioned an artist, Wayne Taylor, to paint this dome in memory of our sons and the other children in our bereavement group.

On June 11, 1994, the Cumberland Inn Dome was dedicated in the loving presence of many of our fellow bereaved parents and other guests. C. M. Dupier, Jr., a professor of Geography and Anthropology at Cumberland College gave the dedication address. Parts of it will always stick in my mind:

I can't think of anything that would have graced this lobby more beautifully or appropriately than a memorial to children loved and lost.

The artist who made this dream become reality is Wayne Taylor, an alumnus of Cumberland College, class of 1972. Wayne prayed over this work of art, asking God to inspire his vision and guide his hand as he interpreted the grief, the hope and the assurance felt by all who have lost children. Thank you Wayne for expressing the inexpressible.

The symbols contained in the painting were suggested by many of you, and each symbol has individual and special meaning. As I gaze upon this heavenly portrait I see things that you have seen, and perhaps some things that you have not. I would like to tell you what I see.

The cherubs are our children who are a little less than the angels, but nevertheless immortal.

The hearts are our hearts, and some have been pierced by the pain of loss.

The bird is the symbol of freedom which we long for to soar beyond doubt to faith.

The lightning bolt is the power that God had loosed in us to overcome and strike down the temptation to give in to faithlessness and hopelessness.

The daisies are for endurance. They live and grow all through the spring and summer, and bloom in the fall, as though they are saying to the chill of winter, "We shall over-come..."

The doves are for peace.

The star is for guidance.

And the roses are God's gift to us on blue and rainy days.

The horse, Pegasus, is our transport.

The rainbow is the promise that pain shall cease.

And the smiley face reminds us to celebrate life and seek joy in every moment; for joy is God's way of lighting the world for other pilgrims.

The butterflies. Oh, the butterflies! They tell us of meta-morphosis, the way life changes through time and eternity.

They show us the stages we must go through, the stages of life and the stages of grief. We start as eggs in mother's womb; we emerge as pupae, in need of mother's milk and the humanizing care of our parents. In the larval stage we wrap the cocoon of life's threads around us. Then, when that day comes, we emerge victorious over death and enter that final, eternal stage which is more beautiful than all the others.

That's what I see; perhaps you see more.

There is a veiled plaque on the wall. The plaque reads:

"What the caterpillar calls the end of the world, the Master calls a butterfly." (Richard Bach)

This dome has been an inspiration not only to many bereaved parents but to all the travelers who have stayed at the Cumberland Inn. God undoubtedly inspired Wayne Taylor in his artistic memorial to all of our children. Upon first seeing a photograph of the two cherubs Wayne was painting to represent Drew and Jeremiah for the dome, I was confused. Why had he given one of the cherubs the face of my deceased mother? How did he know my mother? None of the cherubs were to have the faces of actual children. A coincidence…or was it God's way of letting us know He was with us? Later, I found out that Wayne in fact had no knowledge of my mother. He was as astounded as I was with this revelation. As each member of my family viewed the photos, they all immediately asked why the image of my mother had been used instead of Drew or Jeremiah.

As I contemplated a name for this book, I mulled over name after name…nothing seemed right. My answer came several weeks later after I had a vivid dream about Jeremiah. In this dream he said authoritatively, "Mom, you know you have to name the book, *Children Of The Dome*!" Normally I do not remember my dreams but this one woke me with its importance. Yes Jeremiah, it would be called *Children Of The*

Dome.

Since 1994, Wayne has done another dome for our family. As you enter our new corporate building in Beattyville, a smaller dome towers above, a symbol of our sons and of the children of other parents who have experienced this loss. Yellow butterflies, the symbols of our sons and my mother, surround the cherubs like playmates.

Losing two children should qualify anyone from ever facing another of life's trials but each of us knows that is not the case. Luther and I had struggled with finding meaning in our lives in the three years since the children were killed. We felt like swimmers who had gone down twice but were on the verge of being rescued from drowning. Along with Jordan, we had come to realize that we could live again, we could be a family with hopes and times of joy. Suddenly, we were faced with another hurdle - my diagnosis of breast cancer in May of 1995. Admittedly, I did not handle this well at all at first. How could I face this fight when I was still barely surviving the loss of our sons?

Luther and I went to the beach to await the final diagnosis. We were both shaken to our very roots. As I sat railing at God for handing me yet another crisis, Luther just listened. He knew I needed to get past the initial shock and that I needed him there to support me. We sat in each other's arms facing the ocean, drawing strength from the powerful waves. Words cannot express how we faced this as a couple. When I chose to have a double mastectomy with total reconstruction, Luther supported my decision totally. I knew that my appearance was not what was important to him. We had been married twenty-five years and our love was much deeper than appearance.

My first surgery was performed on July 24, 1995, a day after the third anniversary of the deaths of our sons. At that point, none of my doctors knew about our loss. Only later did they learn that this was not the most devastating event in my life. Indeed, this surgery and the three subsequent ones were a breeze compared to what our family had endured since Drew and Jeremiah's accident.

My cancer was detected very early due to twice yearly mammograms as a result of my family history of breast cancer. Thankfully, I had no lymph node involvement so no chemotherapy or radiation was necessary. Maybe this diagnosis was a blessing in disguise because a later diagnosis, once the cancer was more advanced, may have greatly increased my chances for a recurrence. I can assure you that I didn't think this at first. I was angry…again. Maybe God gave me more time. Maybe I was given more time to write this book. I don't know. I can, however, say now with certainty that I have absolutely no fear of dying. Drew and Jeremiah's deaths have liberated me from that fear that I had harbored for so long. My mother fought for life because she was leaving her three children. Two of my children have preceded me and they are waiting for our reunion. That is nothing to be afraid of.

God works in mysterious ways. A traditional saying I have treasured states, "Coincidence is God's way of remaining anonymous." I have been the recipient of many of God's "coincidences". One blew across my life like the wind of God's spirit. It began as Luther and I were in Marco Island, Florida, for a national pharmacy conference in May of 1996, a year after my surgery. Combining our need for continuing education hours with a need to get away, we flew to Florida for the four day convention. After only attending two days of meetings, we rented a car and on a whim headed for Key West. Our plans did not include a five hour drive through the Florida Keys, but we did and loved it - the sun, the gorgeous scenery, the water stretching for miles as we drove over the bridges.

Since we had not been to Key West for many years, we had no idea where to stay. As we hastily checked out of the hotel on Marco Island, we asked the concierge to recommend a place for us in Key West. The Casa Marina was his favorite, so he made our reservations. The first morning after our arrival, I went to the pool very early to read and enjoy the sun. I have always felt rejuvenated by the sun, somehow more at peace with myself. No one was in the pool at this early hour, so I enjoyed my solitude. Within an hour I heard a splash and turned to see who had joined me. The boy in the pool had his back to me, and as he turned, I almost gasped. He looked exactly like Jeremiah at a young age. I could not take my eyes off him. His mannerisms brought so many memories flooding to the surface. Here was Jeremiah's twin on a day almost four years after his death.

I tried to read, but I could not tear my eyes away from this child. As his mother came over to check on him, I rose from my chair. Never even considering that I might be intruding, I asked her if this child was her son. Indeed, he was her only child, a ten year old from New Jersey. As I blurted out the story of Drew and Jeremiah and our loss, she cried with me. She and her husband had come to Key West through unusual circumstances. They were so kind and compassionate to me that morning.

Luther came down to the pool later that morning and shared the wonder of watching Nicholas romp in the pool. Tears streamed down our faces as we watched him. Later, we thanked God for this brief look back at Jeremiah at age ten. So often we had commented that Drew will never die as long as Jordan is alive. They are so alike. Now, we had caught a treasured glimpse of Jeremiah too. As we walked away from Nicholas, I silently bade him goodbye and said another goodbye to Jeremiah. I had to force myself to leave. I could have watched him for hours. The memory of this "coincidence" has lifted my spirits on many occasions.

Our son Jordan is a survivor. At age eleven he faced the loss of his two older brothers with such courage. He was the glue that kept our family from falling apart, quite a responsibility at his young age. As I wept night after night those first few months, he would try to comfort me by telling me that the boys were safe and in heaven. I know his heart was breaking, but he always tried to help us. Now, he was an only child. The two boys whom he had looked up to all his life were lost to him. Gone were the plans for their future together after his Dad and I were gone. Jordan was now alone. I can distinctly remember him asking me what he would do now that Drew and Jeremiah would not be there for all the holidays like Thanksgiving when he grew up. With whom would he share these family times? I told him that he would undoubtedly marry a girl with many brothers and sisters, and he could spend family times with them. That possibility exists, but I have learned to live one day at a time - not to look too far into the future.

Since our businesses were in Kentucky, Jordan started high school there. He did not attend The McCallie School as his brothers had. We could not let him go. We could not break up the family unit that had survived our loss. Although we felt Jordan was being shortchanged academically, we knew that emotionally he could not handle being a boarding student.

Jordan did well his freshman year, maturing so much as the year progressed. He was never challenged academically, so he just did the minimum required to pass his courses. Nothing was expected of him, so he put forth little effort. Maybe this was our fault, but this young man had been through so much. We admittedly let him slide that year and the first semester of his sophomore year.

By the end of that semester, we realized it was no longer in Jordan's best interest to remain in high school in Kentucky. We decided he would attend The McCallie School beginning the spring semester of 1997, not as a boarding student but as a day student. Luther and I bought a house in Chattanooga, and Jordan began classes in January.

My dream had always been for Jordan to attend McCallie. The natural order would have been for Jordan to follow his two brothers as four year boarding students at

McCallie, but the natural order had already been irretrievably upset. Our only logical choice was to go with Jordan to McCallie. Those first five months were a big sacrifice for Luther and myself. In our twenty-six years of marriage, we had never been apart. Now, Jordan and I would spend weekdays in Chattanooga while he was in class. Alternating weekends between Kentucky and Tennessee, we were able to maintain our close knit family. How hard this must have been for Luther. Being alone and having all the pressures of running our pharmacy corporation could not have been easy, but he did it. He did it for Jordan. We both dedicated all of our efforts to making sure Jordan was in a positive environment where he could grow both academically and spiritually. McCallie was the refuge we sought for him.

Jordan began his junior year this past September at McCallie. Luther is now in Chattanooga on a more permanent basis, and our family is reunited. To say that Jordan has grown at McCallie would be an understatement. Not only has he excelled academically, but he has taken advantage of the many extracurricular activities available. Drew and Jeremiah are smiling down at their little brother, I just know it. How proud they must be that he has done so well after all he has been through.

Being in Chattanooga and at McCallie has been difficult for Luther and me. There are ghosts of so many memories here. As I walk across campus, my mind wanders to those times when we would pick up the boys from McCallie Sports Camp each summer, to those fall Boarding Parents weekends when they were students, to Drew's graduation day. Memories so sweet but so painful. It must be hard for Jordan to walk in the footsteps of his brothers. Hopefully, he realizes that he is a unique person in his own right. Jordan has a maturity that few sixteen year old young men possess, more or less forced upon him by great personal loss.

Our story began as a love story and still is. Through

our years together Luther and I have had great joys and tremendous times of sorrow. When we married, we never dreamed
we would lose two children. I thank God that I did not know
this was to be our destiny. How could I have lived each day
knowing our boys would die so young? We have been blessed
with three wonderful children. Two are now in heaven, and
one remains with us. We are still a family. Death has not
changed that one important fact. We will, I believe, be reunited. We will spend eternity together after all of us have
lived our lives here on earth. Richard Bach once said, "Here's
a test to find whether your mission on earth is finished: If
you're alive, it isn't." Well, I am alive. My mission is not
finished. I will continue to love and support both Luther and
Jordan as long as I live. God continues to push me to help
other bereaved families. Our loss has developed our spiritual
muscles. We have been lifted to levels of understanding that
we may never have reached. We have used our tragedy to find
a way to help others.

Drew and Jeremiah died over six years ago. There has
not been a day that I have not missed them: missed the feel of
their hugs, missed their youthful exuberance, missed their
adventuresome spirit, missed their messy rooms and fights,
missed the promise of their futures, missed their love. I often
tell people that I now live in two worlds; one foot on this earth
and another with them in heaven. I feel their presence daily,
so in a way they have not left my side. Two recent incidences
exhibit their closeness. One took place the day before the sixth
anniversary of their deaths only weeks ago. Drew and Jeremiah
loved a red convertible that has been in our family for years.
In fact, one of our annual Christmas cards shows all three boys
lounging in this car with obvious glee. The clock in the car
has not worked in over two years. It always displays 12:15.
On the morning of July 22nd, I got in the car and for some
reason glanced at the clock. It was not 12:15. It was 9:15. For
some unexplained reason the hour hand had moved. I decided

to test Drew and Jeremiah. I said, "Boys, I am setting this clock to the correct time and if you are here make sure it works." Well, I set the clock for 9:51, the correct time and deliberately did not look at the clock until I reached my destination. When I did the time was correct! It is still working properly to this day nearly a month afterwards. The following morning was the sixth anniversary of Drew and Jeremiah's accident. Luther woke up early and was lamenting that he had awoken at 9:10 A.M., the exact time we had learned of their deaths six years previous. Later, as Luther was putting on his watch, he noticed that his very reliable watch had stopped. The time…9:10! A coincidence? No, our sons had graced us with their presence on another difficult day. Luther's watch started working again the next day. Our boys have little ways of letting us know they are with us.

The following was written by my husband, Luther, on May 16, 1995, in memory of our sons. A beautiful analogy from nature that helps him work through his grief:

The robin builds a nest in a tree outside our door. Why does she build it there? Probably to be near the safety of humans, away from predators such as hawks and snakes. Also, because there is a good food supply in our nearby pool so she can feed her young. I saw the intensity in her eyes that we all as parents have in ours - the protection and well being of our children. At their birth our purpose in life is transferred to their upbringing. That instinct and love totally consumes our lives. Our every conscious act is for their benefit and safety. Knowing that, how do we continue to live after their loss? We are in fact like the robin. We can only make decisions from our instincts. We cannot foresee the loss of our children, and when it happens, we must blame ourselves because their safety and welfare was our responsibility. In fact, we did follow every avenue for the happiness and safety of our children. There is nothing instinctively that can explain this tragedy in our lives, so we must turn to our faith and spirituality. We must develop a sense of destiny that our loss was what was supposed to be. We must allow our faith to become a guiding path for the rest of this life. This in no way means that we can give up or that life ceases to be. Simply, we must approach it from a different avenue from which we began. Our baby robins are about to fly away. They have outgrown their nest, and their Mom and Dad have done their duty. As human parents, our duty is never done - whether our young have flown away or simply left the nest.

Chapter Two
Jim Taylor

JIM TAYLOR

By Dinah Taylor

In the summer of 1967, I met my future husband Jim Taylor, whom I have always called "Taylor." We were both rising seniors, he at Cumberland College and I at the University of Kentucky. Destiny is defined as "what becomes of a person or thing in the end; one's lot or fortune; what will happen, believed to be determined beforehand in spite of all later efforts to change or prevent it." It was as if we were destined for each other and a life together; within two weeks of our first date we were engaged. We each finished our senior year at our respective schools and were married May 24, 1968, the day before Taylor graduated from Cumberland.

It was as if I was also destined to be a mother. I am from a very close-knit family of four children, each who were loved and nurtured by parents who always put the family and children first. I decided early on that I wanted to be a full-time Mom. After working with so many dysfunctional families as a social worker, I felt I was meant to be a "stay at home mom" and do the best that I could for my family.

After trying to become pregnant for more than a year, we were finally blessed with a pregnancy that almost ended when I was three months pregnant. After much prayer and hope for the future, Young Jim was finally born on July 26, 1972 — my sister Elaine's birthday.

Young Jim's birth was such an easy, exciting birth that I felt that having more children would be easy too — In 1976, however, at thirty years of age, I had to have a complete hysterectomy so Jim was our only child.

After repeated visits to the doctors, Jim, two months of age, was diagnosed with bronchial pneumonia. This was to be the beginning of bronchial allergies which would plague him for many years. Several times in the first years of his life

Young Jim almost died. Each time he would miraculously survive, so we became convinced that he was a survivor and would live forever since he was such a fighter. At six months of age, because Jim's legs and hips were not growing correctly, casts were placed on both of his legs. From that time until he was twelve, he wore corrective shoes and had to sleep with a bar between his legs each night. He fought this battle like any other.

When Jim was thirteen, he began having severe headaches, and we took him to every type of doctor imaginable – from neurosurgeons to chiropractors to acupuncturists. None seemed to find the cause of his headaches. When Jim was eighteen, it was discovered that the headaches were caused by tight muscles in his neck. Even though he was in constant pain, he was always quick to laugh, quick with a joke, and always loved life.

In 1980 Taylor became the president of Cumberland College, and we moved to the President's home. Our lives and destiny changed. Young Jim was the first child to live in the President's home which was built in 1906. Jim's first "official act" when we moved was to shoot out the post lights in front of our home with his B.B. gun. He was also a regular user of water balloons to the consternation of many. He loved rubber snakes and spiders and haunted the workmen with them.

Jim became the younger brother of our college students. Who could resist his beautiful, piercing blue eyes and the one dimple in which you could lose yourself? The students were great baby-sitters and became very good friends of his. Once I found a cleverly written essay of Jim's on How to Meet College Students in which he suggested that you throw a rope in a tree and then ask students to help you retrieve it.

Because Jim was such a gregarious person, he always wanted our extended family and others around. We have the good fortune of having the families of my sister and a brother and Taylor's brother living in our community, and so we have always been involved in each other's lives. Jim was very close to his cousin, Wayne, even though there was a twelve year age difference. Wayne was Jim's "big brother" and Jim often stayed with Wayne and his wife, Sissy, when Taylor and I were out of town. After he discovered horses, Jim spent his summers working at the farm. Lee, another cousin, was twenty-one months younger than Jim, and for the first eight years of Jim's life, lived across the street from him. Lee was the brother he never had.

Because of Young Jim's many health and learning problems, he and I became very close. When he was younger, I read to him constantly. Jim was a child that was always in-terested in what others were doing and wanted to be involved. When I cooked, he wanted to learn to cook and became quite proficient. When I made crafts, he wanted to be involved, and we have many "treasures" that he made through the years. After he began school, the evenings were spent in helping with his homework. I also became very involved with his school. I guess I was one of their worst nightmares. The night of his high school Baccalaureate, the principal of the school said that he thought I should also receive a diploma since I was in-volved with every aspect of his education.

Because of Taylor's position as president of the col-lege, Jim was able to see and do many more things than most children. Because he was an only child, he was included in all the many exciting events of the college. He met Jimmy Carter, Willard Scott, Carl Lewis, Helen Thomas, and many impor-tant people who are the "movers and shakers" of the financial world. He was truly blessed by the privileges that were af-forded him because of his father. We have found that memo-ries in our family are not made in front of the TV but are made by doing things unusual and different from ordinary life.

Young Jim's senior year in high school was so special for our family. It was as if we had to cram in as much togeth-erness as a family as we could, and those times together are our most treasured. We were no longer concerned that Jim would miss too much school, and the year was spent making memories. We took a trip to Washington, D.C., and the high-point of his life came when we met President Bush and the Secretary of Education in the Rose Garden of the White House. He also met our congressman and senator from Kentucky. How ironic I find it that we have a picture of him in front of the many crosses at Arlington Cemetery.

The day of his baccalaureate was spent helping Wayne with a roping clinic which was being given by Charlie Daniels' men of the Charlie Daniels Band at the farm. Jim was in hog heaven! When he came home that afternoon, he was filled with excitement and joy for having spent the day doing what he loved the most, riding horses and roping.

Baccalaureate night — Taylor had the great honor of delivering the Baccalaureate Address to Young Jim and his fellow classmates. His advice that night sounds like a premonition in retrospect. *If you make decisions based upon how comfortable, easy and painless your choices are, then don't expect great rewards... Turn tragedies into triumphs, obstacles into opportunities, problems into possibilities... Problems will never leave you where they find you... When a problem comes your way you'll never be the same... It's not the easy times; it's the hard times that make us and develop character. How do I know? I know because my life is a living testimony... Problems will never leave you where they find you. You will either be bigger or bitter.* Little did Taylor know that in less than 24 hours, he would have to begin to practice what he preached.

The following night was Honors Night when the students receive their awards. I made a quick telephone call to Wayne to see if he and his wife were going to the program. When Wayne answered, he told me that his wife, Sissy, had just left him. She had just that moment walked out of his house and his life. When I told Young Jim, he was devastated. Sissy was like his big sister, his partner in crime, the person who signed him out of school when we were out of town so he could ride horses. Jim's first statement was, "I have to be with Wayne." I reminded him that this was his Honors Night, and he replied, "You don't understand — I have to be with Wayne." With that caring statement and the words we always repeated before leaving home, "I love you" Jim left the shelter of our home and was gone.

Within the half hour, as I was talking to my sister-in-law to explain to her why we were not going to Jim's Honors Night, I heard an ambulance with its blaring siren go by our home. I made the prophetic comment, "I hope that isn't Young Jim." Fifteen minutes later Marie Paul, our coroner's wife, came to our home and asked for Taylor. The instant I saw her I knew that it was about Young Jim, and he was dead. She would not confirm my nightmare until I insisted — She said it was true. She had been trying to find Taylor who was out walking around the campus. A few minutes later he came home, and I had to tell this devoted father that our worst nightmare was reality. "Our son is dead." "How can this be? This night, Jim's high school graduation, is a milestone! This night was to end his life in the nucleus of our small town, Williamsburg, and as a student in high school, and it was to begin a life in the great big, exciting world of adulthood! How can his life here on earth end on such a special night? Why can't he live to have this wonderful adventure?" These are just a few of the questions that were asked on the night that our lives, as parents, ended. It would take many months before we realized that Jim is now on an adventure of a lifetime. How ironic that each of our first words of response to Young Jim's death were, "Now he won't have any more headaches." We instantly felt that Jim was safe and happy.

Jim was approximately three miles from home when the accident occurred. He wasn't doing anything wrong. His mission was to go and comfort the cousin he loved so dearly.

He was driving approximately twenty-five miles per hour when the right wheels of his automobile slipped off the pavement. The road had eroded to the point there was no shoulder and huge poles had been placed at the edge of the road to keep it from eroding any further. The police surmised that because of the slow rate of speed, his car had careened over the edge of the road and had fallen onto a pole. The pole had gone through the right front passenger window, out the back, left window and had just, by an inch, grazed his right temple, causing instant death.

The "If onlys" began and continued (and continue to crop up seven years after the tragedy). If only Sissy hadn't left her marriage, if only I had not made the telephone call. If only Jim had not been such a loving, caring person, if only we had gone with him, if only it had not rained that day, if only the state highway department had either placed a guardrail there or had repaired the road. If there had been a guardrail, the police felt that he wouldn't have even been injured. If only! If only! But these "If onlys" cannot change what happened.

Six weeks after Jim's death, I began keeping a journal and continue to write in it each day. It is a time of reflection, a method of recording memories and my thoughts, questions, and frustrations. It is also a "conversation" with Jim and a chronology of my grief. I'm glad I kept such a record because I often felt that my grieving was digressing rather than progressing. During those times, I could reread the first journals and realize that I was much further along than I would have imagined.

In August of 1992, I wrote two new fellow travelers, Luther and Rosemary Smith, who were to become our dearest friends. July 23, 1992, ended the lives of two of their precious sons, Drew and Jeremiah. I wrote them and included a Grief Workbook that had meant so much to me. There are never adequate words to convey your thoughts, but I wanted them to know that I empathized with them and they were in my thoughts and prayers. Luther and Rosemary are action-oriented people, and so Rosemary telephoned me, and we became instant soul mates.

Even from the depths of their own grief, the Smiths began reaching out to other parents who had just recently lost children. Rosemary has the charisma to telephone strangers and to say just the right words that help these grieving parents realize they are not alone, and they will survive as they travel through the agonizing journey of grief. Rosemary continues to do this wonderful work and gives the parents' names to me, and they then become members of this group called "fellow travelers." None of us would have chosen to become members of this shattered group of parents, but we are so fortunate to have each other. I have found that in the loss of a child, all barriers are broken down and your fellow travelers become your support and strength. The Smiths have made a great difference in our lives as they have with all who have contact with them. They are priceless treasures.

As the names of fellow travelers became greater in number, I realized that I would not be able to continue to correspond in this same manner, so I decided to write a letter such as people send to their friends at Christmas. The letter was duplicated and mailed. As I shared Young Jim with them, these parents began to share their children with me. The letter began to grow and took on a life of its own. I then decided to make it a newsletter and, call it LAMENTATIONS, because that was truly what we were doing, lamenting over the loss of our precious children.

Soon after Young Jim's death, I realized that, unconsciously, I was collecting angels and wearing more horse jewelry and accessories. I felt this kept Jim near me all through the day. Soon after this realization, I declared that a Pegasus would be Young Jim's symbol and encouraged other parents to adopt a symbol to represent their child.

The College has constructed a beautiful hotel which is

named Cumberland Inn, and it was a dream of Taylor's many years before it was erected. He designed it, and he and I had the great fortune of decorating and designing the dome which is in the lobby of the lodge. Luther, Rosemary and Jordan Smith gave this dome in memory of Drew and Jeremiah, and it contains cherubs and symbols of our children. It is an awe-inspiring sight as you enter the foyer of the hotel. This dome was dedicated at a picnic in 1994 by fellow travelers. Jim and Judy Rose gave the piano in the lodge in memory of their son, Scott, and Young Jim. There are also bricks at the entrance of the lodge which have been placed there in memory of many of our children. As people enter, they are reminded of our children.

My mother was in a nursing home when our son died. When she was told of Young Jim's death, she wanted to know why it couldn't have been her death rather than his. Mother was hospitalized August 30, 1993. In my journal dated that day, I wrote: *Afternoon Mother had no response, and only once opened her eyes, but she didn't see me. It was as if she were looking through me. Night. Mother was alert and responded to us, but the only word she could say was "Yes." She smiled and kept winking at me, and you could tell she wanted to talk but couldn't.* Mother had had a stroke and could no longer speak. September 3 & 4: *Today we lost our past (both parents are now dead) as we lost our future when you (Jim) were killed. Ralph (my brother) and I were so blessed of being able to talk to mother and share in her dying.*

Prior to this, Mother had not been able to speak, so when she began to speak, I knew she was dying. Mother started pointing and staring to the right of her field of vision. She kept saying "It's impossible", and looked at me and asked if it was possible and I told her it was. I was assuming that she was saying that it was impossible for her to die because we were keeping her here. My brother and I "gave her permission" to die, and close to the end, she said, "It's possible." During her monologue, Mother would cock her head as if she were listening to something, so I asked her who she saw. She responded: "Jim, Jr." She said that he was riding on a horse. She then said, "He is proud of you." I asked her "Why?", and she listened and then said, "For what you do with parents." My mother did not know that I wrote a newsletter for parents who have lost children because our conversations during the last year of her life did not permit that much detail as to what was happening. Yet, now she knew. I am certain Young Jim appeared to her as she had said.

My mother gave me the most prized gift she could have ever given — a dying gift of knowing that my family is together as we will all be for eternity. She also "saw" my father (directly in front of her) and she "saw" her father to her left. Mother kept mentioning "5-20" and so we assumed she thought she was going to die at 5:20. She almost died that afternoon at 5:20, but didn't. Mother stopped talking and lapsed into a coma. I stayed with her all night — the hospital personnel were surprised that mother was lingering. The following morning my brother stayed with Mother while I went home to shower. Mother passed away after I left her room. It was as if she was waiting for me to leave. After Mother's death I was talking with my sister-in-law and telling her of this number, 5-20, and she suggested that it may be a date. It hit me like a lightning bolt — Young Jim died on 5-20-91!

After Jim's death Taylor and I busied ourselves with anything and everything to occupy our time. I have found that the more idle time I have, the more all-consuming and detrimental is my grief. With Jim being our only child, we feel that it is up to us to make sure that he is remembered, and if these remembrances are not permanent, he might be forgotten after our deaths.

Taylor and I have often stated that we have been blessed by loving and supportive family, treasured friends and the honor of being at Cumberland College and receiving all the many opportunities it has offered. In July of 1991, the trustees of Cumberland voted to name the proposed football stadium after Young Jim. Taylor started our football program in 1985, and Jim was the first ball boy. September l0, 1994, The James Taylor, II Stadium became a reality.

The summer of 1993 found both Taylor and I hospitalized at the same time at the University of Kentucky Medical Center in Lexington, Kentucky. Thankfully we were both discharged on the same day which was ironically July 26th, Young Jim's birthday. As we entered our bedroom back in Williamsburg that day, the light on Taylor's side of the bed blinked on and then off. This was the first sign from our son. I remember telling Taylor that Young Jim was telling us that we were both okay and that he was right here with us.

Exactly a year went by before we experienced another light incident. As we approached Jim's birthday in the summer of 1994, I had been feeling that he was gone from me. I felt empty. I knew I'd never forget him but felt like he had forgotten me. As if he knew my thoughts, the light beside Taylor's side of the bed blinked off then on again on his birthday.

Since that day in July of 1994, the light incidents have comforted us on many occasions. Several times my sister Elaine has had similar incidences while staying at our home while we traveled on college business. It always involves the same light, the one by Taylor's side of our bed. Recent occurrences have involved times when our entire family is in our home. Living in the public president's house precludes that our bedroom serves as our private living room on family occasions. Young Jim loved family times and company and invariably lets his presence be known.

Shortly after Young Jim's death, Taylor made the prophetic statement that perhaps Young Jim was destined to have an even greater influence in death than he might have had if he had lived. Destiny has brought us to our knees, but destiny also will help us rise again. Until our own deaths we will do as much as we can to be sure Young Jim is remembered. We are truly blessed to have our family, our friends, the people we know and the good fortune of living at a college where we have many "children." God gave us Jim and each other, and for that we will always be thankful. Young Jim was the best of both of us. When we remember our son, we will always remember him with a smile.

My husband Jim wrote the following letter after Young Jim's death to the people who had extended their sympathy to us:

Dear Friend,
As I write this letter, I'm reminded of St. Barton's Ode: "I am hurt but not slain. I will lie down and bleed awhile — then I will rise and fight again." Since the death of our only child Jim, my wife and I have been sustained by the thoughts and prayers, the warmth and sensitivity of people like you.

At a time like this, the only thing I know to do is to keep extremely busy; it seems to help. During the past week as I talked with one gentleman, he said: "I understand that Jim was your only child and that with his passing you will no longer have any children." I responded gently by saying:. "No, that's not exactly true, for you see, Dinah and I are like Mr. Chips, we have thousands of children and they all happen to be located at Cumberland College." With the passing of our son, our only child, I suppose that is the way it will be for us. We shall never get over our loss, but time helps us deal constructively with the pain. After all, suffering develops character, and I'm told it even helps purify the soul.

I served as the speaker at our son's baccalaureate on the evening before his death, and I mentioned to the graduating class that problems will never leave you where they find you. That once a problem comes your way, you will never be the same. It's impossible because you'll either be bigger or bitter and a person's attitude will be the determining factor. Thank you so much for your warmth and sensitivity, Jim

Chapter Three
Peggy and Denis O'Connor

PEGGY AND DENIS O'CONNOR
"The Inseparable Duo"

By Elaine E. Stillwell

On a rainy, cold January night in 1983, I met my soul-mate, Joe, at a local dance sponsored by Divorced and Separated Catholics. Both of us had survived painful divorces and annulments, his in 1971 and mine in 1982. Because he had been "out there" a while, he jokingly said, "I rescued you!" And he did! His strong, loving presence made me feel so protected and cherished and added such a happy note in the life of my three teenagers, Denis, Peggy, and Annie, that I felt I had died and gone to heaven. After a year and a half of blissful courtship, we were married in our local church on a beautiful July evening, surrounded by our five teenagers, friends, and family. The life we had been searching for seemed to spring alive and all our dreams meshed together in blessed contentment, occasionally disturbed by "teenage syndrome." I continued to teach little third graders in the next town, and Joe kept American Airlines' Air Freight in good shape a few miles away at JFK Airport. Denis and Peggy went off to college; Annie enjoyed the last years of high school; Joe's sons joined us occasionally, and our puppy, Mickey, watched over all of us.

Two beautiful years went by. Life was happy and bright, and the children were blossoming. We were surviving the occasional hand wringing times of teenage hood, and we joked that the honeymoon would begin soon when all three children would be away at college. The phone rang constantly night and day; friends ran in and out; noise and clutter abounded, and the dog checked on each of us and barked at strangers. As I nagged our brood to get their rooms clean, do household chores, drive carefully, come home at a decent hour, get up on time, recycle the cans, and hit Mass on Sunday, I

79

didn't realize how precious each moment was. The laughter, the teasing, and the latest gossip and chatter were exhilarating. Life was wonderful, exciting and loving.

During the summer of '86, my three children were busy with their summer jobs and eagerly trying to save money for college in the fall. Denis, a twenty-one year old lifeguard "on the eight year plan," as he called it, was ready to begin his junior year at Northeastern University in Boston, studying International Relations; nineteen- year- old Peggy was working in the County Probation Department, looking forward to returning to her beloved University of Dayton, where she would be a junior pursuing psychology and enjoying her Lambda Nu sorority sisters. Eighteen-year-old Annie, fresh out of high school, was counting the days to begin her freshman year at Loyola College in Maryland, while she waitressed at Swensen's Ice Cream Parlor making more money than her brother and sister, much to their disdain. I, too, was thoroughly enjoying the summer, teaching two summer school classes each morning and then returning home to enjoy the freedom of my vacation or to catch up on my eternal list of things to do.

On the night of August 1st, Denis had three tickets to attend an outdoor concert at the Jones Beach Theatre about twenty minutes from home. Because Annie had to work that night and Denis' girlfriend decided not to go because she had to work on the 4:30 A.M. shift at the golf course, Denis and Peggy, a life-long inseparable duo, went together. Denis sold the third ticket to a fellow lifeguard. With raindrops on the windshield, off they went at 7:00 P.M. looking forward to a music-filled evening. The night was hazy and drizzly with poor visibility, but the show went on.

Suddenly, at 3:30 A.M., the shrill ringing of the phone woke me from a dead sleep. I was informed by my former husband, Denis, Jr., that our son had been in an auto accident and taken to a local hospital. Would I please come right away?

I inquired about Peggy, but nobody seemed to know anything about her. I figured she had met friends at the concert and gone on with them, as kids do. Thinking Denis had a broken arm or leg, (nothing life-threatening even crossed my mind), my husband and I prepared to leave for the hospital. Annie wanted to come with us, but we asked her to wait at home in case Peggy called.

Fifteen minutes later, the three of us reached the emergency room and found Denis being prepared for brain surgery! He was a strapping 6-foot-3 inch young man in great physical shape. Looking at him as he lay there so still, I wondered if he would be better in time for college next month. He had a few glass cuts, which the emergency team had cleaned, and I thought he was so big and strong that he could come through anything.

As I signed the papers, I asked again where Peggy was, and the doctor said that she was at the scene of the accident. Naively, I said, "How silly Peggy was to stay and guard Denis' car, his pride and joy, when she should have ridden in the ambulance with him to the hospital."

With unbelieving eyes the doctor looked at me and said, "She didn't make it."

It took me several minutes to realize that Peggy wasn't here because she was dead and that she was "at the scene of the accident" waiting to be taken to the morgue! She was the heart of my heart, my precious free spirit, the sunshine of my life. My heart broke as I clung to my husband, but I was soon whisked away to meet the surgeon who would operate on my son.

Standing in the hospital hallway, surrounded by state police, priest, doctors, nurses and other medical personnel, we learned that at 1:10 A.M. our children's car had smashed into an open drawbridge, with no other vehicle involved and no observers present. Knowing that our son knew the road well, driving that route every day to his job at the beach, that he was a good driver, and that no drugs or alcohol were involved, our whole beings screamed for an answer. Was it the dim bridge lighting or the poor visibility due to the fog and rain? We'll never know. The uncanny part was that had they not had the lifeguard friend to pick up and take home, they would never have been on that fateful bridge!

As Denis was rushed to emergency surgery to relieve the pressure on his brain, Joe and I returned home to tell Annie the tragic events of the night and then to proceed to the morgue to identify our beautiful Peggy. The eeriness of seeing Peggy lying there behind a glass enclosure and pull-type curtains, of not being allowed to reach out to touch her or hug her, the awfulness of not hearing her call out, "I love you," as she did each morning from her bed, and of not seeing her smile all combined to add to our devastation. After we left the morgue, we stopped at home to make a few phone calls and then the three of us returned to the hospital to await the completion of Denis' brain surgery. We were told that the next forty-eight hours would be crucial so forces of friends and family took their turns with us at Denis's side in intensive care. Meanwhile, Denis' father, Joe and I made funeral arrangements and I wrote this funeral liturgy for Peggy.

MARGARET MARY O'CONNOR
August 23, 1966 - August 2, 1986

Who would know Peggy and not smile? She brought laughter, happiness, and a sense of humor with her wherever she went. Her sense of caring and concern, her big heart, touched so many in her short life. She reached out to all ages, infants to old folks, and they all felt her warmth and sincerity. She was a beautiful free spirit enjoying her colorful outfits, dangling jewelry, and big pocketbooks. She truly relished life and loved being Irish. Expressing her thoughts verbally or in writing was her forte and choosing just the right card was her specialty. She had a knack for expressing exactly how she felt in a concise, humorous style that endeared her to you. She bared her soul to Denis III and shared her soul with Annie; she spoiled our dog, Mickey, and he was her shadow.

Peggy loved parties, staying up late, shopping, celebrations, Christmas, balloons, crepe paper, and tradition. She was loyal to the core and had an innate sense of fairness. She was a good friend. She made mistakes but would always say, "I'm sorry!" Attending the University of Dayton, living in "The Ghetto" there, being a member of Lambda Nu Sorority, and deciding on a psychology major were joys to her. Whether babysitting, working at the A&P, Nassau Beach, the Probation Department, or just being your friend, she joked and laughed and made you feel the happiness in her soul. People responded to her twinkling green eyes, that impish smile, her famous dimple on the chin, and those unforgettable freckles! We cherish our memories of "Peggy O" and will never forget her sensitive, fragile, beautiful, loving spirit.

A devoted bevy of friends and relatives manned our kitchens, answered the phone, fed us, walked the dog, did errands, ironed clothes, picked up people at the airport, dried our tears and never left Denis alone at the hospital as we raced between funeral parlor and intensive-care unit. The hospital staff kindly looked the other way as Joe, Annie, Denis and I visited at all kinds of weird hours. Denis had been operated on in the early hours of Saturday morning, but as we struggled through Peggy's wake on Sunday and Monday and her funeral on Tuesday, he remained in a coma with no progress noted.

Burying Peggy next to my mother, whom she was named after, helped my heart a lot. The idea of sharing her with my mother who had died eighteen years before eased my pain. I knew Peggy would be in very loving hands and that she wouldn't be alone. It made it easier for me to leave the cemetery that day. Following the funeral, guests returned for lunch to our home, where Denis, Joe, Annie, and I were surrounded by our families and friends, meshing our past and present lives together. As the last one left at 5:00 P.M., we washed our faces and returned to our bedside vigil with Denis, III.

I don't know if the doctors already knew the hopelessness of our son's case and perhaps attempted to give us time to assimilate all that had happened, but early on Wednesday morning, the day after we buried Peggy, they performed some neurological tests on Denis and later that day declared him brain dead.

Denis' college roommate, who had never left his side in the intensive care unit, whispered to me, "I believe Denis chose to escort Peggy to Heaven." That single thought, knowing they were together as they loved to be, kept me going. In an attempt to keep this tragedy from having happened in vain, we agreed to donate Denis' tissue and organs to help other people live. It helped our hearts to know that part of him lived on, especially those piercing green eyes. We only regretted that we had never had the chance to do that with Peggy.

After a prayer service beside his bed and our individual good-byes, we began all over again to plan a funeral and liturgy that would reflect our son's thoughts, feelings and special interests. Again, I dug deep into my soul for words to tell the world how special this son was to me. I was exhausted, in shock, and tied up with a myriad of details. The phone never stopped ringing, but somehow God gave me the strength to meet the 7:00 P.M. deadline for the printing of the Mass booklet. As hard as it was to write my thoughts about Denis, because I never dreamed he would die, it actually helped me to pour out my raw feelings of love in my eulogy for him.

DENIS EDWARD O'CONNOR, III
February 4, 1965 - August 6, 1986

The first born, the big brother, the only son, named after grandfather and father, curly blond hair, piercing green eyes, sun burnt nose, and infectious smile; he made his own mold. Social studies, history, the Civil War, Germany, English Literature, cooking, and concerts were his special interests. Fishing, surfing, skiing, and camping fed his love of the outdoors. Swimming, soccer, and lacrosse filled his life with that competitive zest. But music was his spirit. He had a charm that could move all ages, a wit that could keep you entertained for hours, a smile that could not be forgotten, and a love of life that would make you feel how great it was to be young. He belonged to the fraternity of lifeguards. Friends were his anchors, Samantha was his love, Peggy was his pal, and Annie was the one he loved to tease.

Denis loved life, being on the go, traveling, getting together with friends, and talking 'til the wee hours of the morning. He was a loyal fan of football pools, the Mets, the Islanders, Notre Dame, and the horse "My Boy Dennis." Surf shirts, crazy hats, and sunglasses were his trademark. He was surrounded with golf clubs, lacrosse sticks, stereo tapes, records, and whatever else he could fit into his car. He was getting ready to enter his junior year at Northeastern University in Boston, majoring in International Relations. We will not forget Denis' wit, his talent doing imitations, his fantastic memory of cartoons, his love of gourmet food and of his sisters' homemade cookies, his collection of Hummel Christmas balls, his pride in being in great physical shape, his surfboard, his puppy dog, his bear hugs, and his "gift of life" to others.

With an honor guard of lifeguards and our local priests and bishop at the altar, we buried Denis with Peggy and added his name to the scholarship at the University of Dayton so their memories could remain together.

Again our relatives and friends returned to our home for lunch and mutual support. After serving lunch, cleaning up and restoring things to order, all our caretakers left us. Denis went home and Annie joined some friends. As Joe and I sat in the living room, thoroughly exhausted, we looked at each other and wondered, "Where do we begin?" It was a terrifying feeling trying to imagine how we would go on living, much less make dinner that night. We needed a caretaker to ease us into our new life, but there was no one there as we began our journey. For seven days we had been pampered and ministered to, and now we were on our own, devastated and in pain.

Mustering up all the energy I could, I did some last minute shopping to get Annie ready for college. My heart broke for her as she prepared to go 200 miles away without a support system nearby and surrounded by total strangers, Three blurry weeks later, we drove her to Maryland to begin her freshman year of college. About to begin the honeymoon we had so often joked about, I cried all the way home. The pain went to the very core of my being. My heart felt as if it had been put into a vice. Tears flowed without even thinking about them. Getting up in the morning took every bit of energy I had. Peggy and Denis haunted every thought in my head. It didn't seem possible that my body could endure such incredible pain.

Joe, whom I call my "blotter," dried my tears and gave me strength by listening to my heart's cries and putting no demands on me, letting me work out my own time schedule. As stepfather to my children, he hadn't invested as many years of love in them as I had, but he grieved with me because he loved me so much. My pain became his pain. His hugs made me feel needed and alive. From them, I learned you need four hugs a day for survival, eight hugs a day for maintenance, and twelve hugs a day for growth. Peggy and Denis were vibrant, fun and loving, and we honor them every time we carry on "their traditions." We feel better for it because it keeps them alive in our hearts and keeps their memory from somehow being erased.

Networking by word of mouth, phone, letters, and conferences, we have met people all over the United States. Our story has appeared in a number of books, and by speaking on grief issues and writing articles, we have shared Peggy and Denis with the world, thus keeping their memories very much alive. Though the pain never completely goes away, it does lessen and becomes part of your life. Of course, we never know what will trigger tears or a bad day. They happen. But tears are healing, so we shed them and start all over again. Some days are wonderful and some are the pits; we learn to live with that.

We learn to tell our friends and family what we need to survive because they don't automatically know. We learn to do what gives us peace of mind; we learn the activities that we can handle and how to surround ourselves with the people who make us feel comfortable. We sadly lose some old friends and happily find some new ones who let us set our own time-tables. We do a lot of things differently and make new memories; we talk about our children; we thank God for the good days and live through the tough ones. We learn to turn to our mate and communicate no matter how hard it is so we don't get isolated and lonely. We also learn that "helping is healing", and the more we reach out to other hurting people, the stronger and more at peace we become. We discover we are new people, because we will never be the same again, as we rearrange our priorities.

I feel Peggy's and Denis' presence very much. They live in my heart and are a part of everything I do. When I pray to them for help, they are quick to respond in a very uplifting way. They bring good weather, find parking spaces for me on crowded streets, and send peace when I feel agitated. I've shed my tears and suffered my bad days and even twelve years later find it's not all smooth sailing, but I've built a good life that is meaningful, and the special love I have for Peggy and Denis has not been wasted, but rather reinvested in many ways that come back a hundred-fold to my family and me. By sharing Peggy and Denis with the world, whether by talking or writing, our hearts are deeply touched by the people who have never met them but tell us they feel they know them.

I am teaching a different audience now than the third graders. My time is devoted to writing and speaking on bereavement issues. One special story, The Widows' Chain and Butter, from After Goodbye, by Ted Menten always touches my audiences. *

THE WIDOWS' CHAIN AND BUTTER

One of the most devastating emotions after the death of a loved one is the feeling of isolation. The great loss of connection is very often coupled with a sense of being abandoned by the one most loved and trusted. In this widows' group, each member is in a different stage of grief in their journey back to life. As a symbolic ceremony, they form a chain with those newly bereaved at the end of the chain. Using this chain, they start bringing each other forward with a symbolic tug. Motion is the only way out of grief. When people feel that they want to get back into life, this is a good way to get going. The process forges a strong chain of healing—link by link.

At the end of this group's meeting, they were asked to hold hands and do an exercise of remembrance, which lets them honor the one they love by saying one word that brings back a memory of that person. The memory word did not have to be explained to the group; it was like a secret code word for which only they knew the real, true meaning. The list of "magic" words: hamburgers, ocean, Rover, chocolate, Babe, etc., essentially expressed the same thing - a remembrance that gives both pleasure and comfort, the comfort of release. It is always just one word that says it all. And that word always means exactly the same thing: "I love you and I miss you."

Rachel had been a widow less than a year. After a few months of devastating mourning - she seldom got out of bed before noon and almost never left the house – she reluctantly came to our widows' group. Silently, she listened and observed without joining in. When we spoke our closing words of "remembrance", she remained outside the circle. She left abruptly, with a simple thank you to the group, and I thought that was the last we'd ever see her.

The following week Rachel appeared again as if nothing had happened. Once again she observed the group in silence, and once again she remained detached and aloof. At the end she thanked us and left. I wondered if she would return, and she did.

In time, she became part of the group. But when the chain was formed at the closing, she was always at the end - by her choice. Even after three months, she kept assigning herself the last link. Others who had joined the group after her were moving along. But Rachel insisted she was still at the end of the chain.

One Wednesday night, the subject was honoring and remembering how, after our loved one has died, we can remember and honor them with our life and our living. Susan had just begun to talk about some of her memories of her husband when Rachel suddenly stood up and started shouting.

"Stop it! Stop it!" she screamed at us. "Stop talking about remembering. I hate that!...What's the matter with you all? How can you talk about remembering? Where's your pain?" She stopped suddenly and faced me directly. "Don't you get it? I don't want memories - I want my husband!"

It was a truth we all knew and lived with, but seldom spoke of. It was the very core of our grief. A memory is a poor substitute for the real thing. A memory can't hold you in its arms or fill you with pleasure, or laugh at your jokes or pitch a ball, or brag about your cooking and fight back unfairly, or surprise you on your birthday. In a world where the living are diamonds, memory is a paste imitation - a lackluster copy of the gleaming original. No one wants a memory. We all want the real thing.

Rachel raged on for a few minutes more, and then faced with our stunned silence, she sat down, hands folded primly in her lap, and waited for us to respond. I wondered who would answer her, and hoped it wouldn't have to be me because I didn't believe I had the words. Thankfully, Barbara did.

"For weeks now Rachel, you've assigned yourself the last link in the chain and we let you. We let you because all of us have been there and don't really want to admit that we are moving along - making progress. Moving along seems like forgetting. Moving along seems like infidelity. Moving along says 'I have stopped caring and loving.' So we let you stay there for your own good and your own comfort. But tonight, dear friend, you have moved forward and you have brought us with you. You have said the words we all fear and hate and opened all the old wounds we thought were healing. Your rage gives meaning to your love and to ours."

She reached out her hand to Rachel. "Not one of us wants to settle for less than the real thing, but the real thing is gone. Margarine isn't the real thing. Butter is. But if there is no butter, then you make do with the next best thing. I don't want my life to be dry toast. I want it covered with rich golden butter. But my butter is gone, and all I have left is the memory of its richness, its pure golden quality, its sweet taste. The margarine of memory will never, ever, replace or even approximate the real thing. But, Rachel, it is far better than dry toast!"

"Stewart is dead, Rachel, dead and buried and gone. Forever. Your butter is gone, just like mine is, and everyone else's in this room. All you have to do - all you can do now - is decide if you want the rest of your life to be dry toast."

In silence we all examined the loss of rich, golden butter in our lives and knew that it was the prospect of a life of dry toast that had brought us here together. There, in our group, we shared our recipes for a life, using margarine.

That night as we held hands and closed with our one word memory, I asked Rachel to start.

"Butter," she intoned.

90

"Butter."

"Butter."

"Butter."

And I completed the circle, whispering, "Butter."

* Reprinted with the Publisher's Permission from: Running Press Book Publishers, 125 South 23rd Street, Philadelphia, PA., from the book after Goodbye by Ted Menton (ISBN # 1561382957) pages 107 - 114

Chapter Four
Myra Stamper

MYRA STAMPER

By Peggy Stamper

I met by husband Gene in 1959 while I was working at Wolfinbarger Pharmacy in Beattyville, Kentucky. The fountain at Wolfinbargers was a gathering place for the locals in our small town, and Gene had come in for coffee after his return from the Air Force. After we dated for about nine months, we were married on June 25, 1960 and began our lives together.

We had several moves early in our marriage that took us first to Winchester, Kentucky, where we both attended Vocational school as newlyweds. Jobs were so scarce in Eastern Kentucky that we moved to Middletown, Ohio, afterwards to find jobs. Gene's aunt and uncle lived there, and as many young couples did during those years, we lived with them until we found work. We only lived in Middletown about six months, and during that time I became pregnant with our first child. We both were excited with this pregnancy and decided on another move, this time to Pontiac, Michigan, before the birth of our baby.

Between our move to Pontiac, we had returned home to Beattyville to be with our families during the Christmas of 1965. We were excited about our move to Michigan because there were many jobs available there and we were going to have our first child. On the last day of December, we began our drive to Michigan. Although the winters are cold in Kentucky, we were not at all prepared for the extreme cold that met us in Michigan. I have vivid memories of that trip when at one point our right headlight went out, and I had such a hard time seeing the road signs off to the right. After we stopped and had the headlight fixed, our way seemed much brighter. Full of excitement, we arrived safely at the home of my aunt and uncle who like Gene's family before welcomed us into their home until we found jobs.

Jobs were so plentiful in Pontiac at that time that we couldn't even find an apartment until the beginning of March. Gene had found work immediately at Pontiac Motors where he joined my uncle on the night shift. My aunt and I were left to find us an apartment because the men had to sleep during the day. We would check the newspaper ads early each day and finally found an apartment in a home that was perfect for us. We settled down to wait the birth of our child.

When it came time for me to go to the hospital for the birth, I went with my aunt and not Gene. As most young families do, we needed the money, so Gene went on to work. I tried to be brave and did pretty well at first, but my labor went on for hours. I remember looking up, and Gene was there. I found out later that one of the nurses had called him at work to come to the hospital. After 36 hours our son, Mark Anthony, was born. This was May 6, 1966, and our first born and only son was to live only 32 hours. Even after an autopsy, there was never a cause of death for Mark Anthony. The doctors kept using the term "delayed labor", but we will never know why our son died. I was never allowed to hold my son. My hands physically hurt from the longing to hold him. To this day, I can remember the loss I felt.

I was still in the hospital when Gene brought our son back to Beattyville from Michigan to be buried. The pictures we have of him are my only memories of this precious child. He was a beautiful, dark headed baby who looked so healthy. Back then no one discussed the loss of a child so we were left alone to grieve the loss of our son.

Two months after Mark Anthony's death, I also went to work at Pontiac Motors on the night shift. Both Gene and I wanted a child so badly. We were naturally worried about me getting pregnant again, but the doctors had assured us that there was no reason a second pregnancy would turn out like the first. I did become pregnant again, and we gradually began to quit worrying and enjoy our good news.

Our second child was born on March 8, 1968, in the same hospital in Pontiac, Michigan. Myra Lynn Stamper was a beautiful baby girl born on a March Michigan day so unusually warm that the nurses had to open the windows in our room yet two days later as we were taking Myra home, Pontiac had eight inches of snow! Myra's birth had been so different from Mark's. I had been in labor only six hours with no complications. Our daughter was healthy, and we felt so lucky as we took her home.

Myra was such a precious child. Gene was very protective of her from the beginning. He always called her "Daddy's Sweetheart." Our lives revolved around Myra who was destined to be our only child. She walked late mainly because we had slick floors in our apartment, and her dad wouldn't put her down on them because she might fall. We didn't take her out much after her birth in March because it was too cold and then not much in the summer because of the heat. We thought that if we kept Myra at home with us, we could protect her and keep her safe. The loss of Mark Anthony always played a part in how we treasured Myra.

When Myra was nineteen months old, we moved back to Beattyville. We had lived in a nice neighborhood in Pontiac, but the schools there already had police patrolling them, so we decided to move. Most of our relatives lived in Kentucky, and like most young couples, we were homesick.

In May of 1972, we bought the only dry cleaners in Beattyville which we own to this day. I had not worked at all since Myra's birth but did when we bought this business. I did not like to leave Myra with a baby sitter, so I took her with me to the dry cleaners. We tried to always have her where we could protect her. We did this all of her life. Gene and I had fixed her up an area that had a TV, a small cot to take a nap, and a play area. Myra would color for hours and always greet our customers. Even after she started kindergarten that fall, I would keep her with me every afternoon after her half day at school.

Myra became a Christian when she was baptized at age ten. I had always taken her to church every Sunday and had been her Sunday school teacher when she was younger. She always lived her life with grace and compassion for others. She was the same toward everyone; she truly loved all whom she met. During middle school, Myra began sewing. I had been doing alterations at the cleaners since we opened, so it seemed natural that I teach Myra to sew. She learned quickly and graduated from the eighth grade in a dress that she had made.

Myra met two good friends early in her high school days when the Lacy family moved to Beattyville. Rev. Garland Lacy and his wife Sue came to our town to minister at the Pine Crest Youth Camp. They had two daughters, Michelle, who was Myra's age, and Lisa, a year younger. After only a short time, these three girls became inseparable.

At age seventeen, Michelle Lacy was diagnosed with A.L.L., Acute Leukocytic Leukemia, a cancer of the blood-forming organs. Michelle was transferred immediately to the St. Jude Children's Hospital in Memphis, Tennessee, where she began a two and one-half year treatment protocol. Myra absolutely went wild when she heard about Michelle's diagnosis. She wanted to go to Memphis to visit her but never got to go because of the long distance involved. Michelle would receive her chemotherapy at St. Jude then come back to Kentucky between treatments. During the months of Michelle's treatments, Myra learned much about leukemia and much about the courage of her best friend. Today, Michelle has been in remission over ten years and has been released as a patient at St. Jude.

During Myra's high school graduation practice, she would always save a place for Michelle behind her. Michelle was at St. Jude having chemotherapy but would be there for the graduation ceremony. All Michelle had to do was to follow Myra when the time came, and missing practice would not be a problem. On graduation day Michelle came straight to school from Memphis, arriving as all the other students already had their caps and gowns on. What a joyous day that was to see the girls graduate from high school together.

Myra worked as a clerk at our local Board of Education the summer between her graduation and her freshman year of college. She had a great summer and went to Eastern Kentucky University in Richmond that fall with high expectations. Her first major was Fashion Designing for which she had received a scholarship to study. After this first year, she changed her major to Elementary Education mainly because she wanted to be a wife and have children. She thought it would be a perfect job so she could be with her children in the summer.

The summer after her freshman year in college, Myra worked as a waitress at Natural Bridge State Park close to our home. Her cousin Stephen had taken a job there for the summer and urged her to apply. I remember driving with her for her interview, but she was determined to go in by herself. She was so proud when she got the job on her own. Each day after work that summer, she would go to the pool at the park and take a class to become a lifeguard. She had taken swimming for her physical education course her freshman year in college and had loved it. Myra noticed, however, that she could not swim the laps that summer like she did only a semester before in her college class. She wondered if maybe she had mono like a friend had had a few months before. In July of that summer, Myra called us from work to say she was too ill to drive the twenty miles home and asked her dad to come pick her up. Gene took her directly to the doctor who after blood work said that she was anemic and prescribed an iron supplement. The iron pills made her sick at her stomach, but she went back to her job for the summer.

Back at E.K.U. in the fall for her sophomore year, Myra

had a busy schedule of classes. That year Myra had told us how much she loved the education classes for which she would observe classes at a local school. She was really looking forward to becoming a teacher.

The day of November 23, 1987, will always be vivid in my memory. I had bought the turkey for our Thanksgiving dinner, and it was frozen in our refrigerator. I knew that Myra had had a date the night before, so I called her early that morning to see how it went. She said that she had come home about midnight and woken up about an hour later with a severe backache like nothing she had ever experienced. I wanted to go get her, but she insisted that she had to go to her ten o'clock class, so I went on to work. I must have just left the house when she called back and asked her dad to have me pick her up. Before I left, I made her an appointment with our local doctor, and then a friend and I drove the hour to her university. I knew she couldn't drive home, so my friend accompanied me to drive Myra's car home.

Myra was diagnosed that afternoon with A.M.L., Acute Myeloblastic Leukemia, and life as we knew it changed forever. Myra couldn't believe what the doctor had told her. She was so afraid mainly because she knew first hand all that Michelle had been through during her treatment. How could best friends from a small town have similar leukemia? We were all in a daze that night. Not knowing where to turn, the three of us went to the Lacy's home. Who knew better than they did what we were going through? The previous day we had a healthy daughter, but this day we felt like everything had suddenly come to an end.

After seeing an oncologist the following day in Lexington, Kentucky, we proceeded to Memphis to St. Jude Hospital. Myra was over the age limit for children being treated at St. Jude, but they wanted to study the unusual correlation between the close friends having A.M.L. and A.L.L. so thankfully Myra was accepted. Michelle was going to St. Jude for her last chemo treatment, so the Lacys insisted that they drive us to Memphis. I doubt that either of us could have driven Myra those long ten hours on that first trip that Sunday. Myra was admitted that night. On Monday she had her first chemotherapy treatment, and Michelle had her last. We had always heard how wonderful St. Jude was to both the patients and to the parents, so we felt that this was the best place for Myra to be. Later, I would be scared to death when we would go home between treatments because of the wonderful care Myra received at St. Jude. Could I care for her as well at home?

That year Myra stayed at St. Jude through Thanksgiving and most of December. The two of us flew home on Christmas Eve. Earlier, Gene had gone back home to keep our business going while I never left Myra's side. Myra and I were always close, but we became closer during her time in the hospital. I would spend the day in Myra's room, and at night go to an adjoining room to sleep in a chair that made a small bed. There was a window between our rooms, so I could see her every movement. Both of us had a television, and I had an intercom that I kept in my hand at all times when I wasn't in her room with her. Through this intercom I could hear her breathing and would hear her call for me. Many nights Myra would call for me, so I would quickly leave my small room and go through the nurses' station on my way to Myra. The nurses would ask me what was wrong and wonder why Myra wouldn't press her call button. She just wanted her mother, and that never changed.

The doctors at St. Jude had set up a 6-month protocol for Myra's treatment. She would receive chemo for the first week in the hospital, then be able to go to a nearby hotel for the following week with daily trips to the hospital. The last two weeks of each month would be spent back in Kentucky with Myra regaining her strength.

As a beautiful young girl with long dark hair, it was natural that Myra would hate to lose her hair during her chemotherapy. Myra had just had her dark hair streaked before her diagnosis, so we called Dorothy, the beautician who helped so many girls from St. Jude, to see if she had a wig that was streaked. She didn't, but special ordered one for Myra, and that wig turned out to be her favorite one. One wonderful memory I have is of Myra and Michelle in my bathroom during one of our times at home, and the girls trying on each other's wigs. They decided to go downtown that way which they both thought was funny since Myra was a brunette and Michelle was a blond. The courage of these best friends to joke about what other teenagers would fear made me so proud.

Neither Myra or I cried too much during these first three months of her chemo nor did we ever. We both had to be in public so much that we had to keep up a good front. Myra had so much courage. She always said that she didn't want people to feel sorry for her. We would always say to each other, "I won't cry if you won't cry." Believe me, she had to say that to me more than I did to her. When I was away from her, I did a lot of crying. Myra would say that she was glad that she had her chemo in Memphis because her friends would not have to see her so sick. She could come home after her blood counts got higher and see her friends then when she was stronger.

Myra's goal early in 1988 was to complete her first three rounds of chemo and be home for her 20th birthday on March 8th. We'd always promised to buy her a new car when she graduated from college, and while in the hospital she had said that she would probably never get one now. Myra did come home for her birthday that year and did receive the new 1988 Dodge Daytona she had dreamed about. My brother, Donald, is a car dealer, and he helped us find the red Daytona that she wanted. We treasure the video we made on her birthday when she got her car. She was so proud of the car that she took snapshots back on her next trip to Memphis to show her doctors and nurses. To this very day, I still drive Myra's red

Dodge Daytona.

Our hospital stay in April turned scary when Myra got an infection and was in ICU for ten days. Although the three previous months had been very hard on her, Myra seemed to be following the normal course of her recovery. Suddenly, she was in ICU and in a drug-induced coma because she was on a breathing machine. The nurses encouraged me to talk to her constantly even though I didn't think she could hear me. Again, I never left her side, and Myra came through this crisis because of her courage and the knowledge of her doctors.

The summer of 1988 was a wonderful one for our family. Myra finished her last round of chemo the first of July and came home to Beattyville for a July homecoming, complete with yellow ribbons tied around the trees in our yard. On July 4th we had a large party in Myra's honor with all of our large family and many friends. We served a tremendous variety of food, but the most special treat was that we finally cooked that turkey that we had frozen back in November before Myra's illness. I had been off from work for about eight months by now. Since our family seemed to be returning to normal, I went back to work at the cleaners. Myra and I had a "porch sale" at the end of that summer and made about $800. We used that money to buy clothes and books for Myra as she returned to E.K.U. that fall. She had lost all the credits the previous year, so she had to enter this semester as a sophomore again. It was with high hopes that we enrolled her in college for the second time.

In December of that year, Myra relapsed and had to return to St. Jude. Although she had been given the choice of starting chemo after Christmas, she chose not to put off the inevitable, and thus we were in Memphis that second Christmas. Since we were in a motel on Christmas Day, one of her doctors, Dr. Joe Mirro, came to pick us up that day and took us to eat Christmas dinner with his family. This man was far more than Myra's physician, he was her friend. We were spared a lonely Christmas alone in a motel room by the love and kindness of the Mirro family.

Since Myra had relapsed once, her doctors told us that chances were high that she would relapse again. While she was healthy and in remission, they wanted to perform a bone marrow harvest. She was already listed on the world-wide search for a bone marrow donor, but we knew that a donor may not be found if and when she needed it. We discussed the harvest of Myra's own bone marrow and decided that we should follow the suggestion of her doctors. They had not failed us yet. Myra had the bone marrow harvest soon after her 21st birthday, and then we had to wait six weeks for her to be tested again. If her bone marrow still showed that she was in remission six weeks after the harvest, then her frozen marrow would be good to use if she needed it later. We were so glad when the results were favorable. Everything seemed to be going as her doctors had expected.

In April Myra's doctors had contacted the national bone marrow search organization and again no match had been found. The doctors gave us two choices: one to wait and see what would happen, but this was not hopeful because they knew she would relapse. The second choice was to go ahead and do a bone marrow transplant with Myra's frozen bone marrow while she was healthy and better able to stand the transplant. This was really our only chance for a complete recovery for our daughter, and that was what we decided to do.

April 29, 1989, was the date of the actual bone marrow transplant. Prior to that date, Myra had been hospitalized in St. Jude and had undergone extreme chemotherapy. Watching her take those pills may have been one of the hardest moments of her entire treatment to that point for me. I knew that there was no turning back. Just before the transplant started, the doctors were encouraged because none of Myra's organs had been damaged by the chemo she had undergone to get into remission.

On the day of the transplant, Myra said she thought she was going to die and that she hadn't told her daddy bye. I reassured her and reminded her of her goal to be home by July 22 for her close friend Gena Cornett's wedding. When her doctors came in after the transplant, she told them about her goal, and again we saw how much courage our daughter had.

I called Gene twice a day during this time to keep him up on Myra's condition. He remained in Beattyville to keep our business going. Myra's condition worsened as the days went by. One morning Myra told me that her daddy wasn't going to make it. We both knew that he was leaving for Memphis later that day with his brother and his sister-in-law. They were on their way to Texas and wanted to stop and see Myra. At that time I had not realized what Myra was telling me. I was able to get Gene on the phone before he left, and he immediately understood what Myra was saying. He called the airport and got a flight to arrive about 8 P.M. that night. Myra had grown progressively worse as the day went on, but she seemed so glad that her daddy was coming. She kept asking me, "When is daddy getting here?" When he arrived that night, she was in I.C.U. but sitting up in bed with her legs crossed underneath her. She held up her arms and said, "There's my daddy!" Two hours later Myra had to be put on a respirator, and for the next week could only write notes to us. She died peacefully at 2:40 P.M. on June 14, 1989, surrounded by her parents, her uncles and aunts, and several members of the Lacy family. Her body had finally not been able to overcome the fungal pneumonia that had developed. Myra, our beautiful daughter, had fought a courageous fight for nineteen months and had done it with such strength.

Myra was buried in our family cemetery on top of a mountain in our county. A consolation to me is that one of my brothers and my sister- in- law live directly across from where Myra is buried. From their kitchen window, they can see both

Myra and Mark's graves. Since Myra's death I have worked to make this lovely cemetery a fitting memorial to our children and the other family members buried there. The cemetery is fenced, and we installed a new gate and lamp posts at the entrance. A new sign at the gate was designed by Myra prior to her death. On this sign there is a tree and the words, "The tree of life is the fruit of the righteous - Proverbs 11:30." This tree is a duplicate drawing of a tree that Myra drew while in St. Jude after her transplant. This tree was the center of a fund raising idea Myra had for St. Jude. She planned to implement this idea as soon as she was released from the hospital. Although she never got to use her tree for that purpose, we used it to memorialize her. After her funeral I went to her grave every night after work until the night of December 23 when my aunt died. I missed that night, and after that it became less often that I felt I had to go.

A young man approached me on the day of Myra's funeral. Unbeknownst to me, he had tape-recorded an interview with Myra months before her relapse for a college research paper on courage. He gave me the tape. That night as I sat in my car near her grave, I listened to her soft, steady voice. Myra's unselfish concern was for her father and me. She had no qualms about her fate - she worried only about how we would deal with her death. In the first few weeks after the funeral, I listened to this tape over and over. It was a comfort to hear her voice. After this period of time, the idea of listening to the tape was too painful. Six years passed before I could listen to the tape again.

My life changed drastically after Myra's death. I could not even go grocery shopping because it reminded me of how Myra hadn't been able to eat for so long due to the side effects of her chemotherapy. I told Gene that he would have to go to the grocery. I also couldn't go places where anyone was having fun. Myra loved to have fun, and she should have been there. Our town had started an annual Woolly Worm Festival the October before Myra's death, and she had loved it. This festival, not unlike Groundhog Day, predicts the upcoming winter by conducting a survey of the color of the local woolly worms. If the majority of the woolly worms are black then the winter would be harsh. For the next two years after Myra's death, I had to leave town during this festival weekend. It seemed so trivial to me that all these people could be having fun, while I was so consumed with my grief. Leaving town was just what I had to do to get through those weekends.

I returned to work at the dry cleaners shortly after Myra's death. It seemed more normal at work than it did at home where Myra's absence was so hard. Our house had lost its life. Gone were the nights spent sitting in our family room floor with the three of us playing rummy. Gene and I were now alone with only the memory of both Mark and Myra to sustain us.

To those of you reading this book who are bereaved parents, I want to say that you will make it with God's help. Others do much to support us, but in the end this loss is only ours. No one knows our loss except other parents who have experienced the same tragedy. It is so important to take one day at a time. Myra lived her short life day at a time, so I try too also.

Chapter Five
Brian Penkalski

BRIAN PENKALSKI

By Janice Sevre-Duszynska

Even now as I have finally forced myself to sit down at the word processor to tell Brian's story, I would, without hesitation, rather avoid the pain of reliving the tragedy.

I sensed from the time he bounced in his crib that I could not hold on to him. There was something I knew perhaps even before he was born – his name Brian – a name my mother always liked for a boy. Before I was married I had seen the movie, *Brian's Song*, and somehow I knew that when I had my second baby son, I would name him Brian. That was what he was to be called – despite the foreshadowing of a short life of the football player, Brian Piccolo, in the movie.

There were signs all of his life that Brian would not be with us long. When he was about two or three, swimming in a lake with us in a lifejacket, he paddled away momentarily and began choking before my brother-in-law grabbed hold of him.

At my youngest brother's wedding, just a few years before Brian died, my brother asked Brian to take some additional pictures with his camera. In the church I had this uneasy feeling – that Brian wasn't going to be in any of these pictures – as if he had never been here – as if he'd be leaving us soon. Months before Brian's death, I began to see signs of his transition similar to those that I experienced before my mother died when I was sixteen. I had dreams of him lying on the grass on the side of the road with his eyes closed. I would wake up in a sweat and try to convince myself that he was only peacefully sleeping. Deep down, I knew otherwise.

When I saw him cutting grass the October before he died, I went out on our deck to call to him that his father and I had returned from a ride out in the country. I called him several times, but he was smiling with his cap on and earplugs in his ears. He didn't hear me, but I noticed how content, how happy he seemed. I walked down the deck steps and I was going to let him know we were home and I'd be starting to cook supper. Just beyond the steps, a few feet on the grass I stopped. It was as if there was an invisible wall, almost glasslike and I was not to proceed beyond it. I heard a voice that said, "Let him be. He's happy." I walked up the steps and knew that something beyond my control was happening.

One afternoon that fall, he invited the neighbor kids into the family room and he was roughhousing with them on the floor. I looked in on them and I was struck at how much joy he felt playing with them. As I watched them, I somehow realized in the back of my mind that I would not see him with his own children. When their mother called them to dinner, Brian stood against the family room glass door and said to me, "Mother, I know now what you've told me all of my life: That happiness comes from within."

Inside I knew his fate was sealed. He was telling me he had learned the lesson he was sent here to learn. Somehow I gathered the strength to tell him as I hugged him, "Then you've already learned what it takes many people a lifetime or many lifetimes to learn."

There were more signs and symbols the closer we came to his moving on. I remember once when he lifted me up in the kitchen saying, "Momma, don't be afraid." I sensed in his bones that he'd be going soon, or when I rubbed his back – his muscles, his blood all told me, "not much longer."

He got a card from his grade school friend who was now living in New York, and as I held the letter, I felt the same sensation I had when my mother's old friends came to visit her shortly before she died.

The dreams continued. The last time I drove in his car with him and he got out while I sat momentarily in the driveway, the inside of the car transformed in my mind to the inside of a coffin. I saw the soft, satin ticking bulging all over. My arms moved out and my fingers opened wide and it was as if I was reaching to touch it. I wanted to run out and warn him never to get into his car again. The first part of his body that I was drawn to was the back and side of his head. I knew that I had been told his ending of this lifetime.

The week before his accident, I saw a rainbow as I turned the corner into our street. It ended right by our house. To me a rainbow is a link between this world and the next. There had been a magnificent double rainbow twelve hours after my mother died as my father, brothers, sister and I sat on our front steps. I knew there was no escaping what had already been decided.

You might ask, "Well, if you knew this was going to happen, why didn't you do something about it?" It's more like a mist that you walk through and absorb, but your conscious mind refuses out of abject terror to dwell on. Intuitively, though, you know. There was much more that I heard and experienced telling me that Brian would be continuing on but away from us, even up to the moment he left us in early December of 1990. That day there was such a struggle inside of me. I had to try to let him go.

Shortly after his death I saw him one morning at the foot of our bed, smiling, a golden light passing through him. Then that February I heard him say, "Later," and remembered that was how he'd always say good-bye. The resonance of his voice sifted through me for a few days before I understood its meaning. He was telling me, "I'm okay, Mum. I'll see you again. I love you."

The next month, March, his voice came through a dream in which he told me that he would have been like one of the brain damaged children for the next thirty years of his life if I had interfered with his destiny.

It took me eighteen months to "heal" from Brian's passing – to let him go. What I have learned that may help others is that no matter how much you love someone, he or she has choices, and those are between that person and the

Creator. It may have also helped me that I knew on a spiritual level that his death was going to happen and that helped me get used to the idea.

Chapter Six
Roger Herndon

ROGER ALLAN HERNDON

By Donna Herndon

Oh, dear God, please take this pain away - this white hot pain that sears my soul, that grips me with such a physical force I fight for breath.

"Cause of death: Total Body Trauma."
Those words are branded into my mind. How could a life so full of promise end like this? A life begun in innocence, hope, and love just twenty-one short years ago.

My husband and I made the trip to the U. S. Army Hospital in Berlin, Germany, late on Thursday, June 24, 1970. At 00:35 (military time) on June 25, Roger Allan Herndon made his appearance and was welcomed into our military family: dad, CPT C. W. (Woody) Herndon, Jr.; mom, Donna; and big sister Melissa Kaye, age 2-1/2 years. At 7 pounds and 20 inches, Roger was a small package of determination. At six days of age he managed to roll over in an attempt to escape my efforts to change his diaper. That early display of determination (occasionally labeled as stubbornness!) was repeated throughout Roger's twenty-one years, whether in climbing the drawer pulls as a toddler to get on top of the kitchen cabinets or in diligent study which took him to the top of his high school class.

That same determination, combined with curiosity and wonder about the world led to his study of aerospace engineering at the U. S. Military Academy at West Point.

During those intervening years, Roger's horizons expanded beyond those of many children. During our four years at Fort Knox, Kentucky, following the transatlantic move from Berlin while he was still a toddler, Roger and Melissa were blessed by special friendships with children from Jordan, India, Greece, and Iran as well as with other American children whose dads were in training at Knox.

Roger never met a stranger, nor was he intimidated by anyone or anything. Occasionally that proved embarrassing. While I was serving as the mayor of the VanVoorhis community at Fort Knox, Major General Donn Starry, the Post Commander, was a guest in our quarters on post for a cook-out. Little Roger put ice down the general's back. Fortunately, the good general had a great sense of humor and loved kids. He promptly removed the ice from his shirt and put it in Roger's little shorts.

After three years at Fort Knox, my husband decided to resign his commission to accept a job with Westinghouse in Pittsburgh, Pennsylvania. Life in the civilian community was a major adjustment, and Woody missed flying. After two years there, my cousin Anne Hoke's husband Chuck persuaded Woody to move back to Kentucky to fly for him. We moved our children back to our roots in Murray where all four of their grandparents eagerly awaited them.

It was good to be home and surrounded by a loving extended family. Grandparents along with aunts and cousins enriched Melissa and Roger's lives. They both grew up with a sense of security and family strength that was well nurtured in our rural community.

Melissa graduated from Calloway County High School in 1985. She accepted a scholarship at Murray State where she met Jeff Graves, whom she married in 1988. Roger was absolutely thrilled when he became an uncle on New Year's Eve, 1988, with the birth of Aimee Dawn Graves. He adored Aimee and was elated when her brother, Nathan Dale Graves, was born July 25, 1991. Roger had airline tickets to come home from West Point Labor Day weekend to see Nathan. The tickets were never used. Roger was killed in a plane crash on August 2, 1991, while in an aviation training program. Roger was twenty-one years old and on the threshold of his final year at West Point.

I cannot comprehend how forever changed our lives are. Even the memories hurt.

Roger was neither a born athlete nor a genius. He had to work extraordinarily hard to achieve his goals. It was his positive mental attitude and perseverance that earned him recognition such as "Student of the Week," a Kiwanis prize, Beta Club Boy, Football Coaches' Award, Baseball All-Stars, National English, Math, and Science Merit Awards; more than thirty-five JROTC leadership and service awards, KY Boys' State Representative, Who's Who Among American High School Students, KY Governor's Scholar in 1987 and class valedictorian in 1988.

Roger's life at West Point was enriched by a wide range of experiences. He loved meeting and photographing General Norman Schwarzkopf. He found programs at the academy featuring such diverse personalities as Tom Clancy and Phyllis Diller to be very stimulating. He enjoyed excursions into New York City, especially one where Brenda, his fiancée, was with him. He was exhilarated by the experience of training in the weightless environment at the Space Center at Huntsville, Alabama, in March, 1991. Roger was on active duty when he was killed. He would have been touched by the tribute accorded him in the October 15, 1991, Congressional Record.

Roger's life made a difference. We are forever grateful for the comments of friends and classmates.

"...Roger's death made a much greater impression on me than his life. While he was here I took his friendship for granted. I was complacent to believe he would always be there, day to day, year to year...I've learned to rely on God's wisdom rather than on my own simple logic..." Cadet Jo Phillips

"As I look back...I guess there were times that I was the student and maybe he was the teacher...He challenged me to be a better teacher through the high standards he had for himself and was looking for in others...He was the personification of the Army's slogan 'Be all that you can be.'" --Alan Martin, Sunday School teacher

"Without Roger's smile and eternally cheerful attitude, I would not have made it through last semester intact..." Cadet Tina Schweiss

"An excellent student, a good athlete, a caring person. I guess his smile is the thing I remember most - a smile that was sincere and infectious with a hint of mischievousness."
                    Jerry Ainley, Principal, C.C.H.S.

That first Christmas was a nightmare. We spent part of the holiday with our friends John, Nancy and Stacy Sommer in Rockford, Illinois. The vacuum in our family celebrations devastated us all. Woody left the day after Christmas to return to his job flying helicopters to the oil rigs in the Gulf of Mexico.

The appearance of a Monarch butterfly caterpillar in the yard during the difficult days between Roger's funeral and the West Point memorial service distracted us a little bit when we had to search for milkweed to feed the emaciated little creature. It ate with enthusiasm and grew and then spun a shimmering chrysalis. A beautiful Monarch emerged from that chrysalis the day Brenda and I returned from West Point after the memorial service. Since then, I've periodically seen Monarch butterflies and have been comforted and reassured by their presence.

Our lives limped painfully along as time passed. At the time of Roger's death, I was working as Alumni Director at Murray State University. During a period of time when my work environment at MSU changed, and stress began to overwhelm me, I became despondent, deeply depressed by circumstances that no longer permitted me to be effective at my work. One day, I was astonished to see a huge Monarch butterfly puppet while shopping in a store. Needless to say, I bought it. This purchase sometimes went to bed with me when Woody was away in Louisiana flying. I literally clung to it as a tangible reminder that God had not forgotten me. Within a matter of days, I was offered a new job as Coordinator of the new Family Resource Center for the Calloway County Schools. My job involves working with students and their families on many issues both academic and social. I have found profound satisfaction in ministering to those with special needs, including several parents who have suffered this same devastating loss.

These encounters with Monarchs continue, especially at times when I have become most despondent, have experienced doubts, or have experienced extraordinary stress such as dealing with my mother's (successful) bout with colon cancer. Dozens and dozens of incidents have occurred, incidents that defy reason and rational explanation.

The analogy of metamorphosis is precious as we consider the next stage of our lives. The symbol of hope, the butterfly, is the symbol of the Compassionate Friends. This support group has surrounded us with love and encouragement. A friend helped me design a bumper sticker "I Brake for Butterflies" for distribution to fellow travelers. It serves as a visual link to those of us who have lost a child.

Chapter Seven
Scott Shannon

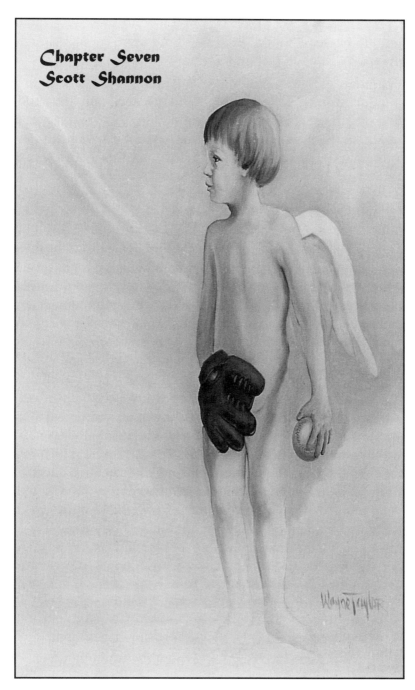

SCOTT SHANNON

By Beverly Shannon

I wanted a brother or sister for Susan, our first child, from the time she was about a year old. It was not so easy as I soon found out through many visits to the doctor. Finally, after months of waiting, Scott Ray Shannon was a born a year and a half later. He had such a sweet, precious personality. Scott became interested in baseball when he was very small, trying to catch a ball with a glove bigger than he was. By the time Scott was three years old, he was steadily focused on playing baseball. It soon became obvious in the next few years that he did have a natural talent as well as a love for baseball.

Scott's developing talent thrilled us. We would attend his games and watch him pitch, with coaches commenting and amazed at "what a great arm this kid had" when he was only nine years old. At twelve years old we saw him pitch in the city tournament knowing that many in the stands and watching along the fence had come to see the kid who could throw harder than any twelve year old had thrown for many years. As I would put each plaque and trophy in his room year after year, I did it with so much pride. I was not proud of what Scott was accomplishing through baseball but how baseball was molding Scott's life: his ideas, dreams of dedication and sacrifice, discipline and learning to follow the rules, to win with your best and to lose with your best. How could he have known that this foundation would see him through his darkest moment - not on the mound pitching for his team but in a hospital bed fighting for his life? Did he somehow know at a very early age that his life was destined to be very short and that he had so little time to accomplish so much? Scott was always so impatient, maybe because his spirit was soon going to leave us. He was so driven to do it all and do it <u>now</u>!

We started looking for his first car when he was seventeen years old. He and I spent several afternoons going from one car dealership to another. Suddenly, there was the car. He saw a black Honda Prelude as we drove onto one lot. He never took his eyes off the car. He wanted this car so much and wanted it now. As I look back on this incident, I am grateful for every second of enjoyment he had with that car. This was so much a part of Scott, the wanting to "do it now." His comment to me one day was, "I hate to stop at a red light. I don't have time to wait!" I think his spirit knew. He wanted to live each moment to the fullest.

Scott signed a baseball scholarship upon graduation from Lafayette High School to enter David Lipscomb University in Nashville, Tennessee. He met the challenge of college as he did everything. He was so determined, so competitive, so driven to succeed.

Music was another important part of Scott's life. His last birthday request was to have small speakers added to the sound system he already had in his car. Scott never lived to celebrate his twenty-second birthday as time stopped on November 5th, six days before we were to celebrate.

The friends that Scott made at Lipscomb were numerous: the guys he played baseball with, the teachers, and his coaches. All of these people became part of his family. After four years of traveling together, spending days and many nights together, he was welcomed by many into their homes. One family in particular became his constant support during baseball season as well as when the more difficult struggle for his life began. Scott's first roommate was Raymond Harvey, and his mom, Carol, and father, Vic, were very close to Scott. In fact, Vic soon became one of the most-loved men in Scott's life. Vic was a quiet, gentle, unassuming, yet very strong individual who was fighting his own battle with cancer. He was always at the games, watching and encouraging the boys. The last few weeks that Scott spent at Vanderbilt University Hospital, Vic would come nightly to the waiting room just a few feet from Scott's room. Scott, being very tired from the day's events would say, "Mom, go see if Mr. Harvey is in the waiting room. Ask him to come and sit with me." Mr. Harvey would enter the room, smile at Scott, touch his foot as he walked past the bed, then go to a chair in the corner of the room. Words were rarely exchanged, but the joy of being together was enough. Seven months after Scott lost his fight, Vic Harvey was also gone.

Our first indication that Scott was ill was at the tryout he had been given for the Oakland Athletics. He had been complaining of feeling tired during the last few months of school and really struggled to finish a game. At the private tryout in early June of 1991, all that Scott had to do was throw the baseball three to five times consistently at ninety to ninety two miles per hour. A contract already signed by the A's management was waiting. He tried so hard but could not. Why? This had always been so easy!

A short time later on Labor Day, Scott was admitted to Vanderbilt Hospital. The day the doctors told us the mass in his chest had been diagnosed as cancer and that the chances of survival were not good, he looked at me and said, "Mom, no matter what, keep me focused on beating this!" He fought day and night for two months with this same spirit.

The days were so difficult with the chemotherapy, the surgery and the pain, but the nights were harder. He would get so apprehensive when I had to leave each night to stay in a hospitality house across the street from the hospital. Early one morning when it was still dark outside, I walked into his room. He was awake. Somehow he was different that morning - not anxious, not worried about the day - very peaceful. He said, "Mom, last night I spent with God. I know now that whatever happens I'm going to be all right. He is here with me!"

There are no words to describe standing by Scott's bed. Each moment would bring a new and more serious problem to solve. However, in the middle of acute and constant fear of what was going to happen, we shared priceless, special times together: a laugh, a hug, a touch of his hand when he needed something, that look in his eye, and saying "I love you Scott," a thousand times each day before his death on November 5, 1991, in the intensive care unit at Vanderbilt Hospital.

I was unable to return to my surgical nursing profession after Scott's death. The joy was gone from my life. Susan was on her own so my major concern became caring for Scott's younger brother Seth. I had no energy for anything else. I spent long hours at Scott's grave, many times lying prostrate on the ground. I didn't eat, didn't sleep, didn't want to be around people. Gradually, I reentered the world. Scott's messages had a lot to do with that process.

I have only had one dream of Scott. About six months after his death, I dreamt that I was waiting outside a large circular wall with other people who had been given a chance to visit heaven. I waited day after day. Finally my name was called and I was led through a gate into an area where many people were sitting at tables in an area with no roof. I instantly saw Scott sitting at a table on which he had writing materials and a stack of books. I ran to him reaching out my hands to grab him. His words were distinct. "Mom, you can't touch me!" He seemed impatient but very happy and content. Uncharacteristically, he was wearing an olive green suit. I realized it was the suit he had been buried in. "I want you to know that I'm okay. I'm fine. Don't worry about me." He kept going back to writing between our one-sided conversation. As he stood up, I was aware that it was time for me to go. I asked if I could kiss him goodbye. He said, "No." I left and as I was passing back through the gate, I looked back and he was already back to writing. Although I was hurt that he didn't seem to be as excited about seeing me as I was him, I was so comforted from the dream. Scott was healthy again! Gone were those vivid memories of my beautiful son ravaged by cancer.

One other episode stands out where both Seth and I

felt Scott's reassuring presence. Each baseball player at David Lipscomb had a brown plastic sign with their name and number that adorned their lockers. The coaches at Lipscomb had given Scott's plaque to Seth which he prominently displayed on a bookshelf in his room. One day, this sign kept falling off onto the floor from where it had been propped against some books for weeks. At first Seth thought this was caused by air blowing in from the air conditioner ducts above the bookshelf, but each time he put the plaque back on the shelf, it would fall off again. Seth mentioned this to me and we both checked out the air ducts - nothing out of the ordinary. We decided to tape the plaque to the shelf with masking tape. Well, a few minutes later it was on the floor again! Never did it fall again after that particular day. We know Scott was sending us a message that day.

I have since returned to my profession as an Operating Room nurse at a local hospital. Susan lives close by and is using her degree in Metal Art Sculpture in her work. Seth is a junior at the University of Kentucky majoring in Secondary Education. He plans to teach History and English and coach baseball.

Chapter Eight
Gretchen Geier

GRETCHEN GEIER

By Jackie Geier

May 23, 1981. On that day I married my best friend, my soul-mate. Bob and I had been introduced about a year before through mutual friends. We connected immediately. He was working full time and going to school at night for his Master's Degree in engineering. I was working full time at a local bank. It was because of our hectic schedules that our weekends together were very precious. Sometimes we would go camping or motorcycle riding; other times were spent at my apartment enjoying quiet dinners and an evening of television. It really didn't matter what we did as long as we were together; and in my heart I knew we would be for a very long time.

The wedding was perfect. All our friends and family were there. Bob's parents were elated, and my dad was happier than I think I had ever seen him. (My mother had died a year before, after a long illness.) My dad loved Bob and thought of him as a son. It was a wonderful day.

Bob and I moved into a small house which Bob owned and had been living in before we were married. I spent endless hours wallpapering and decorating, things I still love to do but with less enthusiasm now. We still enjoyed our weekend escapes, and the honeymoon seemed to go on and on. It came as no surprise when in October of the same year I became pregnant. A very good thing! The next nine months flew by, and I never felt better. Nicholas Evan Geier entered the world June 22, 1982. He weighed 8lb. 5oz. and except for a slight case of jaundice was perfect. Nick was always happy and content, and best of all, slept the entire night from day one.

As the months passed and Nick grew, our little house became too small for our family. We found a new house only two blocks away. It was the perfect location with an elementary school right across the street. I learned I was pregnant again. We were very excited, especially Nick. Even at age two, the idea of becoming a big brother sounded very appealing. Our beautiful daughter, Gretchen Leanne, was born July 19, 1985. We came home from the hospital two days later, and Nick loved his new sister. He was the best big brother anyone could want and a tremendous help to me, even though he was just three. I got such joy out of watching the two of them together, knowing they would always have each other. Because I was an only child, this was especially important to me. Only as a grownup did I realize what I missed growing up without a sibling. Sometimes it was very lonely. I thanked God for giving my children to each other.

The next couple of years flew by. We moved to Richmond, Kentucky, in August 1990, and Gretchen started kindergarten there. After a few idyllic months began that agonizing period of our lives. It started with dark circles and listless behavior and soon escalated to headaches and dizzy spells in the middle of the night. Something was terribly wrong with my beautiful little girl. Following my instincts, I drove her back to Louisville and our old pediatrician. Gretchen was immediately admitted to Kosair Children's Hospital and the testing began. An MRI verified her horrible fate-a malignant brain stem tumor. How could this be happening? Denial immediately set in. I pleaded with the doctors to do whatever they had to do. The next day, Gretchen underwent five hours of life-threatening brain surgery. No one thought she would survive the surgery, but she did. When she returned to her room, she was on a respirator. No one thought she would ever be able to breathe again on her own, but she did. She was being fed by a feeding tube in her abdomen because no one ever thought she would be able to swallow again. But she did. To the staff at the hospital, this was a miracle, and after six agonizing weeks in the hospital, Gretchen was actually going home! She still faced seven weeks of radiation and therapy, but her wish came true. She told me in the hospital that all she wanted to do was be home in time to celebrate her 7th birthday. And celebrate we did. Surrounded by friends and relatives, balloons, cakes, and lots of presents, Gretchen smiled and said, "Mama, this is the best birthday party ever!" All I could do was hug her, and through my tears exclaim, "Of course it is. You're the best daughter ever, and we love you so much!" I will always treasure the pictures taken that day. Because of the radiation and medication, her tiny body had undergone dramatic changes (from 38 lbs. to almost 70 lbs, mainly from fluid retention), but inside was a spirit like none I had ever seen before. The joy and hope we experienced that day would be short-lived, however.

My greatest fear became reality one morning as Gretchen and I were getting ready for another of our all-too-familiar trips to the doctor. As I was helping Gretchen put her shoes on, she said in her softest voice, "Mama, my head hurts." I froze for a moment, but quickly regained my composure, not wanting her to see the fear that had overtaken me. I assured her that after a couple of children's Tylenol it would feel better. We were going to see the neurologist this morning, and he could take a precautionary look just to ease our minds. Surely this was normal. She could still get an occasional headache, couldn't she? We arrived at the doctor's office, and Gretchen seemed to be feeling better, but when asked if she had been having any pain, she simply replied, "Well, this morning when I got up my head hurt. Just a little. But I'm feeling better now." His look of concern did not go unnoticed. He thought another MRI should be done, just to rule out any chance that the tumor may have returned. It was scheduled for the following day, August 13th at 6:30 p.m.. Knowing that we lived about thirty miles away and the procedure could take a couple of hours, the neurologist took the liberty of getting us a room in the hospital for the night. After getting Gretchen settled in the

MRI wing, Bob and I went to the cafeteria for some coffee. We kept reminding each other that this was nothing to get alarmed about. Purely a routine exam. Why was I not believing the words coming out of my mouth? Before my imagination could completely take over, a nurse found us and said Gretchen was ready to go up to the room. We all went up together, and Bob and I tucked our little girl in. We talked for a few minutes, and after a good-night hug and kiss to both his girls, Bob left for home. Nick was spending the night with our friends, the Adkins, but Bob wanted to be sure he was home in time to tell him good-night too. It was important not to abandon Nick or his feelings, and I was thankful that Bob was aware of this.

I settled into bed next to Gretchen. We snuggled close together, my arms wrapped around her, protecting her, making her feel safe. As she drifted off to sleep, I snuggled even closer and listened to her breathing. I hadn't been this tuned in to it since she was a baby, but since her illness it had become a necessity. We were told early on by the doctors that because of the tumor affecting the brain stem, Gretchen could simply stop breathing. I could feel myself slowly drifting off, listening.

It was just before midnight when the silence came. The sweet sound that had lulled me to sleep, the sound I had listened for so intently, had stopped! I remember leaning over and listening and praying for the sound to return, but the room was dark, and painfully silent. I sat up in bed and shook her, "Gretchen, Gretchen. Please wake up!" The sound was gone forever. There was no struggle, no pain, no crying out, she simply went to sleep. For this, I am thankful.

I held Gretchen in my arms for a few moments, and then walked to the nurses station to inform them that my daughter was dead. How could I be doing this? I must be dreaming. Did I really say those words? I must have been in shock at that point. Everything was a blur: Doctors, nurses and machines working on this little girl, frantically trying to revive her. At one point, a doctor came out to inform me that they had gotten a faint heartbeat and by putting her on a respirator, could possible keep her alive. Without hesitation, I said "No, she's been through enough." With that, the machines were brought out; the bed was straightened, and it was over. I saw a nurse go back into the room, and after a few minutes came out and walked over to where I was sitting. "You can go in and be with your daughter now." I could see the tears beginning to well up in her eyes. Mine were yet to come. I knew Bob was on his way. During the futile attempt to revive Gretchen, I had quietly slipped away to a pay phone to call him.

I remember the drive home that night. It was quiet. I don't recall any conversation at all. What do you talk about when your life suddenly crumbles around you? It wasn't until we drove past the neighbor's house and pulled into our driveway that I remembered Nick. Dear God! What was I going to say? Somehow I had to put my overwhelming grief on hold and be strong for my son. Where the words came from is a mystery to me. I recall saying something about no more pain and becoming an angel, that she would always be in our hearts and watching over us. I assured Nick it was okay to cry, to be angry or sad. We did cry together for a while, consoling each other and remembering.

The days following the funeral seemed surreal. It must be what an out of body experience is like. Bob and I both walked around like two ships passing in the night, both consumed by our own grief, our own emotions. Mine were very visible; Bob's, on the other hand, were not. It was during this time that I first met Rosemary Smith. I recall the phone ringing (as it had a thousand times already) but this time the voice on the other end didn't sound familiar. A woman with the sweetest, softest voice asked if I was Gretchen's mother. I hesitantly answered, "yes," and she then explained that she had read the obituary in the paper and just wanted to talk to me. As she continued to talk, I could sense that she knew what I was going through. It was then that she told me her heart-breaking story. Two of her own children had been killed in an automobile accident just the month before. I guess we (Bob and I) didn't have a monopoly on grief and heartache. Other people have already been there ahead of us. Thank God those people were reaching out to us now.

It's been six years now since we lost our beautiful little girl. The pain has lessened and laughter has found its way back into our lives. I still have moments when the tears come without warning. I found it's best just to let them happen. I always feel better after a good cry.

We also have the "Gretchen Moments." These have occurred periodically since about four months after Gretchen's death. The first one happened as I sat in the living room staring at Gretchen's picture and wishing I could see her "one more time." The phone rang and a man's voice asked for "Gretchen." I nearly dropped the phone and then told him he must have the wrong number. He apologized and hung up, only to call back seconds later. Again, he asked for "Gretchen." This time I asked what number he was calling. It wasn't even close to our number, not even in the same area code. I explained that he had reached a number in Richmond, Kentucky. He was completely baffled. He said he was trying to reach his daughter Gretchen in Illinois. Again, he apologized for the inconvenience and hung up. He didn't call again, but I felt so uplifted after hearing that name.

It seems when I'm down or sometimes when I least expect it, I get a nudge from my daughter. Keep in mind Gretchen is not an extremely common name. You don't just hear it everyday. Since that first experience, I have kept an open mind to such happenings. Sometimes things just jump out, other times they are more subtle. Just the other day, Nick and I were at the mall. I had been looking for a pair of clogs. I tried on every pair in the store (I thought). Nick was getting antsy so we were just about to leave when I turned around and on the shelf behind me was one other pair of clogs. Very cute! I tried them on and they felt great. This was the one. I started to scan the shelf looking for the box when Nick and I both stopped and looked at each other. We realized that these "perfect" shoes were made in Germany and the style was called "Gretchen." Nick, being a man of few words simply said, "Well Mom, you know you have to buy these!" And I did.

Even though our family has found ways to move on since Gretchen's death, it hasn't kept us immune from tragedy. In February of 1993, almost six months to the day after Gretchen died, Joan Adkins, our neighbor and dear friend, lost her husband Wayne. He had been diagnosed with Non-Hodgkin's lymphoma several years ago and went periodically for treatments. The family always seemed to be very positive and upbeat. I always felt a little inadequate as a parent when I thought of Joan and Wayne. They were always taking family trips and making them fun and educational for Ian, Caitlan and Brendan. I can remember when they surprised the kids with a trip to the Bahamas for Christmas.

It was after the Adkins family returned home from their vacation that Wayne got sick. He started running fevers and Joan got concerned enough to convince him to see his doctor. Wayne was admitted to the hospital but the fevers continued. He was receiving platelets in an attempt to get his blood built up enough to fight off whatever infection was causing all these problems. After several weeks, it seemed hopeless. Joan was spending every minute at his side, and the kids would spend hours in the waiting room, waiting patiently for the chance to go in and spend time with their dad. I remember driving the kids to the hospital several times, just to save Joan a trip. I was not the only one. There was always someone doing something, anything to help. The same people who came to our aid in time of need again responded to the Adkins family. That's what friends do, and we share many wonderful, giving friends.

Our families are truly blessed to be surrounded by friends, neighbors and a whole community that rally to help someone in need.

It was one day while I was visiting Wayne in the hospital that we really talked. Joan was going to spend some time with the kids, out to lunch or something, so I came to relieve her for a while. I knew she needed a break, and I looked forward to spending some time with Wayne. He had always been a quiet man, very friendly, but quiet. His job took him out of the country frequently, so I got to know Joan and the kids much better. On this day, however, Wayne shared something with me that he knew I would understand. He told me that he had seen Gretchen the night before. He said she appeared over the top of an angel sculpture I had given him. I can't remember the conversation, or even if one occurred, but I do believe she came to him, and he seemed very grateful for her visit. Within days after that visit, Wayne passed away. Joan called us with the sad news early in the morning. I could hear the sadness in her voice, but also the relief.

In reflection, I suppose I could be angry, bitter or question my faith, but I don't see any of these as productive or realistic options. If anything, I've grown stronger in my faith and learned to live life as it comes to me. Nothing is guaranteed and your life is what you make it. There is room for tears and sadness, but these emotions have to be balanced with joy and hope. You must allow yourself to grieve, but also allow yourself to laugh. I know my daughter wants me to laugh. And in my heart, I know we'll be together again one day.

Chapter Nine
Kellie Carpenter

KELLIE CARPENTER

By Judy Carpenter

I don't remember when I didn't know Dennis Carpenter. His parents Dennis and Cordelia Carpenter owned a farm about two miles from my parents, Ed and Mary Hollan in Jackson, Kentucky. I remember when we rode the school bus together. I thought he was very obnoxious. He usually had the honor of sitting in the front seat because of behavior problems. Each day when I was in the eighth grade and he was a senior at Breathitt County High School, he would always have a smart remark to make to me as I got on and off the bus. He wasn't easy to ignore. After he graduated that year, the bus ride was much more enjoyable.

In 1963, Dennis started Lees Jr. College, and I started high school. He attended Lees for two years then transferred to Morehead State University for his last two years. After graduating from high school, I enrolled at Morehead State. At this time, Dennis was a senior in the education department and ready to start his student teaching the next semester.

Since my roommate (also from Jackson) and I were at Morehead without a car, she asked Dennis if we could ride home with him on the weekend. He said yes and that seems to be how it all started. Dennis and I had our first date that first weekend and continued to date for a year until August 10, 1968 when we were married.

In January of 1972, I went to the doctor. I thought I was terminally ill. I had no energy, slept all the time, etc. I remember telling my doctor that I thought I had leukemia. He promptly started running tests and did blood work. After about three hours, he came back to my room and proceeded to tell me that I would be fine in about nine months. I was in shock. When I told Dennis what the doctor said, I remember him saying, "You mean you are pregnant?" I said, "No, we are!"

At six months, my doctor ordered x-rays to see if I was carrying twins. He found out it was only one big one! On September 8, my son decided to be born two weeks early. After forty-eight hours of extremely hard labor, we had a beautiful 9lb. 13oz. boy, Dennis Edward Carpenter. I had never in my life seen a more perfect, gorgeous little person.

In May 1973, I graduated from Morehead State University with a degree in elementary education. That August, I was hired to teach first grade in Breathitt County. I remember crying for several days as I was driving to work. I missed my son. This was the first time I had been away from him except to attend classes.

Dennis and I decided that since we were becoming financially secure we wanted to move out of our mobile home and buy a house. In March 1975, we bought a huge four bedroom house on Picnic Hill in Jackson, Kentucky. It was a few months later that Dee had his first accident. As I was rocking him to sleep one night, he gave a lunge and completely flipped over my shoulder onto the floor. I just knew I had killed him. He didn't even cry until the next morning when I tried to lift him out of the crib. Then we headed to Good Samaritan Hospital in Lexington, Kentucky, where Dennis met us. Dee was fine except for a broken bone.

In April of 1975, I had another attack of "leukemia." I returned to the same doctor in Lexington who had delivered Dee three years earlier. This surprise was due on January 20, 1976. Being the prompt, punctual person she proved to be, Kellie LeAnne Carpenter was born on January 20, 1976, during a thirteen inch snowstorm, the biggest of the season. She was beautiful! Remember, our son was blonde, blue-eyed and a whopping 9lb. 13oz. Well, Kellie was almost bald, had huge brown eyes, and was a scrawny 7lb. 7oz. She looked like a baby bird compared to our son as a newborn, but she was beautiful and very fragile in appearance. We soon learned that she was not fragile in temperament. It did not take her long to get us to conform to her schedule.

In 1980, Kellie started her school career at La Grange Elementary where I teach. This is the school she attended from kindergarten through the fifth grade. During this time, she was involved in school plays, Brownies, jazz and tap dance, basketball, and student council. If there was an activity available, Kellie was there! Her out of school activities included horseback riding lessons, ballet, gymnastics, and piano lessons.

After La Grange Elementary, Kellie attended Oldham County Middle School. She kept up with Girl Scouts, piano lessons, horseback riding, dance, and gymnastics as well as Beta Club, manager for the football team, band, and statistician for the basketball team. It seems we were constantly out the door, in the car, and on the road. I remember several times in those years thinking how great it would be when she could drive. As I recall that thought now, my eyes fill with tears.

In 1990, Kellie entered Oldham County High School. Immediately, the busy schedule resumed. Once I asked Kellie if she ever planned to slow down. Her reply was, "When I am old!" If she wasn't actively involved in something, she was reading or on the phone. Her freshman year whizzed by full of successes. Despite all her extracurricular activities she managed a 4.0 grade point standing.

In January of Kellie's sophomore year she turned sixteen. For her sixteenth birthday she asked for flying lessons. I suppose looking back on the occasion, Dennis and I were as excited as she was. We could not imagine a five foot two, ninety-eight pound ball of fire flying a plane. She began her lessons that month and by May had made three solo flights. Maybe this was why we never worried about Kellie when she drove her car. Surely, if you can fly a plane you can drive a car!

I remember the last lesson I went with her to fly at the airport in Clarksville, Indiana. Up to that point, I never thought of premonitions. On that Wednesday, Kellie had taxied down the runway when I heard the radio tower summon her to bring the plane back to the hanger. I raced out to see what was going on only to hear the commander tell her she could not fly that plane, the engine was malfunctioning. She asked what would have happened if she had gone up and his reply was, "If you went out in that plane, we would be picking you up all over Indiana." This must have frightened her because she asked me to drive her home, something never allowed since she obtained her license to drive back in January. In the car she was extremely quiet. I recall her looking at me and asking, "Mom, what would you do without me?" Later, the day after Kellie's accident, we received a letter from our congressman that would get Kellie commissioned to go to the Air Force Academy in Colorado.

On August 10th, our wedding anniversary, Kellie sent Dennis a card that at the time just seemed like a card from a very grateful daughter. Now, as we read it, it sounds more like good-bye!

Just four days later on August 14th, I attended an in-service meeting for teachers at school. Dennis was out of town, and Kellie had to work from 4:00 to 6:30 at a local pizza restaurant. At 6:30, she came home, changed clothes and informed me she was going to pick up Carrie, her best friend, ride in to La Grange and be home at 10:30. I was watching television and did not walk out to the car with her which was a first. At 10:30, Dennis got home and asked about Kellie. I replied that she would be home any second because she was never late. Five minutes later, the doorbell rang. Thinking Kellie forgot her key, Dennis went to the door. There stood two policemen and a man we later learned was a coroner. I can never explain all the emotions I felt in that one split second—fear, hatred, anxiety, anger, devastation, you name it. In about two minutes, these three men told us our daughter and her best friend had been killed in a car wreck. Almost at once, our house was filled with neighbors and our minister. Every time the doorbell rang, I would run to answer it because I just knew it was all a big mistake. I knew Kellie would be standing there with a big grin saying, "Hi Mom, I'm home! Did you miss me?" She always asked that same question whether she was gone five minutes or five hours.

The next three days are a blur. Oldham County High School held a memorial service at the school for both girls. I can recall only bits and pieces but what I do recall was a wonderful tribute.

Kellie's funeral was held on Monday, August 17th, 1992. Gradually I realized whether I wanted it to or not, life does go on, and I would not die with a broken heart. Somehow I had to pick up the pieces, find my purpose and try to move on.

I, as well as Dennis, have had several dreams about Kellie since her death. I recall about a week after her accident, Dennis bolted upright in bed one night and said, "Judy, I just heard Kellie! You know how she could say Daa-aaD and make two syllables out of it? She just called my name!" Did she have his number or what? She had him wrapped around her finger with that Daa-aaD word. He also dreamed about her being on a plane with him once, and she was where else, sitting on his lap! I dreamed that I was going with her to the high school to have pictures made. I kept looking at her, and she was so beautiful and so happy. She kept smiling and laughing at me with such a serene look on her face. As we entered the parking lot, I asked her how long this would take, and her reply was, "Mom, I'll be back before you know it!" My last dream involved the door bell ringing, and when I answered the door, there she stood. I immediately asked where she had been and told her that we were worried to death. She answered that she had gone to school and if she had told me before, she was afraid I would not let her go.

Following the funeral, Dennis' sister June spent the week with us. I wanted to go to the cemetery—the fact was I didn't even remember the exact location of the grave, but I knew with all the flowers, it would be easy to spot. I recall sitting on the ground beside the fresh dirt and asking that ultimate question for the hundredth time, "Why Lord, why my baby?" It was about that time that a beautiful yellow butterfly lit on my hand. Many times from then on when I would go to the cemetery, I would see fluttering butterflies everywhere. I would sit on our sundeck and start to get teary-eyed and there, too, a yellow butterfly would flutter by again.

Many of Kellie's friends and teachers had the memorial service I mentioned earlier at Oldham County High School the day after her funeral. Afterwards, they wanted to go to the site where she had wrecked. (I had never been there). As we were all sitting there, each choking on our tears and lumps in our throats, two yellow butterflies fluttered all around us and soared off toward heaven. Silently, I whispered, "Hi, Kellie. I know you are there, just stay by my side, or I will never make it and neither will Dad. We need your help and the assurance that you are with us."

Many of Kellie's friends kept us busy for a long while after that. I remember one day, C.J. Wallace, a very special friend dropped by. I recall him saying, "Mrs. Carpenter, I don't think I have ever seen so many butterflies in my life. They are even up there when I am taking flying lessons!"

On the first anniversary date of Kellie's accident, Dennis' sister June was with us. (Bless her and all she has done to keep us out of the trenches). Dennis insisted on cooking out on the grill. June came into the house and told me to come outside. There on Dennis' shoulder was a tiny, beautiful butterfly. By the time I got the camera it was gone, but I DID SEE IT!

Now I suppose it is safe to tell you about the tattoo! I called Dennis at work and told him I had made up my mind and not try to talk me out of it. Of course, he had no idea what I was talking about. I told him I was getting a tattoo on my ankle and no one could stop me. The tattoo shop being in a racy part of town, he would not let me go alone. He drove me to the shop, and all I can say is that we were the best dressed people there and also had on the most clothes! Being a teacher and probably considered rather conservative, my behavior shocked my friends, but they understood why my butterfly tattoo was so important to me. Cathy Barnard, my principal, announced the fact at our first faculty meeting, and it was total pandemonium. No one could believe it. The comment was, "Now all the students will want to be in the tattoo lady's class."

As I look at myself as I am today and as I was six years ago, I can safely say I would not be where I am without the assistance of all my friends. I can remember Dennis coming home from work and saying everyone wants to know how you are. Our society dwells on the fact that men are strong; they don't cry, they get over it! I am here to tell you, fathers are human too. This perfect little girl that we brought into this world when I thought I had leukemia was very much a Daddy's girl. Remember, I said she had him wrapped around her finger. We are not unique; we are like so many parents who have lost children, trying to keep sanity and remembrance in perspective.

Chapter Ten
Christopher Freundorfer

CHRISTOPHER FREUNDORFER

By Pam Freundorfer

Eddie and I met in the summer of 1982. We married in 1984 after we both graduated from high school and had jobs. Five years into our marriage we decided it was time for children. My pregnancy was both exciting and scary as we thought about the responsibilities that go along with being a parent.

On February 16, 1990, our son, Christopher was born. Eddie was with me as he was delivered by C-section. It was an incredible experience. We felt blessed that he was healthy after my doctor told us that the umbilical cord had wrapped around his neck. Natural childbirth might have been a disaster for our son.

Our first year with Christopher was sleepless. I was working full-time during the day while Eddie worked the night shift. Chris was up almost every two hours every night so Eddie and I saw little of each other. We had a few scares during this period of Christopher's life. Once he fell down the stairs in his walker, luckily landing upright so he was not hurt. Another time, Eddie put Chris in the truck on the driver's side and he immediately ran across the seat to the opposite side so he could wave goodbye. Before Eddie could reach him, Chris tripped on the seat belt and flew out the passenger's side window. Again, he was not seriously injured.

When Christopher was two our daughter Stephanie was born. Chris was excited about the baby and was constantly playing with her. Our family was happy and complete. Eddie had finally moved to day shift so our schedules settled into a comfortable routine.

The morning of August 12th, 1993, was another normal day. Eddie had to be to work at 5 A.M. so we had all turned in early the night before. At about 4:30 we heard Christopher cry out like he was having a nightmare. Since Eddie was already getting ready for work, he put Chrisopher in bed with me. I had another hour to sleep so Eddie left for work and Christopher and I went back to sleep.

My alarm woke me and I got up to get ready for work. After I showered, fixed my hair, put on my makeup, and dressed, I went to wake up Christopher. As I pulled down the covers, I instantly knew something was wrong. I saw his arm first and it was spotty gray. Turning him over I saw that his lips were blue. I fell back against the dresser and froze. Finally I was able to get up to call 911. They calmly talked me through CPR until the emergency unit arrived. When they took over I was able to call Eddie so he could meet us at the hospital.

We had only been at the hospital about thirty minutes when the doctors came to tell us that they had done everything they could but that our son was gone. Christopher was only three and a half years old. Stephanie's first birthday would be in four days and her brother was dead. Doctors determined that Christopher had died from Acute Cardiac Dysrhythmia, an abnormal heart rhythm. A tumor on the left ventricle of his heart had gone undetected because it couldn't be heard in a routine exam with a stethoscope. Our child had died in his sleep right beside me.

Being in our house without Christopher was scary. I don't know why, but I would look around every corner. Was I expecting to see him? I really don't know. I went right back to work but had to take a week off two months later because I was not doing well. During that week I finally dreamed of him. He and I were walking up our street. I was trying to figure out how he was with me when he told me I didn't need to explain anything, I just needed to let him go. Needless to say, I cried most of that day. I was glad to have seen Christopher but couldn't bear the thoughts of letting him go. I still haven't learned how to do that.

For the first three or four months I was unable to wake

Stephanie. I would lie in bed until I heard her make a noise or cry. Finally, Eddie and I let her sleep with us. Each morning I would listen for her to breathe or to move before I could find the courage to wake her. I still do this.

After Christopher's death I felt like curling up in a corner and staying there. If it hadn't been for Eddie and Stephanie I might have done that. Stephanie was so young and depended on me entirely. It is so sad that Stephanie will probably not remember her brother. One day I asked her if she wanted to talk about him and she said, "I remember him playing with me very gently."

Christopher's two favorite things were his pacifier and his tractor. He learned to flip his "passy" in his mouth. I would turn it upside down in his mouth and he would instantly use his tongue to turn it back. Being curious, I tried this myself and believe me, it's not easy.

Santa brought Christopher a jeep at Christmas when he was two. It took him a couple of months to learn how to drive it, but once he did we were amazed at how well he could maneuver it. His love for tractors went hand in hand with his love for his Pap-Paw, my Dad, Jim White.

My Dad had this to say about Christopher:

Chris and I had a bond that formed the first time I held him. There was something special that I can't explain. When he first started to talk and I was at Pam's home, he would not let me out of his sight. He would yell "Pap-Paw" until he found me.

Chris was very active and loved to play with his friends. Every time he came to visit, he came running from the car to show me his new scrapes and scratches that he called his "Boo Boos," thus his nickname "Boo." Boo's love for a tractor went much farther than any child that I have ever seen. When he was about fifteen months old, Pam brought him to the farm. I was working on the tractor doing some fencing. Boo ran out and was standing in the field watching me. I stopped and motioned for him to come over. You have never seen two little legs move so fast! After that experience, he would not let me leave the house without him if he thought I was even going to be around the tractor. Boo loved to come to the farm and stay with Pap-Paw and Nanna.

One day he started a new thing that at first took us awhile to figure out. As you leave our driveway there is a high bank along the road for about 100 yards. After that point the bank drops off so our trailer was visible from the road. We were living in a trailer while building a house on the farm. Well Boo called this last area the "Bye-Hole." Pam and Eddie would have to slow down so he could wave bye.

Boo never talked a lot until he was about two and a half. While we were building the house most of our belongings were in the barn and tobacco stripping room. In October of 1992 we finished the house and began moving the furniture and unpacking boxes. When he saw me unpack a wall clock that Pam and Eddie had given us for Christmas in 1991, he looked at me and said proudly, "My Mommy and Daddy gave you that." Surprise! No one ever knew he noticed.

Boo spent a lot of weekends with us and Saturday mornings were special. While I was shaving, he would have to sit on the vanity and let me lather his face. I would then shave him with the back of the razor. Boo would run to Nanna so she could smell the shaving lotion. Everything in the vanity drawers of mine was also his, even the denture powder. Pam and Nanna found him under the kitchen table with the powder all over him and took a picture that got a lot of laughs. Saturday mornings will always bring memories of Boo.

Chris had an ever increasing hunger for knowledge. In the beginning he would question everything and then respond with, "Why?" One day a single trip to the barn resulted in the starting of every engine that he could find; two tillers, three lawn mowers, and two tractors. Each one was singled out with, "Does that one work?" After a reply of yes came a very positive, "Show me."

One trip to the garden was Nanna's favorite. After showing him how to pick the corn, peppers, tomatoes, and cabbage, came the squash to which he replied, "I don't want to!" After she handed him a squash and explained what it was, he threw it to the ground and said, "Them hurt me." It took a few minutes for us to understand his comment. Pam and Eddie had taught him very early that if he ventured into the street a car would "squash" him.

I have tried to give all four of my grandchildren nicknames but with Stephanie it has been impossible. After several attempts I always come back to "Stetnie," Boo's name for the sister he loved. In many ways Stetnie is a carbon copy of Boo. Her speech, looks and even eating habits are constant reminders.

In 1993 I had left a small patch of wheat for the birds to feed. Boo and I were mowing it down. We finished in about three and a half hours so I told him we needed to put the big tractor in the barn. He could not understand why we should put it in the barn until I told him that it was tired. He looked at me and said, "My tired too Pap-Paw!" He then asked for a ride to the house.

That day working in the wheat was the last for Boo and me and the big tractor. On August 12, 1993, Nanna and I left the farm at 4:00 A.M. for a day of fishing on Lake Cumberland and a surprise birthday party for her with friends in Burnside, Kentucky. We had docked at Burnside Island and about 2:00 P.M. returned to the launching ramp to find our friends waiting. They had the never easy task of telling someone that they have lost one of the most precious things in life - a grandchild. Boo left us that morning, Nanna's birthday.

I still look to the heavens every morning for that brightest star and say, "Good morning Boo. Drive the big tractor good."

Chapter Eleven
Shelby Warner

SHELBY WARNER

By His Loving Family

Shelby Allen Warner was born on February 13, 1974, at Wallace Memorial Hospital in Irvine, Kentucky. He came home to Beattyville, Kentucky, with his parents Shelby and Rowena Warner and was greeted by two older brothers and two older sisters. His oldest sister Teresa was a fifteen year old freshman in high school and remembers being so embarrassed. She thought her mother was just too old to have another baby. After all, her youngest sister was already eight, and they didn't need another baby.

Shelby was born with a head full of thick dark brown hair, chubby cheeks, and all smiles. Since Rowena did not feel well after the delivery, Teresa, being the oldest, helped her dad take care of the baby. That may have been God's plan to let the bond between this baby and his big sister begin so early. From the day he came home until the day Teresa married, Shelby slept with her.

Tiny, the sister eight years his senior, remembers Shelby as such a cute kid, even if he was her little brother. Often she and the other children would jockey for position to get to kiss him just to have Shelby wipe them off and try to escape their flurries of love and affection.

The year that Shelby started school was also the year that his sister Teresa married. Both brother and sister missed each other very much, so much that Shelby spent almost every weekend with Teresa and her husband, Drexel. Drexel understood how important Shelby was to Teresa, and he loved him as she did.

When Shelby was in the third grade, Teresa became pregnant. This was not a joyous development at all in Shelby's mind. He cried for days because he thought that if Teresa had her own child, she would not have time for him. After many days of explanations and a few bribes, Shelby finally realized that this child would not change the love that his sister felt for him. He let himself become excited about being an uncle at the young age of seven.

When his niece Andrea Camille Noe was born, Shelby was so excited. This child became the little sister that he never had. In fact, they grew up together. Andrea was an only child, so she considered Shelby her big brother. They were inseparable. When anyone brought something for Andrea, they also bought Shelby something. When Teresa fixed an Easter basket for Andrea, she likewise fixed one for Shelby even when he was a high school student. Andrea wouldn't have it any other way.

As Shelby matured through grade, middle and high school, he became an excellent student. Very early, his artistic abilities were evident. He displayed a keen ability to design clothing. Many recall that Shelby could turn a simple pair of blue jeans into an exploding piece of artwork.

High school became a time of wonder for Shelby. His Journalism teacher, Jamie Stickler, said about him:

"Shelby loved school, and it showed in his work, in his attitude, and in his heart. I'll never forget the last time I talked to him. It was several months after he graduated, and the illness had returned. He was preparing to leave for Louisville to have a bone marrow transplant, and I saw him at a local restaurant. It was a huge step for Shelby to take, but he wasn't scared, at least he didn't seem to be. He looked so healthy, so full of life, and the smile on his face told me that he would be fine."

Shelby was excited about beginning his junior year at Lee County High School. As usual, he loved his classes and joined every extracurricular activity offered. His grades were excellent as was his attendance. He was so proud that he had not missed a day of school in several years. Looking back, we all agree that Shelby did not seem himself those first few months of that semester. He seemed to tire easily, but we put this out of our minds because he was involved in so many different activities.

As the holidays rolled around, Shelby seemed to brighten up. He loved Christmas, especially the shopping that went with it. Shelby would start making his Christmas gift list very early. He loved shopping for the special presents that he wanted each of us to have. Shopping was a favorite pastime for Shelby. Not only did he love shopping at Christmas, but he enjoyed it anytime! Shelby began planning for Christmas Eve when everyone would go to Teresa's house and he would play Santa Claus. When it was time for him to play Santa that year, he just couldn't because he was so sick. He had a sore throat and a cold. Those were the first symptoms of what would be Shelby's terminal illness.

A few days after Christmas, Shelby's dad took him to the doctor. He was diagnosed with a bronchial infection and given some medication. For a day or two he seemed to feel better, but then his back and side began to hurt. On January 2nd, Shelby made a trip to a doctor but this time a different one. This physician did blood work after finding blood in his urine and put him on a new medication. After several days, the doctor called and said that the results were negative for any urinary problem and that he wanted to just watch Shelby for awhile.

Since Shelby was not one to complain, we all knew that there was more to this when he told us that the pain in his back and side had not stopped. The pain got so severe that he would often call his dad to pick him up early in the afternoon and then he began going home at lunch. This is the point when all of us really became concerned because school was the love of Shelby's life. Looking back, Shelby had been losing weight and just picking at his food.

Shelby made his third trip to the doctor, and this time his sister Teresa went with him and his dad. This time the doctor thought it was his appendix because of the pain in his right side and his nausea. We were sent home again with Shelby still in pain and no closer to a true diagnosis. Several trips to hospital emergency rooms followed with either an inflamed appendix or a virus being blamed for Shelby's condition. Finally, our local physician who had conscientiously tried to find out what was wrong with Shelby put him in the hospital as a last recourse.

After a week in the hospital and being examined by many specialists, Shelby's diagnosis was finally made. It was February 13, 1991, and it was Shelby's seventeenth birthday. He was told that he had Hodgkin's disease, a cancer that affects the lymph nodes and bone marrow. We had all spent the night before at the hospital. The physicians had told us the diagnosis but not Shelby. They had removed a tiny knot from under his chin for a biopsy, and it was malignant. We all knew that he was sick, but we had all hoped and prayed that his diagnosis would not be this.

Teresa had been sitting with Shelby as he slept the night before his seventeenth birthday. She remembers slipping out of the room and just slumping down in the hallway in tears. Shelby would know that the doctors had bad news when he awoke the next morning and saw her face. They were so close. They knew each other's feelings just by looking at the other's face. A wonderful nurse saw Teresa and kneeled down and took her in her arms. They both cried for the young man who slept close by, innocent of the diagnosis that would change his life. That night this nurse reminded Teresa that she was Shelby's strength. She said, "He depends on you. In the morning when he gets this news, if you are upset, then he will be too."

The next morning Shelby asked Teresa over and over about the biopsy results, but she told him that the doctors would be in soon. She feels that God gave her the strength to get through that night and to be with Shelby as he got the dreaded news. About 9:30 A.M. his specialist, Dr. Walton, came in and told him that he had Hodgkin's disease. He took the news better than any of his family and said only, "What a wonderful birthday present." Dr. Walton asked him if he had any questions after he had thoroughly gone over his plan of treatment for Shelby. Shelby answered, "Yes, I have a lot of questions but give me some time to think first." This was the way Shelby approached everything. That day, he began the fight of his life, and he was always informed and a part of his treatment. As the doctor left, Shelby broke down and cried but only for a few minutes. He made Teresa promise him that she would always be honest with him. He said, "If it is bad news, tell me. If it is good news, we'll tell everybody." Then he laughed. From that moment on Shelby lived every day so bravely as he fought this disease.

Shelby was allowed to schedule his treatments around his still busy teenage activities. As his brother Caleb noted, Shelby was a young, college bound student who was suddenly faced with a situation that would not only jeopardize his college dreams but would leave him wondering if he would even see his senior year. After several misdiagnoses, Shelby had finally been taken seriously about his medical problems and at last had a diagnosis. Unfortunately, he was in the fourth stage of the cancer by the time the correct diagnosis was found.

Shelby began the long road of chemotherapy that would take him on a roller coaster ride changing his appearance, his attitude, his personality, and his life forever. He would get sick, go through mood swings, be socially withdrawn, and even without anyone knowing it, be planning his future. Shelby's dream was to stay ahead of the cancer at least long enough to finish his senior year in high school. About half way through the chemotherapy, Shelby seemed to feel like he would beat this monster that had attacked him. He not only made plans to finish high school, but he even went as far as to plan his collegiate future. Shelby matured very quickly during this first battle with cancer.

Shelby really enjoyed his senior year. He was involved in everything he possibly could be. Even though he was still undergoing chemotherapy treatments, he attended his prom, senior trip, and finally his graduation. His last chemotherapy treatment was just one week before he graduated in May of 1992. Within that week we were all told that Shelby was in remission! What wonderful news to begin the summer of 1992. We all thanked God.

The months of May, June, and July were happy ones for Shelby and for our family. Shelby lived every day as though it was his last that summer. He had finally achieved his dream of graduating from high school and now he looked forward to college.

On the morning of July 23rd of that summer, Shelby received some very bad news. Two very good friends of his had been killed in a car accident near Clay City, Kentucky, on the Mountain Parkway. Shelby was crushed. He had gone to school with Drew Smith, and he knew his brother Jeremiah. Shelby had visited the Smiths' home many times as they all were growing up, enjoying every visit. He was very close to their mother Rosemary who would always call to check on him during his illness and send him special treats. He was so upset to think that this tragedy could happen to their family, to lose two sons. The Smiths were always doing good things for others, never thinking about themselves. Shelby went to console this family at a time when he was very sick himself. He spent many hours with Rosemary, the mother of Drew and Jeremiah.

In early August of 1992, Shelby's brother Caleb remembers that he and his wife Terri were home from Ohio for a visit and saw Shelby at the local supermarket. He seemed so excited when he showed them the car that he had recently purchased. He seemed happy, but he was concealing the fact that lumps had formed in his shoulder area. He showed them the lumps, and they told him to have them removed immediately and tested.

Shelby had already decided that he did not want to undergo chemotherapy again. He did not want to have the lumps tested for he feared that the Hodgkin's had returned. As time went on, the family convinced him that he needed to be checked by his doctors. He agreed and just as before, the cancer had reappeared after only a couple of months in remission. This time, the only alternative was a bone marrow transplant, and it needed to be performed as soon as possible. Shelby carefully considered this transplant. He appeared to have returned to good health and had only had three months off chemotherapy. How could this have returned? All of us had thought he had beaten this disease. Shelby finally agreed to the transplant, and it was up to the siblings to be tested as possible bone marrow donors. As fate would have it, Caleb, the middle brother was the only one of the children to be a perfect match for Shelby. Of course Caleb agreed to be the donor.

Shelby was admitted immediately to the University of Louisville Hospital for the transplant. All of us knew the risks involved with the transplant, but it was his only chance to live. Both of Shelby's sisters took turns staying with him in Louisville. They stayed at the Ronald McDonald House a few blocks from the hospital at night, but during the day they remained at Shelby's bedside. Before the transplant Shelby had to undergo intense radiation and chemotherapy to destroy his own bone marrow so that when Caleb's healthy marrow was infused he would be free of the cancer cells.

Caleb arrived in Louisville on October 1, 1992, and went to see Shelby. He appeared normal except he complained of being sick to his stomach. By his bedside, he had a book as usual. He was reading *Misery* by Stephen King, of all things! He told us that his dear friend Rosemary Smith had given the book to him. Caleb asked Shelby if there was anything that he wanted to talk about, but Shelby said no. Caleb underwent the painful marrow extraction in hopes that he might have some part in saving his brother's life.

The bone marrow transfer was a success in that the blood cells regenerated and were accepted by Shelby's body. As the days and weeks went by, all the family at home relied on Teresa and Tiny to tell them the daily reports from the doctors. Since there was no immediate threat, most of the family did not make the long and tiring trip to Louisville on a regular basis. Shelby had instructed his mother to stay at home and not try to make the trip. Looking back, he probably did not want her to see him as he valiantly fought this disease. As each day passed, the desire to hear good news seemed to evade us like a field mouse escaping from a hawk.

As often happens, Shelby's transplant was a success, but his body had been through too much with the chemotherapy and radiation. He developed pneumonia and began retaining fluid. Finally, after the doctors had held out for so long, they decided that it would be beneficial to put Shelby on a respirator. Shelby was intelligent enough to know from studying this disease that this was one of the last efforts that physicians would do in an effort to save the patient from dying. He had put up such a valiant fight! Nothing more could be done. The family was notified that they should come to see him.

The person all the family members saw lying in the hospital bed was not the handsome, blond- headed little brother they all loved. This person was a stranger to their eyes. Shelby was very swollen, had lost so much hair, and had been subjected to so much radiation and chemotherapy in such a short time that his body was almost burned from within. The doctors had little hope, but the family gave Shelby twenty-four hours on the respirator before removing it. Rowena had not come to the hospital, but after seeing how serious Shelby was, two of the children went to bring her to Louisville. Around 5:30 P.M., everyone agreed that Shelby had suffered too long, and he was taken off the respirator. His mother said that he had fought a good fight and had trusted in God for his healing but now he was suffering no more.

Shelby's death devastated each of the family members. His brother Caleb said, "I have never completely gotten over the death of my brother, and I guess I never will. He visits me in my thoughts on a regular basis; sometime happy, sometime sad. I find what peace I can in believing that God had a plan for Shelby, and we are all just a part of that plan. What we were to learn from all this may have already been realized by some and is waiting just around the corner for the rest. I deal with Shelby's death not as never getting to see my little brother again, but instead, I try to live my life as he would have wanted to live his had he lived longer. I know that I will see him again on the other side. So, I live each day the way that Shelby lived his short life, seizing each day by the tail and riding it wherever it takes me. Who knows what tomorrow holds?"

Wise beyond his years, Shelby had tried to make his death as easy on his family as he could. A few weeks before he went to Louisville for the transplant, he told his sister Teresa that he had planned his funeral in case things did not work out as planned. Shelby had been keeping a journal and that was where he had noted all these details. No one was allowed to look at the journal that he would have with him at the hospital unless he died. After his death we did look in his journal and he did have everything planned including the list of pallbearers and what they were to wear, the flowers, the type of casket, and the music he wanted played. Shelby's family tried to fulfill each of his requests. What courage it took for an eighteen year old to plan his own funeral.

Shelby's sister Teresa said: "Shelby was a very warm, understanding young man who was also very set in his ways. If he ever gave you a card, he had put a lot of effort into purchasing that card. I remember going with him to get a card for the Smiths when their sons died. He went to every store in town and stayed at least an hour in the store where he finally found the perfect card. He wanted it to be very warm and soothing. He chose a card with "The Rose" poem written on it. I never understood how touching this card was until I received the same card from a friend after Shelby's death."

"Shelby and my daughter, Andrea, were very close and just before he left for his transplant in Louisville, he took her aside for a private conversation. Andrea had experienced a hard time dealing with death since her grandmother died of cancer three years before. Shelby knew this and as usual was not worried about the ordeal facing him but about how it was affecting Andrea. He explained the pros and cons of the transplant and that he loved her very much. He then gave Andrea his prized class ring and asked her to keep it for him until he got back home. If something were to happen and he didn't return, the ring was to be hers. He told her that if the worst happened, he may not be there to watch her in person, but he would always be with her in spirit. To this day, Andrea and I both feel his presence."

Chapter Twelve
Michael Price

MICHAEL PRICE

By Nancy Kathleen (Terrill Price) Hannon

The few years after my first two children, Denise and Chris, were born were like a roller coaster, fast and up and down. In July 1971, my nineteen year old brother-in-law, Mike, was killed in an automobile accident-my first heart wrenching experience with the death of a loved one. In June 1973, my doctor confirmed that I was pregnant with my third child, a joyful turn of events for us. The following month, my father was diagnosed with lung cancer and started treatment immediately and by November was in remission. We tried to make it a memorable Christmas because we were worried that Dad might not be here for another one. We pushed ourselves through the festivities: the shopping, the wrapping of presents, the sharing and the love that goes along with Christ's birthday. Being eight months pregnant, I needed a big push to celebrate my favorite holiday.

On January 28, 1974, Michael was born. He was like an angel sent from heaven to help us work through our grief. He was a ray of sunshine to our household. Even my mother, who had given so many loving hours to nurturing all of us, felt the healing effects of a little baby's presence.

Six months later, my husband surprised me with a new car - and two weeks later left town for another woman! I was in shock. I had no idea what I was going to do with no job and three young children. With help from my family and friends, we made it through this crisis very well with the exception of Chris. He became depressed and even violent at times. After several months of exhausting every possibility, we decided it would be in the best interest of all of us to let Chris live with his father for a trial period.

This arrangement seemed to work out well for Chris. He began doing better in school and seemed less depressed.

For me, it was very hard to accept that my children had to be separated. It was as if I were losing my son. Again, I was grieving the loss of a loved one, even though the child was still alive.

Denise, Michael, and I had to sell our house and move into an apartment. It was a big change but during this time, the three of us were in the process of forming a very special bond that would last us a lifetime. There were no fights or arguments. We now had a peaceful home.

One year after our divorce, Albert left town without a word to anyone, disappearing without a trace. With him went my son and the child support payments for Denise and Michael. He would appear sporadically over the years, even kidnapping Michael for two weeks when he was five, but his checks never did arrive as he promised. Although I didn't want to leave my children, I knew I had to get a job. Joining a Management Training Program, I was able to make a decent salary and to adapt my work schedule to fit my children's needs. My mother, my best friend, was always there to help, living nearby and willing to baby-sit for me anytime.

When Michael was in sixth grade I married Mike Hannon, a man I had been dating for ten years, since Michael was eighteen months old. The following year, 1986, my fourth child was born, and we named him Matthew. Our lives went well for over a year, and then a wall began to rise between Michael and my husband. I began to resent the way my husband ignored my son while paying attention to our son, Matthew. I soon realized that Mike was jealous of Michael.

Michael went on to high school, played football, got his driver's license, as I prayed a lot and said, "*I love you, Michael. Please be safe.*"

That August my mother moved from our locale to a retirement home in Indianapolis, Indiana, a plan orchestrated by my brother to take control of her finances. We were devastated by this heartless act. She was such a big part of our support system. How could we live without her physical presence in our lives?

Michael was getting mail from colleges now. There was only one college that Michael wanted to hear from. I remember the first letter he received from the University of Kentucky. He took the mail out of the mailbox and was waving a letter above his head with a huge smile on his face. After reading the letter, he gave me a big hug and said, "Mom, I need not look any further for the right college. The right college has found me."

That next fall, Denise, Michael and I loaded up the car and headed for Lexington, Kentucky. I had mixed feelings of pride at his accomplishments and sadness that he would be away from home for good. We kissed Michael goodbye, and I said, "*I love you Michael. Please be safe.*"

Michael had a great first semester at U.K. He made many new friends and seemed to always be running into old friends on campus. He came home almost every weekend, many times bringing friends with him. He seemed happy. It wasn't long before Christmas was upon us and it was a pleasant one for the family. My husband and Michael seemed to get along well as they assembled all the toys, helping Santa with his work.

In January, it was time for Michael to return to college. He seemed apprehensive - about what we never figured out. To his dismay, he was informed that his roommate had moved to an apartment. I tried to make the best of it by telling him he was lucky to have a private room, but that thought did not seem to quell his uneasiness. The days went by; he called each night and seemed to settle back into the routine of college.

Michael's birthday was on January 28th, and we had a "Big 19" party for him at a local country club on Sunday afternoon. Everyone had a great time, including Michael. However, as he bid his goodbyes that night, his hugs were tighter and longer. He seemed reluctant to leave. As we kissed and hugged goodbye, I said, "*I love you Michael. Please be safe.*"

I didn't get a chance to talk to Michael until Thursday night of that week because Matthew had come down with chicken pox, and I was busy with him. Michael was full of news, and we spoke for two hours. He just didn't want to hang up. He was so excited, having just been notified that he had made the lacrosse team. His first game was to be March 6th, and I assured him that we would all be there. I asked him if he would be coming home for the weekend, and he said, "No." He had tickets for a Metallica and Guns n' Roses concert on Friday night and a UK football game on Saturday. He couldn't wait for the concert and was going with David Bell, a fellow he didn't know very well, but he was sure they would run into lots of friends there. He ended by saying he'd call me Saturday afternoon at work.

My mother's intuition told me something was not right. I felt uneasy but didn't know why. I finally went to bed and prayed my usual prayers, with an extra one for Michael.

I couldn't get Michael out of my head. That Friday night, February 5th, I kept thinking about him and the concert. My stomach was quivering deep inside. After fretful hours I fell asleep. I didn't go into work until early afternoon. I hoped I hadn't missed Michael's call. Surely he would have called home if he could not reach me at work. I worked about four hours and accomplished virtually nothing. About six o'clock, I called it a day and went home.

I heard our doorbell ring. I yelled for Mike to answer the door. Normally, I always answer the door. This time I didn't. Off in a distance, I could hear Mike's voice and that of another male. I couldn't make out what they were saying. I hoped that it was Michael and that he had decided to come home after all.

So sadly, I was wrong. Mike came to me and said, "Nancy, there is a state trooper in the front room with Michael's girl friend. He wants to see you." Mike's eyes had a fearful look that I didn't understand. As I walked down the hall into the living room, I wondered why a state trooper had brought Julie to me.

The trooper faced me and in a robotic voice he stated, "I am sorry to have to inform you that your son, Michael Anthony Price, was killed in an automobile accident in Central City, Kentucky, today at 9:30 A.M." "What?", I said. "No, you have this all wrong. Michael's not in Central City. He's in Lexington at school. He's at U.K." The state trooper replied, "Ma'am, I am sorry, but Michael Anthony Price was involved in a fatal automobile accident in Central City, Kentucky, at 9:30 this morning." I then lost it completely.

Mike was trying to comfort me. He told me that there may still be some hope. I had not heard the trooper say that there had been a fire and that the car and passengers were badly burnt. They did not know for sure if it was Michael. Though distraught, I heard bits and pieces of the trooper's conversation with Mike and Julie. He asked the name of Michael's dentist so that the coroner could make a positive identification. I couldn't speak. I couldn't utter a sound for several minutes. Finally, I was able to tell them the name of our dentist. I can't believe I remembered his name because at that time I didn't even know my own name.

Next, I remember the trooper telling Mike more details of the accident. He said that there were two people in the car: Michael, supposedly, and a young man named David Bell who was the driver and registered owner of the car. Both had died and were burned beyond recognition. At the moment when I heard Mike ask about the driver of the car, I perked up enough to hear the answer. I had had the feeling that the driver was not hurt and that my son was the only one with injuries. When I heard that he, too, was dead, my first thought was, "Good. He is dead too. That's the way it should be. If Michael is dead, then he should be too. He has taken away my son." Now, years later, I know that was a terrible thought, but in all honesty that was my first thought.

Why was Julie here with the state trooper? For some reason, neither Michael nor David had any form of identification with them. No sign of a wallet or driver's license was ever found at the accident site. The car registration was partially burned but legible, and the license plate on the car wasn't destroyed. The car was registered to David Bell. His address was listed as the University of Kentucky campus. State troopers had been dispatched to the U.K. campus to question students about David Bell. They came to the conclusion that David had been driving his own car and that Michael was the last person seen with him. The state trooper then went to Julie's address after finding an identification card in Michael's room.

We clung to the faint hope that the passenger in David Bell's car was not Michael. Throughout the night, I had called Michael's dorm room hoping that he was there to answer the phone...no answer. My best friend Laverne and my daughter Denise also called his room off and on that night and the next day...no answer. Late on Sunday evening Denise called to see if I had called Michael's dorm room lately. I said I had not because I was afraid someone else would answer and that would dash my hopes. She said she would call, and a while later she called me back. A male voice had answered Michael's phone, but it was his friend, Greg. He told Denise that he and other friends of Michael's could not believe he had been with David Bell and that they were waiting in his room for him to return. The circumstances seemed suspicious to them. Denise told Greg to call immediately if Michael returned.

Michael did not return. After five agonizing days, the coroner called and said that despite inconclusive evidence, he had confirmed the identity of both occupants of David Bell's car - David Bell and Michael Price. We had to face the inevitable and prepare for the funeral.

With the help of the funeral director, we managed to

make all the necessary arrangements. Obviously this would be a closed casket, so we would bring in pictures of Michael....lots of pictures. I still wonder how I was able to plan my son's funeral. Inner strength seems to surface when least expected.

I wished with all of my might that I could die. I guess that would have been the easy way out. All I could think of was being with my son. I didn't want to play the game of life anymore...it was no longer fun. In the solace of my room, I prayed to God to let me die. "I should known better than to ask you for anything. You didn't listen to my biggest prayer of all; you didn't protect my child from harm." I was furious. Why had God *let* this terrible thing happen to my son? For the next few weeks I questioned my faith in every way imaginable.

So many people came to pay their respects the next day at the funeral home. We needed the support of these people, and to this day I am so grateful to each of those who came. In retrospect, I do feel that I was forced into being a hostess in some respects at the worst possible time in my life. I could not be by myself, even for an instant, without someone "having to speak to Nancy". My mouth felt like it was full of cotton. In order to talk, I had to have a drink of water every few minutes. Members of Michael's father's family came for the visitation and the funeral. Many had not been in touch with us since the divorce years before.

To add to my heartache, Chris and I had words when he accused me of keeping his father, who was Michael's father too, away from the funeral home. I had not done this, but Chris felt I had since there was a current arrest warrant out for my ex-husband because of his nonpayment of child support. How could Chris choose this time to argue a painful subject? I could not deal with this situation at Michael's wake.

The first six months after losing Michael passed in a daze. I returned to work, but my grief consumed my every thought. I soon realized that bereaved parents learn to be the best actors and actresses. To walk out the front door, they have to begin playing the part: put on a straight face, hold back the tears. My first encounter with other bereaved parents came five weeks after Michael's death. Dinah Taylor and Rosemary Smith organized a small meeting for about thirty bereaved mothers in a private dining room in Lexington, Kentucky. I was intrigued by Dinah's and Rosemary's ability to laugh and also by the love they generated. This meeting began the bonding of a special group of women. We shared stories and pictures of our precious angels. I have come to know and love each one of these children. Their memories will always live on because we share their loss.

When I thought nothing else bad could possibly happen to me, I was contacted by my attorney and told that Michael's father had filed a lawsuit against Michael's estate. As far as I knew, Michael had no estate, but that proved to be wrong. The cash value of the basic automobile insurance policy that David Bell had carried was placed into Michael's estate. This insurance money was to be used to cover funeral expenses and to erect a monument. How could this man, who never knew his son, never made an attempt to see his child for twelve years, and never once paid child support have the audacity to file suit against his son's estate? Well, after several court appearances, the court denied Albert Price's claim to Michael's estate and ordered him jailed for back support payments. He was released only after signing an agreement to make weekly payments to fulfill his parental obligations. Finally, this sickening mess was over!

The rest of that first year went by...somehow. Thanksgiving was awful. I couldn't wait for that day to end. Christmas, always my favorite holiday, was so painful. I knew I would have to do a good job of play acting for Matthew and my grandsons. I wanted no part of the festive activities but did buy three Precious Moments angels in memory of Michael.

Like many bereaved mothers, I was now into collecting angels.

I was grateful for the company of the other bereaved mothers, because with the exception of Laverne, my old friends have avoided me. When I happen to run into one of them, they seem on edge. If I dare mention Michael's name, they look like I just slapped them across the face. They say they are afraid they will make me sad, but the exact opposite is true. Can't they see I need to talk about my son, know that he has not been forgotten?

Michael's death has left scars on my young son Matthew. We began counseling for Matthew the first week of Michael's accident. For the first three years, Matthew didn't show much emotion about losing his brother but wouldn't let me out of his sight at all. He seemed to be doing better until the death of his beloved dog, Joe-Joe. We had boarded him at a reputable kennel while we were out of town, and somehow he had escaped. We rushed home to search for our dog. After putting up more than two hundred flyers, offering a reward, and searching for hours, my husband and Matthew found Joe-Joe lying dead in the road. We all were utterly distraught. I'm sure this affected us worse because our feelings were still very raw from the past three years.

It has now been over five years since I last kissed my son, Michael, goodbye and said, "*I love you Michael. Please be safe.*" My life has changed tremendously. I was divorced two years ago, not as a result of Michael's accident, but as a culmination of years of problems. There came a time when I could no longer handle being alone and lonely while living with my spouse. Matthew and I moved from the house where we had all shared so many wonderful times. That was hard, but in many ways I needed to make this move.

I feel sorry for Matthew. It is so hard for me to let him be a child. I catch myself making excuses as to why he can't go out to play or ride his bike. I know I have to let go, but he is only ten years old. I know I will be frantic when it comes time for him to drive a car, go out with friends, or go away to college. I'll let go when he is thirty-two! - just joking. Seriously, I pray that I handle this problem in a positive way.

None of us ever "gets over" losing a child. We learn to live with the grief a little better with each passing day. I am learning to "live" without Michael. As long as I am alive, I will work to keep his beautiful memory alive as well. I have been severely wounded, but I continue to heal. I will never make a full recovery because I do not have my son, but I thank God every day for bestowing his blessings on me. He gave me the opportunity to have known my precious son for a total of nineteen years and nine days. *"Dear Michael, my son, my hero, I will love you for eternity, my baby. Please be safe. Love, Mom."*

Chapter Thirteen
Frannie Smith

FRANNIE SMITH
" A Spirit Set Free"

By Frank Smith

Accepting a dinner invitation from my friends Barbara and Chuck Crume one Sunday afternoon in 1967, I got more than dinner. I met my future bride, the hostess' sister, Sharon, who was visiting from Texas. I didn't see her again until the spring of 1968 when I heard she had moved to Shepherdsville, Kentucky, and was living but a few blocks away from me. Wisely, I decided to stop by and say "hello". As I knocked on the door, she came around from behind the house and took my breath away with her beautiful eyes and smiling face. Since we both had recently broken up with old flames, we followed our hearts, started dating, and ended up getting married the day after Thanksgiving in 1968.

A year and a half later Sharon and I were thrilled to welcome our first child, a son we named Todd. In 1974 I began my years of community involvement with the Jaycees, Red Cross, and politics. I was elected by the people of Kentucky to the House of Representatives for the first of what turned out to be three consecutive terms. On July 6, 1976, a miracle baby was born. We named her Francine Nicole Smith, which quickly shortened to Frannie. A beautiful premature girl, born 2-1/2 months early and weighing only 2 lbs., 6 oz., she had to be kept in an incubator for the next 2-1/2 months before we could take her home.

Because our baby was so delicate, my wife, Sharon, was tense in those early days, and her breast milk was slow to appear. A neighbor hinted that if she would drink beer, it would relax her and enable her milk to flow. Sharon was a little skeptical, especially since she didn't even like the taste of beer, but she tried it anyway, and it worked! We were very much relieved because we knew how desperately our tiny baby needed the nutrients of mother's milk to hasten her development. I would get up each morning at 4:30 A.M. and carry the precious milk to the hospital before I went on to work. I felt Frannie sensed my presence even though her sight hadn't developed yet.

Little did we know how special she was, except that she came into this life with a lot of zest and desire to live. We didn't know until we were ready to take her home that the nurses used to parade her all around the nursery, naked, just to show off her perfect little body. She had fingernails, hair, all of the attributes of a fully developed body but she was very small. Her heart was still a little weak but nothing to be overly alarmed about. Fortunately, thanks to a lot of special care, Frannie was able to be brought home in September.

During her childhood years she progressed very rapidly. By about the age of three, she had pretty much caught up with the rest of the kids. She was always an active little girl, quick to learn and eager to get into things. Busy as a Brownie, Girl Scout, and cheerleader, she maintained a hectic schedule of school activities at St. Aloysius Grade School. She excelled at whatever she chose to do, receiving various awards, trophies, and academic honors.

Her high school activities continued to keep Frannie busy after she graduated from grade school and middle school. A National Honor Society student and a Governor's Cup winner in math, she also joined numerous school clubs and delighted in drama and tennis. For me, as a father, in addition to being my friend and companion, she was my confidante and future, a genuinely loving daughter who fulfilled the greatest expectations I could ever hope for in life. She was a part of me, a reflection of the best of her father, the best of her mother, and then she was Frannie. We felt blessed to have such a wonderful daughter.

Going back to a few years before Frannie began high school, Sharon experienced the first of three upsetting premonitions that came to her in her dreams. In 1988 she dreamed that her best girl friend had died. She described what she saw so vividly to me - a coffin with Linda Jane's picture on it. Within a month of that dream, Linda Jane, her husband, Marlin, and four others were killed in a private plane crash in the Ozark mountains in Batesville, Arkansas. When Sharon went to Orange, Texas, to our friend's funeral, there was the coffin and Linda's picture, just as Sharon had described it before the accident.

A year later, in November of 1989, Sharon had another dream. This time it was of her brother Tracy's death. She told me about this dream right after she had it. Within a month of that dream, her fifty-five year old brother died of a heart attack.

Then, in January 1993 Sharon had another dream. This time she woke up horrified and very shaken. When I asked her what was the matter, she replied that she had a terrible dream. I begged her to tell me what it was. "I need for you to tell me," I pleaded.

"No, it's too horrible. I can't tell you," she moaned.

"You've got to tell me," I implored. Sharon then explained that in her dream an angel had come to her and had told her that "it was Frannie's time". That startling message about our precious sixteen year old daughter frightened Sharon to the very core of her being. I tried to comfort her, telling her that I would hope and pray that our Frannie would be safe, but we couldn't put Frannie into a glass bowl to protect her. We were both badly shaken by that premonition.

Within a month of that dream, Frannie was killed in a freak skiing accident at Paoli Peaks, Indiana, on Sunday, February 7, 1993. On a ski outing with her friends, she lost control coming down a slope, skied off the trail, and hit a wooden fence. Her head hit the cement base that was exposed around the fence post, and she never regained consciousness.

At Frannie's wake, the night before her funeral, her

fourth grade teacher, Sister Madeleva, came up to us and shared an essay Frannie had written some seven years earlier. Sister had asked the class to write an essay on a famous person, a movie star, or someone they admired and would want to interview if they had that opportunity. Some of the class chose the president; some chose rock stars; some chose movie stars, but Frannie chose to interview God. This took her teacher somewhat by surprise. It wasn't really out of character for Frannie, yet it made a tremendous impact on the teacher, who had saved the essay all this time. We weren't aware of Frannie's interview with God. She asked, "What was it like when Christ was hanging on the cross? Did he suffer? Was He in much pain? What was heaven like?" - and other basic fourth grade questions. Her teacher was impressed by the fact that, in her thirty years of teaching, Frannie was her first student to interview God.

Later in the same evening, a very unusual thing happened. I was talking with my brother's wife's sister, Judy, telling her about Sharon's three premonitions, when she told me that she was a medium. She said that she did not advertise, never charged for her services, nor did she like to go to funeral homes where, if she was "open," she could take on a bad spirit as well as a good spirit. Judy told me some things that impressed me and took me by surprise. One of the things she told me was that my father, who died of cancer at the age of forty-seven and who had been dead for twenty-five years, was there to greet Frannie as she passed into the light. That thought had never even entered my mind, even though I have always believed that there is a heaven and that there is a life after death. I found the idea very comforting.

Judy then told me something which had an even greater impact on me, given the fact that she had never been to my home. She informed me that in Frannie's room under her bed there was a box, and in that box there was a message. "You will know it's for you, what it means, and what you're to do with it," she advised. I didn't know if there was a box under Frannie's bed, but I repeated the conversation to my wife who told me that she was aware of the box's existence, but not of its contents.

That night when we got home, as I checked some office messages, Sharon went directly to Frannie's bedroom to look into the box "under the bed". She knew it contained personal things, but we would never have opened it under any other circumstances. Even when your child is dead, you feel the instinct to respect her privacy. As Sharon was searching through the box, she found a folded piece of spiral-bound note paper. In Frannie's handwriting there was a message.

Pray for me my fellow man on the day of my death.
Pray for the world I'm entering that you may enter too.
Let your minds be at ease, for I love you, and know that you love me.
Don't worry about goodbyes for I am still with you.
I am watching you and guiding you just as before, only now you don't see me.
Let it be remembered that I know you and am praying for you.
Now...I am free...a spirit gliding in beauty.
Every time you see God's beauty, you see me.
I am with you...travel with me.

This loving message brought a sense of peace to our hearts. It didn't take away the hurt, the grief, the pain, and the sorrow of losing Frannie, but it reflected the beauty of her soul and gave our hearts strength to go on with life. We didn't know when she had written it. Her grandmother claimed that she had written the poem about four months before her death. Frannie had asked her grandmother if there was anything she should change about it and her grandmother had said, "No, it's absolutely beautiful the way it is written." She hadn't picked up on her message, thinking it was only something

Frannie had written for school. Then, we asked her boy friend if he had seen it, and he said, "Yes." He had asked her why she had written it, and Frannie had replied that she just wanted to have it. Obviously, she did sense that her time was short, and it seems that she was guided by God to write that poem that she so carefully left for us. I read it at her funeral service.

About three months after Frannie's death, our twenty-two year old son, Todd, who had his own place, came home to spend the night. Even though he was six years older than Frannie, she had helped him many times with his studies, which came naturally to her but were difficult for him. His room was across from Frannie's, and we had kept her room pretty much like it was. Todd needed an alarm clock to get up in the morning, so he went into Frannie's room, got her clock, set it, and went to bed. At about midnight the alarm went off, and Todd, who sleeps like a log, never turned it off. I got up and went into his bedroom and looked at the clock which was ringing for no reason. The time was set properly for 6:30 the next morning. It quit ringing, and I went back to bed. About thirty minutes later, it went off again, with my son still sleeping away. Once again I got up and checked the alarm clock, finding no apparent reason that it should be ringing. I went back to bed and went to sleep. Perhaps an hour went by before it went off again. Because I was exhausted and had to get up early for work, I asked Sharon to check the clock. I was worn out. Inspecting the clock, she, too, found no explanation why it should be ringing. She shut it off, reset it, and came back to bed. The next morning at 6:30, the alarm went off, and Todd got up!

Afterwards, Sharon told me that on the day before Todd arrived back home, she had been praying for a sign or symbol from Frannie to let her know she was around. I'm not too sure how to interpret the alarm clock ringing indiscriminately. It could have been a message to let us know that Frannie was present, or to let my son, who had not been in the house for some time, know that she was close. Or maybe, she was just upset because he took her alarm clock from her room and put it in his room. Like most brothers and sisters, they had their private spaces and their own routines. Whatever the reason, we feel it was a message from Frannie and that my wife's prayers were answered.

Sharon and I took different paths to ease our pain. I spent hours pouring out the love in my heart while designing Frannie's monument for her grave. We wanted it to be a reflection of her warm personality and spiritual beauty. For about eighteen months, I worked relentlessly on that, and finally, it all came together. In order to be able to afford it, I bypassed the monument company and went directly to the granite company to study the process of monument making. I learned the necessary techniques and incorporated them into her monument. In fact, the whole process was a work of love. Fortunately, I was able to find Al Fantoni, a very special man who had sculpted and worked with granite all his life. He had emigrated from Italy and lived up in the East. I worked with him and several others in the design and development of the monument. A year and a half later, the day came to set up the 6,000 pound monument. Working along with a crane operator and a thirty ton crane, I ended up setting it up myself, which was frankly quite an accomplishment. It is an absolutely beautiful monument.

Sharon found comfort in collecting angels and filled our home with every type of angel memorabilia you could think of. Angel mugs, napkins and placemats adorn the kitchen, framed angel pictures, needlepoint pillows, angel sheets and towels, knick-knacks, music boxes, candles, an angel blanket throw, and an angel fountain decorate our home with a loving presence. A welcoming angel hangs over the front door, and outdoor angel lights announce the Christmas season. Sharon even discovered angel sweaters, blouses, vests and pins; I have given Sharon a lovely angel necklace and matching earrings, and she once surprised me with a gorgeous angel tie.

Leaning on each other, and learning more about each other, our healing was beginning. Sharon and I were motivated to reach out to others, like others had done to us. In the early stages of our grieving, twenty-one months after Frannie died, we began hosting an annual bereavement seminar, choosing the weekend before Thanksgiving each year to help bereaved families prepare their hearts for the holidays. We have found that in soothing others, we ourselves are refreshed as well.

Reinvesting the love we have for Frannie, knowing it's never wasted, enjoying all her special signs to us, and being surrounded with dear friends and all Sharon's angels, has given us the strength to take each day count and to bring us one day closer to seeing Frannie again.

Chapter Fourteen
Kristie Kauffmann

KRISTIE KAUFFMANN

By Susan Kauffmann

Kristie wasn't the fastest runner on the Sacred Heart Academy cross-country team, but the fact that she was part of the team at all was a miracle to us. Our daughter, Kristine Marie Kauffmann, born on February 22, 1977, with a dislocated hip, spent two weeks in a hospital, her legs suspended in traction. Additionally, surgery was performed to place her hip back in its socket. After Kristie's surgery, the first year of her life was spent in a body cast from her chest to her feet to allow her small body to completely heal. Although Kristie couldn't remember, her early experience most probably set the tone for her "never-give-up" attitude.

Kristie, (also known as Krickles) though perfect to us, was a normal kid by other's standards. An average student, Kristie's interests peaked in student activities and sporting events rather than studies. Krickles' coordination skills sometimes had a hard time catching up with her rate of growth—Krickles was 5'10". She loved softball, basketball, and volleyball. Many times Kristie was not the starter, but she faithfully showed up for every practice and was a fervent supporter of her team.

Kristie's transition from lanky childhood to princess was almost complete when she turned sixteen. She had become very pretty - a face framed by long, beautiful, blonde hair and set alive by sparkling blue eyes. After her braces were removed, a slight discoloration remained on her front teeth which left Kristie in tears. Her smile showed how proud she was once the dentist took action to remove those stains. The bill for his services arrived after her funeral.

Friday, March 5, 1993, was typical of most Friday evenings around our home. Kristie's brother Mikey was spending the night at his friend's house; her sister Lisa had stayed home, and Kristie attended the Louisville Ice Hawks hockey game at Broadbent Arena in Louisville, Kentucky. Kristie's father and I spent a relaxing evening at home. I was in bed reading and had just finished painting my fingernails when Kristie came home from the game. She bounced up the stairs to say "good-night". As usual, she had a great time at the game, and before she went into her bedroom, she pulled my blanket over my feet, so I would not smudge my wet fingernail polish.

Michael's job as a certified public accountant required Saturdays in the office during tax season, so he left early that morning of March 6, 1993. Mikey was still at his sleep-over. Lisa had caught a ride to her modeling class and telephoned afterwards to let me know she and a friend were attending a grade school basketball game. Kristie always slept late on Saturdays, but I noticed the time approaching 12:25 p.m. (late even by Kristie's standards). A few of her friends had telephoned during the morning, and I did not think it unusual that the telephone didn't awaken her. I went upstairs to rouse her, but I knew the moment I entered her room that would never happen. She was lying on her back with her arms stretched out. An open container of lipstick and eye shadow used the night before still lay on her bedside table. Kristie had died during the night, just feet down the hallway from our room, feet from Lisa's room, and Mikey's room, and no one knew it. I ran to her bedside…her body was cold, lifeless. I ran to my bedroom and called "911"…and then ran back to Kristie's room and started performing CPR. This was a part of my training as an RN but it was futile. I couldn't bring her back!

The emergency technicians arrived, along with a procession of police, detectives, a coroner, and our parish priest; still, we had no answers to the cause of Kristie's death. A detective, upon leaving Kristie's room, advised me it was not suicide…a thought that had never crossed my mind. The coroner advised that an autopsy would be performed to determine the cause of death. The lack of an answer left us empty and afraid for our other two children. Later we learned that Kristie died of hypertrophy cardiomyopathy, a genetic abnormal heart condition which often has no symptoms until the first symptom, sudden death.

Losing our beautiful daughter as we did left us emotionally overwhelmed. Being alone at this time was unthinkable, and friends and family arranged it so they were with us constantly. Their presence did not suppress the burdensome feeling of loneliness. Our hearts longed to have Kristie with us. We worried about Kristie - was she all right? We needed a sign...and signs started coming.

In December, 1993, following Kristie's death, our local newspaper the Courier Journal did an article about bereaved families coping with the loss of children during the holiday season. We had a display on our porch of an illuminated angel (symbol of Kristie for us since her death), and Kristie's story was part of that article. Shortly thereafter, we received in the mail a package and letter from a family named Shepherd. In the package was a gift of an angel. Their letter told us that they had passed a storefront and for some unknown reason this particular angel in the window caught their eye. They purchased it. When they arrived home, they read the article in the newspaper about Kristie and our angel display. The Shepherds felt the angel should be for our home. We, in turn, wrote back expressing our heartfelt gratitude for such a gesture from people we had never even met. As we became acquainted with the Shepherds, similarities in our families began to surface. The store where the angel was purchased was called 'Susan's Corner' - my name is Susan. Mr. Shepherd's father and brother were both born on February 22 (Kristie's birthday also). Mr. Shepherd's brother died in 1977 (the year Kristie was born). Mr. Shepherd's eighty-one year old mother surprised us with a pastel portrait of Kristie she had painted from the wallet size photo we had given them. Although her hands were not very stable at this point in her life, the pastel was a perfect likeness of our daughter Kristie. In the corner of the picture is a small white rose. No rose appeared on the wallet size photo nor was she aware of our tradition of the white rose and its significance. Our special painter stated there was no reason for the rose-only that something guided her hands.

Michael, Kristie's father, has been blessed with three extremely vivid dreams of our daughter. In Michael's first dream, an older-looking Kristie and he were in the kitchen of our former house. She had the most beautiful smile and appeared radiantly happy. He felt so peaceful, especially after she said the only three words she spoke, "Dad, I'm okay". In the second dream, she was younger and they were playing together in the basement of Michael's mother's house. When I questioned Michael about what she was wearing, he recalled her red plaid dress even though Michael normally does not notice that kind of detail. I was amazed. The dress he vividly described was a special Christmas dress she had as a baby. I knew this was a message to me. She knew I would remember this special dress. And lastly, in the third dream, she appeared to be about sixteen years old but had a different hairstyle. Kristie had no words for her Dad that night but they danced and danced in each other's arms!

My one and only unusual experience with Kristie occurred about three months after her death. I was writing in the kitchen after everyone else had gone upstairs to bed. Suddenly I felt someone enter the room. My back was to the door so as I was turning around I was already calling out Lisa's name. I fully expected her to be standing there but the doorway was empty. In my thoughts I said, "Are you there Kristie?" Still feeling a presence near me, I went upstairs to see if anyone was awake. Both Michael and Mikey had gone to bed and their lights were off. Lisa's light was on so I entered her room. I asked if she had come back downstairs. She said, "No Mom, I'm washing my face getting ready for bed." Now I was certain Kristie was with me. So she'd stay, I decided to read for awhile on Lisa's bed. "Kristie, are you there?" I kept repeating this thought until I realized I was whispering out loud. Suddenly I saw a filmy form move across the room. There was no figure to it. I didn't actually see Kristie but knew it was her. Within seconds I no longer felt the presence. Kristie was gone but I was greatly comforted.

Five years have passed since Kristie's death. The healing has begun but still a part of each of us died when Kristie died. Her name spoken aloud by others is comforting to our ears and hearts. We need to hear and remember the funny things that she did and said. She was a special person. We continue to watch for signs. I wear one of her rings always. I wear her clothes occasionally, and to this day have not allowed those garments to be cleaned. In my heart and mind they still have the sweet aura of Kristie.

Emerging from the grieving process, Michael and I discovered the desire and need to have another child. This child would not replace Kristie - she is irreplaceable. We, having reached our-mid forties, found that we were both experiencing a strong desire to adopt. Our feelings grew even stronger as we began the application process. For various reasons, an American adoption would be impractical. However, we were guided to "World Child", an international adoption agency.

Michael, Lisa, Mikey and I welcomed our new Russian daughter and sister, Nikki Barinova to our home on August 21, 1996. Did Kristie assist in this? We don't know, but when we arrived at the orphanage in Russia and entered the room that held so many babies, Michael pointed Nikki out as ours even before the officials introduced us to our new daughter. Nikki even has "our nose"! Was it coincidence that Michael selected her? What directed us to go to Russia to make this baby a part of our family? We don't and won't know, but Nikki's transition to her new home and family has occurred so simply and completely. Nikki feels to us as though she has been with us forever…it's as if she were born into our family.

Each day, since Kristie's death, we still take carefully, one by one. Gradually, we've become stronger, healing little by little. Our thinking process has slowly changed from feeling that the burden of another day was too heavy, to believing once again in tomorrow. Three children in this family have futures ahead of them, and we all must go on, for each other. Our home now has the echoes of laughter within it again. Music is part of our household. Memories are again being recorded. Kristie is forever in our hearts and minds.

Chapter Fifteen
Mitch Warren

MITCHELL J. WARREN

By Carol Warren

The story of our Mitchell begins with a nursery decorated with pink and white hearts. We'd had our son Michael four and a half years earlier and we were ready to bring home a baby girl. Mother Nature was not to be second-guessed, however, and we found ourselves the parents of another wonderful son. My friend hurriedly painted splashes of blue throughout the pink nursery, and we settled into raising our two sons.

Being an athletic-minded person, my husband was ecstatic over having two boys to coach for the next fifteen or sixteen years. Then, three years later, I became pregnant again, and this time we did bring home a "pink" bundle from the hospital, and we named her Mallory Lee Warren. Mallory was a baby clone of her two big brothers, and now we had a dream come true family. I was sure no one felt luckier than I.

Mitchell was the middle child and was the most temperamental as well as the most affectionate and lovable. I could always count on a hug when he bounded in the door after getting off the school bus or when he would see us at school doing volunteer work. He would always beg us to take him home whenever we finished whatever project we were working on, rather than waiting for the school day to be over. I miss touching him so much. Every night when we lay down to read books at bedtime, he would twist my hair around his fingers, a habit he developed as a nursing baby. It is ironic that Mitch had this habit of twisting my hair; the mannerism most people remember about him is the way he would run his fingers from the front of his hair through the top. There his hair would remain standing tall and straight. After his hair was in its vertical position, he would usually rest his hands lightly on his waist. This is a visual image which will forever be cemented in my mind.

As he grew, Mitch was very social and had a beautiful smile. He always wanted to go out to play with his friends as soon as he arrived home from school. His friends thought he was very funny, and his favorite style of artwork was just as entertaining…he drew every kind of silly monster that his big imagination could conceive. One of his favorite activities in third grade was to put dead flies into the vents of the heating system in his classroom. Aside from his mild mischievousness, he was very intelligent, and although still very young, he had the undeniable speed and strong competitive spirit that would make him a fine athlete. One week before he passed on, he had swished the winning basket for his YMCA basketball team.

The day before Mitch turned nine years old, we left on a family trip to Panama City over our spring break. We were going to meet our friends, who also have two sons and one daughter, and share a condominium. We started driving late at night and around 5:00 A.M., my husband dozed off and lost control of our vehicle. Mitchell was killed instantly when our mini-van landed on its side after rolling over an undetermined amount of times. The rest of us were totally uninjured and climbed out of our van, wishing that we had been the one to die instead of Mitch. A preacher and her husband took us to a motel where we spent the day waiting for our family to drive down to Alabama where the accident occurred and take us back home to Indiana. Horrifyingly, we spent Mitch's birthday in a strange place in a total state of shock instead of celebrating at the beach, one of Mitchell's favorite places. As we drove back from Alabama, our older son Michael cried, still wishing he had been the one to die, but since then we have not seen him cry at all. He was thirteen at the time of the accident and has kept the grief of losing his brother harbored deep inside himself, among all of the other emotions teenagers have to learn to deal with. He doesn't bring up memories and only responds when directly spoken to about Mitch. He attended a bereavement class for siblings at our local Hospice agency, and our hope is he knows he has permission to grieve whenever he needs to. I think Mitch's death has been very hard on him.

Mallory was five and in preschool when Mitch died. Her innocent age seems to have enabled her to grieve and hurt for her brother. She expresses her feelings and has what we refer to as "Mitch attacks" when she has to cry. She becomes upset because she can't remember everything about him, but she talks frequently about Mitchell's laugh and the games they played in the bathtub together. We try to reinforce the memories she has and to create more by telling her stories about Mitch. She is in the third grade now and has the same teacher, Mrs. Funk, as Mitchell had at the time he passed away. Mrs. Funk is very quick to recall a memory of Mitch and still carries the hat he gave her in her coat pocket. Mallory also had the same teacher as Mitch, Mrs. Lang, in second grade. Mrs. Lang, like Mrs. Funk provided love and support to Mallory in dealing with her brother's death. Every day when we walk into the school building, the first thing we see in the lobby is a plaque memorializing Mitch and two benches which were placed there as a memorial to him. This is the year that Mitch would have gone to junior high, so it is easier for me to be involved in school because I don't have to see his classmates growing into adolescents without him bouncing alongside them.

As for myself and my husband, after the shock of the accident and Mitch's death dissipated, the pain, despair, and loneliness arrived. A huge chunk of our family was missing, never to be replaced. Someone we talked with and hugged every day for nine years was gone and never coming back. I remember a three week period after Mallory was born when Mitch had severe headaches and vomiting. The agony I felt as we tried to diagnose and correct the problem was so painful that I knew nothing could ever hurt that bad again. Now we were also facing an unbelievable and unending battle of guilt and shame because we had failed at the parental task of keeping all of our children alive and well. I know it's very hard for my husband knowing that he was driving the car when the accident happened. In all honesty, the only reason I survived the initial time period after Mitch's death was the fact Michael and Mallory were depending on me to make everything okay.

By force we are learning to live this new life we have inherited. Unfortunately, my thoughts often turn to wondering if Michael and Mallory are also going to die, and panic quickly sets in when I am not certain of their exact whereabouts. We no longer look to the future since a big part of ours is missing but instead take each day as it comes and try to make it as good as possible. A huge hole will always remain in our hearts. Our thoughts are continually about Mitch, but we can laugh and feel some happiness. We hope and pray that his heavenly spirit is with us while we are still here on Earth, but the real strength that keeps us adrift is knowing that we will spend an eternity of time with Mitch when our time comes to die.

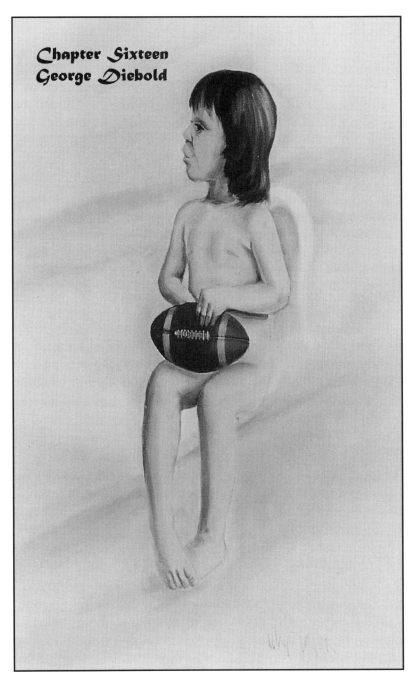

Chapter Sixteen
George Diebold

GEORGE DIEBOLD

By Don Diebold

George was our first born child. We learned how to be parents quickly. We made mistakes but also learned from these situations. Our children meant everything to my wife and me. We often hear how many people, if they had a chance to do it over again, would have remained childless. What a mistake that would have been for us. I can't imagine living without children. When George was taken so violently from our lives, part of our future died. I truly believe those people who say they would have rather been childless would see things differently had they experienced the loss of a child.

George attended Catholic schools all his life. This was a sacrifice both his mom and I felt was worthwhile. He always knew this and did his best to make us proud. He was pretty much a "B" student in grade school and later in high school he mostly made A's. Grade school brought so many changes in his physical and emotional development. He constantly battled weight problems until his 7th and 8th grades. Then he starting growing taller and developing an athletic body that made him proud.

George loved football, but at first this wasn't the case. As I said, he battled weight his early years. He went out for football in the 5th grade at my coaxing. After he went through two weeks of wind sprints and conditioning, I wasn't sure if George would stay with it. He was always last in the sprints. My heart ached at times as I felt I was pushing him to do something he was not comfortable with. But he decided to stick with it, and he grew to love it. The week before he died, six years of football later, he was timed by the high school staff as the fastest offensive lineman in the sophomore/junior classes. He was also in the top five in several weight training classifications. George had a goal to be the best he could be, but his true ability will never be known due to his untimely death.

George had a hobby he shared with his Dad. He had other interests - music, girls, and other sports- but what brought us very close was baseball cards. George started collecting baseball cards when he was ten years old. I became interested and together we would go to card shows, flea markets, card shops, ball games, wherever we could find cards. George got a few autographs, but collecting the cards was his true love. Now that he is gone, his cards are priceless to me. I look through them and remember how he got the Kirby Puckett Rookie card or the Cal Ripken Rookie card. There are a thousand more cards not worth nearly as much to any other collector as they are to me. These cards are memories that I will never sell or forget.

March 31, 1993, has to be the worst day in our lives. It started out okay, just like any other normal day. It was the first day of vacation for me and the Wednesday of spring break for our children. George was sixteen and he was in his second week of a new job as a bagger for Kroger supermarket. This was the first day he had been off during his spring break. The night before, he had worked until 8 P.M. and wanted to spend the evening overnight with a friend. Linda, his mom, wanted him to stay home, but we both felt like he deserved some time to play.

That Wednesday Linda and I woke up to rainy weather. We went to Kentucky Kingdom, an amusement park, to buy George and his brother season passes. We bought those, went down to get Bob Dylan concert tickets for Bobby and me, and came home. It was around lunch time when George called, and I talked to him for the last time. He thanked me for the pass and wanted to know if I could pick him up around 6 P.M. I planned to go to a card shop to trade some baseball cards, and I invited George to go along. George did not want to go this time. This was one of the many "What ifs?" that we constantly torture ourselves with. Had I insisted on his coming home, would he still be alive?

About 3:30, we got a phone call from the hospital. There had been an accident, and we were to come immediately. While we were on the phone, our doorbell rang and two city detectives were there for the same reason, to tell us about the accident. George's mom kept asking these officers, "Who was driving?" This is when we learned that George wasn't in a car accident—he had been shot. My wife, our two other children, and I got in the car and headed for the University Hospital, hoping that our worst fears were unfounded. Somehow, I knew while driving downtown that my son was dying. Everything seemed to be going in slow motion. My wife kept muttering, "Please don't let it be in the head." The kids, Bobby age thirteen and Sharon age seven, were in tears in the back seat, saying nothing.

We got to the hospital about 4:00 P.M. and a chaplain took us to a small room. An ER doctor came in and asked me if George was right or left handed. With these words, I knew that he had been shot in the head. I replied that he was right handed. The doctor then said that the worst thing that could have happened has happened. George had been shot in the head. His prospects were not good. I called my younger brother to come to us. He is a pediatrician, and I suppose I felt he may have been able to give us some advice in what was a hopeless situation.

I'll never forget going into that emergency room and feeling so helpless. There on a gurney hooked up to IV drips and monitors was my sixteen year old son. His brown hair was red from the blood. His body convulsed, and the pain was evident in his face. His mom began talking to him, which seemed to have a calming effect, yet we both felt so helpless. For the first time, we knew we could not do anything to make it right, to make him whole again. I saw things most parents only dream about in their worst nightmares. I saw CAT scans of my son's head showing bullet fragments from the front to the back of his skull. The gun that the other boy used to kill my son was loaded with Hydra-shock shells which explode on impact. We were told that if George lived, he would be like a severe stroke victim.

Nothing could be done to relieve swelling until the bleeding could be controlled. This would take ten hours before any other options could be considered. At this time, his pupils were fully dilated, and the only thing he could do on his own was breathe. This is one of the first things George did as a baby and was the last thing he would do thirty-three hours after he was shot.

As I said earlier, March 31st was the worst day of my life. April 2nd was a peaceful end to George's suffering. I know that there was physical pain for George and emotional pain for all of us. At one point on Thursday in the early afternoon, the clouds outside his hospital room broke and a ray of sunshine seemed to bathe the room. My wife felt this was when he left his body to go to a higher place—a better place. She was telling him it was O.K. to let go. We knew that he could not return to his battered body. You have to believe there is a better place because if you don't, the loss of a child would truly be unbearable.

Funeral preparations are never easy but saying goodbye forever to your sixteen year old son is devastating. George's thirteen year old brother Bobby picked out the oak casket and read at his funeral service. Walking into the visitation room and seeing George's body there was such a kick in the stomach. So many well-wishers were there including the Archbishop of Louisville, the EMS attendant, teachers, friends, and family members. You wonder what inside you keeps you going through two days of this tremendous onslaught of well intentioned people. Three priests co-celebrated the funeral mass for George on Monday of Holy Week. They tell me that the procession to his burial plot at Saint Michael's was over two miles long. I did not want to leave George there, although I now know it wasn't him that we were leaving. As one of the priests would later tell me, "Now you have another Guardian angel watching over you."

Once the wake was over at our home, we were back to being a family, not of five, but only four. We were survivors. The house was so empty now. How would our two surviving children cope? How would we handle this? We had learned to be parents from George, now we would be put to the test. We poured ourselves into our other two children. We went to family counseling because it was "the right thing to do." We soon realized that for us, this was not true. Someone suggested a group called Compassionate Friends and we tried this as well, but something was missing. Linda had received a call from Rosemary Smith from a town near Natural Bridge in Kentucky. Later, we received some grief therapy books from her as well. Her network of fellow parents who had lost teenage children was the best support we could possibly have received. We became members of a fraternity of sorts, one that no one wanted to belong to, but one that we were glad to have on our side. These were people who had been where we were at that time. When you really needed someone to talk with, this group of friends was always there or a phone call away. This group has been our lifeline when times have been really bad.

Immediately after George died, we threw ourselves into pursuing his killer in the juvenile court system. Little can be said of this part of our story due to juvenile secrecy, but it was established that George at no time touched the weapon that killed him. As the homicide detective told us, your son was in the wrong place at the wrong time. George was talking to a girl on a cordless phone when he was shot. He said, "I need to check on (the other boy)." George walked into the room where the boy was sitting, gun pointing at George. He pulled the trigger and George lay dying. One minute George was a happy teenager with a new job and a girlfriend; the next minute the life was ebbing out of him.

George's death helped rewrite Kentucky's law involving parental responsibility when their child uses a handgun to commit a violent act. This law was passed on July 15, 1993, too late to have made a difference in George living or dying but this outcome has brought us some satisfaction. Since George's death, I have spoken to nurses and students at the college level about our tragedy and how we have coped. We have been interviewed by numerous T.V. stations, radio stations, and newspapers and have in other ways too spread the news about how guns can dramatically change the lives of others. George's image was also used in an MTV music video to dramatize how final and tragic gun play is in the hands of a juvenile.

We cope day to day. That's what we all do as bereaved parents. It's all we can do. We try to push the thoughts of his pain and suffering out of our minds. We try to think of all the good times we had. Memories can never be taken away from us. These are the only treasures left, and we savor them like the sweetest dessert you can imagine. Almost two years after George died, we were blessed with the birth of our fourth child, Garrett. My wife felt George's presence with her in the delivery room. She saw his face above her after Garrett's birth. George was smiling down on all of us. Garrett has been a joy. He does not replace George and was never intended to do so. He is a unique individual who has helped us through many hard moments.

Garrett, or "Wild Man" as we lovingly call him, began talking about an imaginary friend when he was about two years old. "Dirder" always had to have an extra chair at Garrett's small table. Garrett spent a lot of time conversing with his friend. We were somewhat worried until we started noticing some amazing similarities between Dirder and George. Then we were stunned rather than worried. One night as I was drying Garrett after his bath, he hid behind the bathroom door. I told him we had to get him dressed and asked him what he was doing. He said, "I'm putting a hole in the wall like Dirder." I froze, speechless. A month before George died (and two years before Garrett was born), George had stormed upstairs after a minor disagreement with Linda and me and punched a small hole in the wall.

A second "Dirder" incident shook the whole family. We were on vacation in Chimney Rock, North Carolina, hiking on a steep downward slope. I decided to put Garrett on my shoulders until we reached a more level area. Garrett said, "Dirder said, 'Dad used to carry me on his shoulders like this too!'" Each of us stopped dead in our tracks. I <u>had</u> carried George exactly like this, many times. Very recently Garrett amazed me with yet another "Dirder" revelation. I was babysitting him while Linda took Bobby and Sharon shopping. We stopped at McDonalds for a picnic lunch. I decided to take Garrett to a local park. As we sat down on a bench he casually commented, "Dirder said he sat here before." I knew I had never taken George to this particular park, but Linda later told me she had been there with George on many occasions. Does Garrett hear the voice of his brother? It certainly seems like it. We think he does.

Our family has lost a vital member, our firstborn child. We have found ways to fill our lives with new memories while holding on to the treasured ones of George.

Chapter Seventeen
Anna Beth Burnett

ANNABETH BURNETT

By LuAnn Burnett

On May 9, 1993, a beautiful, sunny, spring afternoon that happened to be Mother's Day, our lives were changed forever. My husband and I had been married nearly twenty-three years and our lives were moving right along. We had recently moved to an older, established neighborhood where the streets were never busy. We loved our newfound peace and quiet. The big old trees and large lots were just what we had been looking for. We had an almost twenty-one year old son living on campus at the University of Kentucky. Our middle son was getting ready to graduate from high school, our youngest son was graduating from elementary school, and our daughter was finishing up second grade and was a delightful addition to our family of men! God had blessed us in so many ways and we were very grateful.

We had just returned home from a family brunch at my sister's home where the family had gathered to celebrate Mother's Day. Our-eleven-year old son had stayed to play with his cousins, and our middle son was leaving in our car to pick up his older brother on campus. AnnaBeth followed him outside asking questions about a phone call he had taken for her. He was in a hurry to leave and she wanted to play, as they often did; this was her favorite brother. As he pulled out of the driveway, she grabbed onto the car, using her elbows to hold on to the inside open right front window. "Look! I'm still here!" she quipped. Then, in a split second, an utterly freakish accident occurred. AnnaBeth's feet touched the pavement, and she was jerked down onto the driveway. Her head hit the pavement before her hands, and she died almost immediately of severe internal head injuries. She was bleeding from her mouth, ears, and nose as we rushed to the fire station a few blocks away. She was unconscious from the beginning, and the EMT

198

could not find a pulse. I was in complete shock as we raced to the hospital in the Emergency Life Support truck. About half an hour later, the doctor came in to tell us that she had died.

When someone tells you that your child is dead, has to be the most horrible gut-ripping experience. I remember blurting out, "No! It can't be! Not my baby! Why not me? I've lived my life! Take me, not my baby!" But we don't really have that choice or any control over our lives. When things like this happen, you spend the rest of your life trying to come to terms with your loss.

Going through the grief process is very hard and it takes a long time. Each person grieves in a different way, so it is very important to take your time and listen to your heart. Don't try to do what some well-meaning friend or family member may tell you to do. You must walk this way alone. Others can be there for your support, but you must do the work. Feel all the feelings; cry as often and as long as you need to. Scream, be angry, be physical, pound on something, let it out, and keep on letting it out until you feel you have poured out your soul. Then, be still; be still and hold on, hold on to life, as you slowly let go. You must let your loved one go. They are no longer in need of their bodies or this earthly life. We are still here, wrapped up in this physical world. Theirs is now a world of spirit.

When AnnaBeth died, I was in shock for at least a year. Time had no meaning. Fortunately, I was able to quit my part time job at the pre-school. I was allowed the luxury of staying home and being able to take the time and energy it takes to work through the grief process. Having the time to work through your grief is very important. I think if I had not been able to take the time, the effect on me would have been much more detrimental, both emotionally and physically, and the healing would take much longer.

During the first year, many things continued to happen. I read all the books about grief that I was given by friends and found more on my own. I took care of myself first and then the rest of the family. They were all very supportive and understanding. If I just felt like crying or if I stayed in bed with a headache, it was all right. Most of my crying was done when no one was at home. I could scrub or mop or dig in the garden and let the tears fall. I felt numb and sort of dull for the first few months. I could sit for a long time and just stare into space, something I never used to do before. Journal writing was another therapy I adopted. It is very healing to be able to put feelings into words and then to be able to transfer them to paper. When you read them again, you begin to see that you are changing, growing, healing.

Another "tool" that helped me deal with the loss of my daughter was exercise. When AnnaBeth died and I stopped teaching pre-school, my activity level went down considerably. After about two years I realized that I was feeling lethargic and depressed. I joined a nearby gym and began to work out with weights three days a week. Soon after that I started going to aerobics class and found the physical exertion to be exhilarating. For me it was the first time that AnnaBeth was not in the forefront of my thoughts. When I was pushing myself physically, I had to concentrate on that and somehow it was a relief. I began to sleep better, eat better, and feel more energetic. I think that making your body stronger somehow makes your mind stronger. Exercise has done that for me.

I was also blessed with having a very strong extended family. My father died in 1979, but my mother, two sisters, and my brother all live nearby. They were all with us from that first horrible day, calming, planning, soothing, and working at holding everything together for us. Our families and friends surrounded us with love, food, faith and the courage to go on. To this day, my mother and I go every Sunday to visit AnnaBeth's and granddad's resting places. It is a very healing ritual that we share.

Five months after AnnaBeth died, my oldest son fell

twenty-five feet off a roof and survived. He did break his upper left arm and elbow and was in the hospital for a week after surgery. It seemed so ironic that our daughter fell less than three feet and died while our son's life was spared. Two months later, in December, we had gathered the family together in Snowshoe, West Virginia, for a skiing weekend that would mark AnnaBeth's ninth birthday. My husband had a mild heart attack and when we returned to Lexington, he was hospitalized until after Christmas. I'm sure AnnaBeth's passing had much to do with his illness. He gained weight after she died and although he was able to cry and express his emotions more than many men, he was still expected to get back to business and "be over" the tragedy much too soon. Because men are usually the main income producers in a family, they don't usually have the time to spend on grief work that many women do. I think this is a real problem for many bereaved fathers.

This is the ending of our fifth summer without AnnaBeth. She left five years ago in May. I still miss her terribly, but now that this much time has passed, it is not as hard as the first year without her. You get stronger. The pain of your loss is dulled with the passing of time, but the scar, the hurt, the empty, missing part never goes away. Really, you don't want it to; it's all you have left. That and all your memories of all the wonderful time you did have with your sweet child.

Our sons are moving on in their lives as we are all trying to do. Our oldest sons, Chap Jr., and John, are both working in their father's roofing company. Both are college graduates and express interest in building the family business. They both seem all right. Our middle son Seth is the one I am most concerned about. On the outside, he appears to be doing just fine; going to U.K., active in his fraternity, working at the Student Center. Somehow, I feel that he has not yet dealt with all of this tragedy and his part in it. He knows that no one blames him for AnnaBeth's demise, yet he knows that he was directly involved in it. I think that somehow he feels that he has never been punished for his lack of good judgment - yet his punishment is in his awareness of it every day. I pray for him every day to be at peace about this and for him not to risk his safety or tempt fate concerning his own life. We have had several good talks and cries about all this over the past three years, and I only pray that he will be all right. Daniel, our youngest son, is a sophomore in high school, an honor student and football player.

We still talk about AnnaBeth all the time. At dinner when we pray, I always thank God for sharing her with us. We have planted an evergreen tree in the back yard and started a flower garden in her memory. Each year on her birthday, December 19th, we invite her cousins, friends, and family to come over for a tree trimming party. We decorate the evergreen with treats for the birds, rabbits, and squirrels. Her classmates planted a tree at school in her memory, and the high school football booster club planted a pink dogwood in the cemetery in her honor. We plan to honor her memory in other ways as time goes on. Our home is filled with her pictures, art work, and poems. She has left us in body but not in spirit. You must search for the spiritual presence of your loved one. It is there waiting for you to become aware of it.

I would have to say that the first year, the first time you go through all the birthdays, holidays, and little family celebrations and vacations without your sweet child is the hardest year. Passing those milestones and then the anniversary of their death is very hard, but you can do it. You have no choice; you will survive; you will succeed; you will smile again; you will find meaning in life again, but it is hard work.

AnnaBeth was such a bright, outgoing, vibrant spirit. You always knew when she was around. She loved to be silly and laugh and take chances. She lived life to its fullest and had all the confidence in the world that she could do anything! She was a cheerleader for her brother's basketball team;

she loved jumping on the trampoline, bike riding, and dancing around and acting out songs. She made friends with many people, old and young, adopting extra grandmas and grandpops along the way. She was becoming a good reader and won a creative writing contest at school. Of course, I could go on, but I will conclude with this one last story.

AnnaBeth always loved her kittens. She had one that disappeared a few months before her death; in fact, we had just replaced the first "Mitten" with "Mitten-Too" about two weeks before the accident. I'm not sure what inspired her, but she had drawn a huge picture of a cat and had colored it in with all the colors of the rainbow. This "Rainbow Cat" has become our symbol for AnnaBeth, and we have given many people who knew and loved AnnaBeth framed copies of this wonderful drawing. I also had it reduced to two inches and made it into a pin that I wear every day. In her room, I also found a self portrait she had drawn. It is a picture of her smiling face, and these words are scribbled in a cloud above her head, "Forget about those things down there, look at this, I love you mommy." I'm so thankful for that short sweet message and the advice. I try to remember it and live it every day.

PINK SNOW
(Or a Day with AnnaBeth)
 By Lu Mattone

"Grandma, look! Pink snow!" As I peek out the back door, I can see AnnaBeth, my eight-year-old granddaughter, scooping up handfuls of pink, flowering crab apple petals from the grass, throwing them up and letting them fall on her head, completely entranced with her "find." This is one year the blossoms haven't been frostbitten and are at their fullest and loveliest. I could smell their sweet fragrance drifting across the yard. What a perfect day.

"Bet you can't see me!" I hear from the branches of

the dogwood tree (the grandchildren's favorite as the branches are low). Tousled curls flying as she jumps from a limb, she stops next at the statue of St. Francis in the flower bed close by, and I can see her talking to the saint of the woods. All the grandchildren seem to have a special affection for him and went up to hug him as toddlers. "How sweet," I am thinking.

Now she is swinging on the rope swing hanging from the tree and asking, "Grandma, could you get the 'trick' mattress out, please?" I keep the camper mattress where I can get to it easily and place it on a grassy spot. She is happily doing somersaults, headstands, and cartwheels for the next hour. This is one of our special days together, and I am enjoying every minute.

Some days she wants to embroider and will make up her own design using the brightest thread, often making little pincushions for her favorite people. Some days she wants to draw, color, or paint. Her multicolored "Rainbow Cat" has become quite famous in the family circle, and we all have a copy. AnnaBeth loves animals—especially kittens—so when her kitten Mittens was to be a year old, she decided there should be a birthday party. All her young cousins and aunts and I came to the celebration which was complete with horns, hats, and balloons.

About a month after our "pink snow" day, our family was gathered again for a Mother's Day brunch at my daughter Mary's, with good food, laughing, teasing, and picture-taking as usual, and the four boy cousins talking AnnaBeth into getting a plate of doughnuts for them before the "healthy stuff." Her "But, Mom, it is Mom's Day!" was so appealing, who could refuse? I had to leave early to meet our senior group to go to the Opera House to the musical *42nd Street*. We enjoyed it thoroughly and returned to the church parking lot about 4:40. I was very surprised to see my son waiting for me. "Why?" I wondered. He looked so sad.

"Mom, there's been an accident—it's AnnaBeth."

I felt a huge weight in my heart. "She's okay, isn't she?" (Dear Lord, let her be! Please!) But I knew it was serious.

"No, Mom, she died," he said.

I can remember the intense pain and sadness that went through my whole being at that moment. <u>Children</u> <u>aren't</u> <u>supposed</u> <u>to</u> <u>die</u>. Not AnnaBeth! That little whirlwind of endless energy who danced through our lives and made us feel good just to be around her? Not to hear her come bounding in from school with a "Hi, Mom, what's for a snack?" as she turned on the stereo to hear her favorite song, "I'll Always Love You." Not to have her come in from her room outrageously dressed up in different colored socks and lipstick just to make us laugh. Not to watch her cuddle Mittens. Not to watch her swim like a little guppy. Not to tease her big brothers John and Seth and twelve-year-old Daniel who was really her buddy and she was so proud to be a cheerleader for his basketball team. Not to climb up into Dad's lap or Mom's arms and say, "Gee, I love you!" Five years have gone by since the Mother's Day our family can never forget. We're all still healing and their home, once so full of AnnaBeth, is now so quiet.

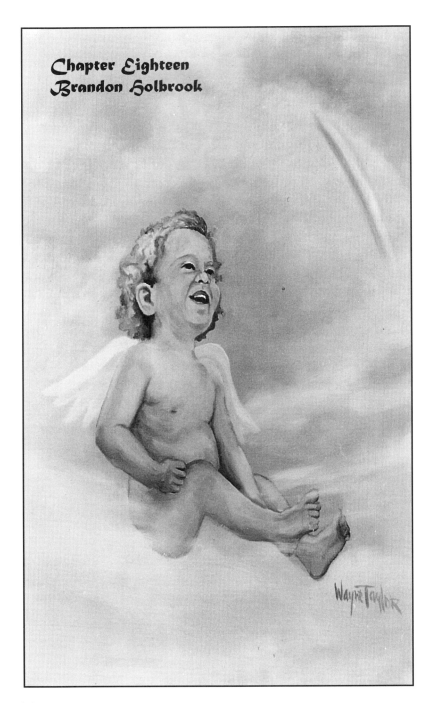

Chapter Eighteen
Brandon Holbrook

BRANDON HOLBROOK

By Linda Holbrook

I wed my high school and college sweetheart, Dennis Holbrook, in a small, country church in Wheelwright, Kentucky. We had enjoyed a four year courtship and postponed marriage until we had college behind us and were financially secure to ensure that everything would be just the way it was supposed to be. We continued our professional careers successfully as teacher and administrator, but there was something missing, and we both knew what it was - a baby. On October 7, 1976, we experienced the joy of the birth of Dennis Brandon Holbrook. Our lives changed gears quickly as parenthood became the central part of our lives. It was an easy decision to put my professional career on hold and devote myself to being a full time mother. Brandon was such a happy baby, always smiling and never wanting to sleep. He especially enjoyed being read stories and nursery rhymes, his favorite being "Little Boy Blue." We never did get him to repeat the line, "Will you wake him?" He would just always answer, "No". We thought he would never learn his ABC's. He kept saying that the letter after K was Mart!

The house was so full of laughter and excitement. Somehow Brandon always managed to get the last laugh, like the time we were playing cops and robbers. He handcuffed me and happened to forget where he had put the key. My neighbor had to cut them off my hands! Another time he locked himself in the bathroom, and we had to remove the door to get him out. Three years after the birth of Brandon, we had a second son, Justin Kyle Holbrook. Brandon was a little disappointed when we first brought Justin home. He said we had promised someone to play with, but this little baby couldn't do much of anything! But, as the story unfolded, the two of them would become great friends over the years. When you saw one of them you would see the other. The names Brandon and Justin became synonymous. Everything was going just as we had planned.

Early on, athletics played an important role in Brandon's life. If for no other reason, Brandon liked to have the opportunity sports brought to associate with people. His first experience as an athlete was Pee Wee baseball. When he came home from his first game, he explained every detail to his grandmother, and when she asked him what position he played, his reply was "the batter". He played all sports, and according to all his coaches, including Dad, he would always give everything he had whether it be in practice or in a real game. We always wondered if maybe he loved football the most because he got the opportunity to be a little rowdy, hit someone, and not get into trouble! On the other hand the incident that most reflected his true personality occurred at a district track meet. Being an accomplished runner, Brandon had won the 800 meter run almost every time in the previous two years. At this particular meet he finished second to a teammate. The local newspaper did a story of what team spirit our school exhibited after the reporter heard Brandon yell to his teammate to "kick it in" as they turned the last turn. Later, when we asked Brandon what happened that made him lose the race, we were humbled by his answer: "Well, my teammate is a senior and to win that race could mean that he could get a college scholarship. I am just a sophomore and to win that race would have been important only to me." His teammate did receive that college scholarship.

The story moved along just as if it were scripted. Our lives consisted of a wonderful marriage, loving families, two happy, healthy sons, successful careers, and a beautiful home filled with lots of love and the smell of chocolate chip cookies. Then, on June 17, 1993, the unthinkable happened instead of the "all lived happily ever after" ending. Every parent's nightmare is that they will receive a telephone call that their child has been in an accident. Well, we received that dreaded call and immediately thought we would find a broken arm, stitches, or maybe even surgery when we arrived at the hospital. When we pulled in, I became anxious when I saw about a hundred people standing outside. We ran to the emergency room and asked to see Brandon Holbrook. The nurse just gave us a puzzled look. We asked again, and we heard the words that will ring in our ears forever, "I'M SORRY!" Her eyes provided the rest of the explanation. How could everything so right suddenly be so wrong?

The next days, weeks, months, and years would be a journey filled with pain, heartache, and numerous obstacles to overcome. A turning point came in our lives when we met Rosemary and Luther Smith, another grieving couple who had lost two of their sons in an automobile accident a year earlier. Until the accident, it was very important to me that people would perceive me as a good cook and hostess. I had invited the Smiths to our house for dinner. When I arrived from school they were already there so I had no time for last minute changes. When we entered the house the ham had burned, which seemed manageable. We would just scrape off the burned part. When I took the baked beans out of the oven, they looked like the little black rocks in the aquarium. They were beyond help. Before, I would have panicked, but by then I thought, we have buried children, what is a ruined dinner? I have learned with great difficulty that often the situation may be beyond our control. It is, however, our own reaction that we have some control over. To accept our fate was not our choice but how we reacted to it would be. Even this, however, is much easier said than done.

Up until we met Luther and Rosemary, we had shared our loss of Brandon only with others who knew him personally. The Smiths never knew Brandon but they were the only ones who really understood our pain. Somehow both Dennis and I found it easier to discuss our loss with these total strangers. After recovering from the embarrassment of my ruined meal, Dennis opened up for the first time since Brandon's death. I saw Dennis in a different light that night. I thought he wasn't grieving as much as I was because he wasn't outwardly grieving. At that moment I knew we both felt the same pain but had different ways of showing it.

One day, shortly after Brandon's death, we were standing at the cemetery and looked up and saw the most beautiful rainbow. Immediately we smiled at each other despite our sadness and knew that it was a sign we would see Brandon again someday. Rainbows came to symbolize Brandon's presence for us. Two years after his death as his class assembled for part of the graduation ceremony, Brandon's football coach spoke through tears as he awarded the scholarship we had set up in Brandon's name. Unbelievably, at that very moment, a rainbow appeared in the sky over the school. There was no rain in sight. Another two years after that, a dear friend was certain the young man she met on a campus sidewalk was Brandon as he appeared from nowhere with a smile and a "How are you doing?" This encounter left her speechless. When she turned to acknowledge the boy, he had vanished. She went on to her class and unwrapped the brown paper seal on her new textbook. A rainbow was on the cover. My friend called me crying. She was absolutely certain that the boy had been Brandon. Coincidence? Maybe so to those with little faith who never knew Brandon. To us, it is our reassurance of God's promise that we will see our son again one day.

Chapter Nineteen
Tiann Wilson

"WHEN THE CREEK RAN RED"
By Sue Wilson

The afternoon of August 31, 1995, was my youngest daughter Taiann's second day at school. She was a sophomore at Southwestern High in Somerset, Kentucky. Taiann was really looking forward to the school year. She had written in a personal narrative for one of her classes, "This is going to be my best year yet!" Taiann was excited that afternoon. A young man by the name of Matthew Coomer had asked her for a first date. I learned later that he had waited three years for the chance to date her. Taiann was going through her closet trying to decide what to wear. She picked out three tops and asked me which one I thought looked best on her. Of a green, yellow and red one, I picked red. She said they were going on a picnic. As we talked, she was getting ready. I told her that I would drive her to meet Matthew half way so they could have a little extra time together for their picnic. Taiann thought that would be a great idea and called Matthew to tell him. We left the house at 7:30 that evening to meet Matthew at 7:45 at the Blue and Gray Restaurant. Taiann was so excited. She was the happiest I had seen her lately.

When we arrived at 7:45, Matthew wasn't there yet. We sat in the car and talked. He pulled up at 7:55, apologizing for being late. I told him, "absolutely no big deal." He had hurt his ankle while helping his Dad put tobacco in the barn. I asked where they planned to go on their picnic, and he asked, "Mrs. Wilson, do you care if I take Taiann to the most beautiful and peaceful place that I know?"

I said, "No, Matthew, I don't mind, just please have Taiann home early as it is a school night."

"Yes, Mrs. Wilson, I will." Matthew walked Taiann

around his parents' dark green mini van and opened the door for her. I walked around and motioned for her to roll the window down and told them to be careful and be home early. The last words that I spoke to Taiann were, "I love you, see you in a little bit." In less than 45 minutes they were both dead. It is a nightmare beyond anyone's comprehension.

I returned home, went for my evening run, watched some news and waited for Taiann's return from her date. I heard a knock on the door. When I opened the door, I saw five police officers. I instantly knew something was wrong. The sheriff blurted out, "Taiann's been MURDERED!!" I asked them to come in. My knees started shaking. My back felt as if someone had hit me on the lower spine with a baseball bat. My hands were wet with sweat. The sheriff began asking me questions. I was trying to answer them, but couldn't because the words wouldn't come out. I asked them where Taiann was. Could I see her? How was she killed? Where was she right then? Please let me see her! Was she raped? Did they know anything about who had done it? I asked again if I could PLEASE see Taiann. Where were they taking her? What kind of vehicle were they taking her in? They told me Matt had been shot, and then asked if I knew anyone who owned a sheaf knife. I remember getting a drink of iced tea as my mouth was cotton-dry. I was trying to focus on their questions to help in any way I could. They told me that Taiann was on her way to Frankfort for an autopsy and that I would not be able to see her until she was brought back here to Somerset to the funeral home. I remember the look of horror on their faces that night. They were in a hurry because they were looking for the suspect. They asked me if I would be okay. I said yes.

They left. I ran outside and ran up and down the street in the dark saying, "This is not happening. What am I going to do? What am I going to do?" My son and other daughter had spent the night with friends. I knew that I had to call both of them. I got them out of bed and told them it was an emergency, to come home as quickly as possible. By this time, I was wild. As soon as Stephen walked in the door, I shouted, "Taiann's been MURDERED!" I told him what the police had told me and Stephen ran out the front door. I didn't see him for a while. Tonya, my oldest daughter, came home next. She went berserk. I was in shock. I said over and over again that I had no idea who could have killed them. "Who" seemed to be the main question on everyone's mind. Taiann had dated another boy and had recently broken up with him. He seemed to be the one everyone suspected, but I knew he could not have done it. I loved the boy and treated him as my own child.

It seemed like a thousand people came to the house that day. There were TV cameras, reporters, flowers, food, people to mow the lawn, to clean the house, more food and flowers. I was taking care of it all. The phone never stopped ringing. I wanted to answer each and every call.

My family came. It was around 2:00 in the afternoon when I looked at my sisters and said, "It is Labor Day weekend. We need to get to the funeral home and make arrangements." We grabbed our purses, and with my oldest and only living daughter, went to Pulaski Funeral Home. Have you ever had to go to the funeral home to make arrangements? I hadn't. I remember the staff being so kind as I raced around the room with all the caskets in it, saying things like, "Taiann would like that one," or "that is not her color." They stood calmly by the door waiting for our selection. We finally decided on a pink coffin with roses carved on the handles. I felt like I was in a nightmare. I expected to wake up at any time. We selected the songs, the program, her favorite Bible verses. The man gave me the bill and I left without even looking at it. I returned home to the same chaos I had left earlier. I was concerned about the police capturing the killer. We made several phone calls to the police station. Each time they said no information was available yet.

Sometime the next day the phone rang. It was the funeral home. The man said, "Mrs. Wilson, you can't use the dress that you brought up here for Taiann." I said, "Why not?" He said, "Ma'am, have you not talked to the sheriff?" I said, "He has been too busy trying to catch the murderer to talk to me. Please just tell me why you can't use the dress. I can take whatever you tell me." He said, "This is not my job. You need to talk to the sheriff." Well, after several reassurances that I was really okay, I talked him into telling me why he could not use the dress. He said, "Mrs. Wilson. Taiann had over 100 knife wounds on her body. Her neck was slashed open making it impossible to use the dress. We need something with a high neckline and long sleeves." I told him I would see to it that we got another dress as soon as possible. I hung up the phone. I screamed, "Taiann had over 100 knife wounds on her!" My legs went out from under me. My son picked me up and carried me to my bedroom. My family was trying to help but what could they possibly do? I got up, fell on my knees, and told God that I could not take this, I was not going to take this, and that I wasn't going to the funeral or anything! I remember feeling so helpless. I didn't sleep that night. As I lay there I thought about Taiann and what must have happened that night. The police had told me that Taiann was found lying in the water on her side and Matthew had been dragged over to the sand bar. He was found lying face up in the weeds with a bullet hole in his chest.

Tonya, my twenty-three year old, decided that she was going to the funeral home to fix her sister's hair and do her makeup. We argued back and forth for awhile with everyone in the house telling Tonya that she did not need to see her sister, that Taiann would not want Tonya to see her in that condition. But Tonya's mind was made up. I felt like a coward because I was unable to go with her. Some unseen force was holding me back. By the time Tonya arrived at the funeral home, the two morticians had all of her wounds concealed except for a few on her arms and face. When Tonya arrived,

Taiann was lying on the preparation table. When she saw Taiann she thought her legs were going to buckle. She said she asked the Lord to give her strength to make it to Taiann. Tonya's friend who was a hair dresser had accompanied her. I don't think Tonya will ever get over seeing her little sister like that. She said she placed a kiss with her fingers on each wound that was still showing. She noticed that she had something wrong with her eye. The cosmetologist told her that Taiann had multiple wounds in and around her eye.

We cried a lot that night. I didn't know how to help my two remaining children. I was hit with a whole series of emotions that I had never experienced. I don't know if shock is an emotion, but I do know that something took over and gave me insurmountable strength to do what I needed to do. I was still talking to the police, the news media, friends of the children. I tried to take care of everyone, welcome them into our home, and encourage them to help themselves to whatever they needed. We had more food than we could eat.

My nephews, brother-in-law, brother and a friend took their guns and went to the creek where the murders occurred. As the murderer had not yet been found, tension was running high throughout the community, especially among our family members. They found a pair of white female socks at the little bridge where the children had parked the mini van. They found blood on some rocks. This evidence was collected and taken to the coroner. I looked at the socks and recognized them as Taiann's. We became fearful for our own lives. The police questioned the boy Taiann had dated. The community was ready to hang him. The murders had been so vicious it appeared to be a hate-passion crime. I called Taiann's former boyfriend and told him not to go anywhere by himself. The police tested him for powder burns, questioned him and released him. They did not make a statement to the community that he was cleared of suspicion.

Day 3, Sunday, arrived without my being able to sleep

or eat any food that I can remember. Everyone tried to get me to eat. I would take a bite or two to appease them so they would leave me alone. The viewing was to start at 2:30. The funeral director told us that we could not let anyone touch Taiann. I asked Tonya to stand at the head of her casket, Stephen to stand at the middle, and I stood out away from it. It was important to me to talk with Taiann's friends. I felt like this would be the last chance I would have. The people stood in line for four or five hours. No one complained, even the elderly. Some people who were my school teachers when I was a little girl came. Taiann's teachers, friends, family, and neighbors were all there; it seemed like the community was grieving for and with us. We stood in line until 10:30 that night. The police had asked if they could put a hidden video camera and recorders in the casket and around the funeral home in case the murderer came to the viewing. I was truly touched by the reverence of the people who came to the viewing, but I could not shed a tear.

Day 4 arrived. It seemed like a nightmare that was never ending. I remember looking at the clock around 4:00 A.M. and wondering again what Taiann must have felt before her death. I must have slept, because I woke up around 8:00. I felt compelled to go to Matthew's funeral which was at 10:30. Taiann's was scheduled for 1:30 that afternoon. I did not know where Matthew's church was, but I knew the little community that he lived in, so I knew we could find the funeral. My sister and I drove through the countryside until we came upon the funeral procession. I parked the car and ran to the front of the little white country church. The hearse was backed up to the door of the church. The pallbearers were taking the coffin out. I had a picture of Taiann with me as Matthew's Dad had requested. I handed it to the funeral director and asked him to put it in the casket. I found Matt's Mom and Dad and walked in with them. I sat in the front row with his family. I had met his parents for the first time the night after the murders. I sat by his grandmother. She introduced me to the people that walked by as 'the little girl's mother.'

We didn't have time to go home before Taiann's funeral. The funeral director met me at the door and told me they had lost the music I had selected. I calmly went with them to reselect the music. It was truly a beautiful service. I had poured out every ounce of my energy that was supplied by adrenaline or shock into making the funeral beautiful for my daughter. As I sat there listening to the ceremony, I wondered if I had done everything that I was supposed to do. One of Taiann's friends came up and fell on her knees. She put her head in my lap. She was crying and trying to tell me something about Taiann. I sat through the whole funeral without a tear. When the time came for the family to go up to the casket, I still could not cry. I told my children to get the Bible from her casket that I bought her as a little girl. Stephen said, "Mom, she might want that." So I left it in her casket.

When we left the funeral home, the TV cameras and reporters were there asking if I wanted to say anything. I made the statement that, "I am asking the Lord to put whoever did this into such a state of guilt that they cannot eat, sleep, drink, walk, or function until they come forth and confess." Eleven days later the murderer was captured. After questioning, he said, "Get your tape recorder, I want to tell you everything." He gave a thirty-five minute detailed confession.

Matthew had taken Taiann to a little creek near his house called Housefork Creek. He and his family had spent many happy outings there fishing, camping, swimming and wading. Matthew and Taiann left at 7:55 P.M. It took them twenty minutes to reach the creek. The confessed murderer said that they were sitting on the little bridge, laughing and talking, dangling their feet in the water. He decided to cross the creek on his four-wheeler and splashed mud and water on them. Matt yelled, "Hey! Don't be doing that." Taiann and Matthew had waded about 150 yards down the creek, carrying their shoes. Jeff Coffey, the confessed murderer, said, "The farther up the creek I went, the madder I got. I turned around, went back and shot the boy." Coffey said on the witness stand that Taiann went over to Matthew, got down on her knees, and put her hand over the hole in Matthew's chest to try to stop the bleeding. He tried to shoot the girl, but the gun jammed. He said she said, "Stop, quit. Please don't hurt me." A lady and her father who lived sixty yards off the creek testified that they heard Tai say this. He confessed that he knew that he couldn't leave any witnesses. Taiann fought Jeff Coffey with everything she had: his shirt was torn, her shirt was torn, and she had numerous defensive wounds on her arms and hands. He stabbed her in the back, over forty times in the chest, slashed her neck from ear to ear four to five times and broke off the knife blade in her eye socket. They were both dead by 8:30 P.M. Coffey left Taiann lying there in the creek.

Jeff Coffey did not know the children. We had never heard of him. He took his rage at someone else out on my daughter for no reason. We asked for the death penalty. The jury gave him life without the possibility of parole for 25 years. He has shown no remorse. He bragged about their murders in jail. He said he wished he had done more to the little girl before he had killed her, that her blood felt warm, and that he wished he had "done her before he had killed her," meaning have sex with her. An inmate gave this testimony against him at the trial.

The trial was ruthless. Defense attorneys did not care about me or my daughter. I did not know they would go to any extreme to protect the murderer's rights. I learned very quickly. There were people sitting in the courtroom that did care and I knew they were praying for me. I knew that with the Lord beside me and them behind me, I was never alone.

Our lives have been changed forever. I have seen everyone in my family suffer. Three years later, I still see them suffering. People say that you experience some kind of closure with the funeral - we were hurting too bad to even begin to understand what lay ahead of us. Then we waited two years for a trial. The prosecutor asked me if I felt some kind of closure after the trial. I told him that I felt that closure was something you might get when you bought a house. I still don't have closure. We still obsess about Taiann's horrible death. I don't think it is humanly possible to imagine what she went through, but I have spent night after night awake, thinking about what happened to her. I have unresolved pain that I think I will always carry in my heart.

If you want to know how you can help, I ask that you call the Attorney General of Kentucky in Frankfort, and tell him that we want the law returned to the law abiding people of the Commonwealth. You may contact the Office of Victims' Advocate at 1-800-371-2551. You may also write a letter to the parole board about never allowing Jeff Coffey out of prison where he might murder another child.

Chapter Twenty
Don V. Drye

DON VICTOR DRYE, IV

By Janie Drye

I grew up in a small community called Forkland in the town Gravel Switch, Kentucky. My husband, Don, also grew up in a small town named Bradfordsville, ten miles from Forkland in central Kentucky.

Don and I began dating in October of 1971 and married on August 16, 1972. I worked at Peoples Bank in Gravel Switch while Don worked at his grandfather's funeral home, the Don V. Drye Funeral Home, in Lebanon, Kentucky. After the death of his grandfather, Don went to work at Whirlpool in Danville.

Our young married life was spent always doing something on the weekends, just enjoying our time together. It wasn't long before we began talking about a little Don Victor Drye IV. On June 2, 1977, an 8 lb. 10 oz. boy was born and our dreams had come true. It was one of our happiest days. From the beginning we called our son Don V.

As a baby, Don V. was very friendly. He never met a stranger. At just fifteen months old, he won the baby contest at Ham Days in Marion County. He began helping take up money for Crusade for Children. Everyone thought he was the cutest little thing, so they gave him money. He was always involved in any local activity such as plays, parades, and Christmas caroling.

Oh, how the years flew. Before we knew it, we were registering Don V. for kindergarten. He was so excited to go to school and ride that "big bus". He wanted to ride the bus that first day. As the bus approached to pick Don V. up, it looked to me like a big yellow monster coming to get my son. I followed the bus to school and met him there. We found his room and met his teacher and teacher's aide. Don V. began to work the puzzles at the table and instantly started making friends. Then, he was ready for me to leave. He wanted to be big for everyone else.

The years went quickly and Don V. entered high school. He was very active in R.O.T.C. and was a drummer in the Marion County Marching Band. Like all teenagers, Don V. loved loud music. Whether it was playing in his car or in his room, it was very loud. He and his Dad would argue over what kind of music to listen to. Don V. loved rap music, but his Dad could not stand it. He disliked it as much as Don V. loved it. Don V. was a mama's boy. We were very close. If he had a problem, he would always come to me for the answer or just to talk. He was my only child.

The year 1993 was an exciting one for Don V. He would be sixteen and get his license. In May we bought him a 1992 red and black Mustang convertible…his sixteenth birthday present. He was the happiest kid in town. His dreams were coming true. On July 20th he got his drivers license. He already had a job working as a bus boy at the Steakhouse, a local restaurant. Don V. was all set - a car and a job for gas money. What more could a sixteen year old want?

On a Tuesday morning during this time, Don V. went to work, and his Dad and I went to Lexington for the day. When we returned home, I paged Don V., and he called me right back. He was at a friend's house. He asked if he could spend the night, but I told him no because he had to work the next day, and his Dad would want him to come home. He was told to be home by 10:30 P.M. At about 10:25 P.M., the phone rang. Ashley, Don V.'s friend, was calling to see if Don V. was home. When I told him that he wasn't, he told me that there had been a wreck on Hwy. 337, and they thought it may be Don V. I rushed to tell Donnie that we had to go check on Don V. The site of the accident was about one mile down the road. It was Don V. Just as we arrived, the rescue squad also arrived.

Someone got Donnie and me in a car and took us to

the hospital. I prayed all the way to the hospital. There we had a long wait. Every few minutes I would ask the nurses if Don V. was going to be all right. The nurses would only say that they were doing all they could. About an hour later a nurse came out and told us that Don V. was gone…the most terrible news any parent can receive. I wanted to see Don V. for myself to make sure he was gone. As I reached to touch him, I knew his spirit had gone to heaven. There was only a body there.

The next three days were hectic, but family and friends pushed us through it all. All my family came in that night. All we could do was cry. At about eight o'clock the next morning, people started arriving at our house bringing food and supplies to take care of everyone. Donnie and I stayed in the bed most of the day even though our house was full of people. Late that afternoon, they got us up to go make the funeral arrangements. They helped dress me and got together Don V.'s suit and other items for his funeral. After making the arrangements at the funeral home, we went to the cemetery to pick out our lots. There were only two grave sites left of the Drye plots, one for Donnie and one for me. Since Don V. went first, we had to choose another plot so we all could be together. We chose three lots just behind our previous lots and placed Don V. in the center of the two of us.

Since Don V. was our only child, we spent a lot of time at his grave site. We would go first thing in the morning, at lunch, then back in the evening. After I went back to work, I could only go in the evenings. We placed a solar light at his grave because he was the light of our world. I didn't think I could go on without Don V. and really did not want to. Each day I would pray for God to give me the strength to get through just one more day. Somehow, I was able to make it those first months. When I was at home, I spent most of the time in bed. Nothing interested me at home. The empty house had lost all joy and meaning for me. When we would go out, I would always tell Donnie that we had better get back home. He would tell me that we now had no reason to go home to that empty house.

About two or three weeks after Don V.'s death, I got a phone call from Rosemary Smith. I will never forget what she said that night. Donnie and I were getting ready to go to the cemetery; in fact, Donnie was already in the car. As I answered the phone this lady said, "I am Rosemary Smith, and I don't know you and you don't know me, but I read about Don V.'s death in the paper. About a year ago I lost two sons in a car accident." My answer to her was, "And you are still living?" I knew how I felt and could not imagine losing two sons at one time. At that point I did not think anyone else knew how I felt. My world was gone. I could not function. All I could do was cry. I never realized any one person could cry so much as I had.

Rosemary and I cried and talked for about an hour. She was a wonderful listener. She told me about her friend, Dinah Taylor, and said I would be getting some information from her. After talking to Rosemary I felt like I had known her for a long time. There was a special bond there. In a few days I received a package from her. Included were books on grief, a short biography of her sons Drew and Jeremiah, and their pictures. It seemed as if I already knew these boys from just talking with Rosemary.

Donnie and I were unable to go to the stores where we had once shopped like the grocery store, the beauty shop, and the Wal-Mart in our hometown. We would drive to Louisville or Lexington to avoid seeing anyone who knew us. Even when we drove to those larger cities, I would see someone who looked like Don V. and start crying. Just seeing young boys having a good time would start my tears. Nothing was right anymore with Don V. being gone.

I also got involved in Compassionate Friends in Danville, Kentucky, which meets the first Tuesday of each month. This group has helped me so much. My only hope is that I have been able to help someone else in our group. Being a good listener is a good quality in groups like these. I love to talk about Don V., so I know others like to do the same with their child. I love for other people to mention Don V. I tell them that it is okay if I cry when we talk about him. They haven't made me cry by remembering him. I cry because of the love I have for him.

In the spring of 1994 we went to a meeting at Rosemary and Luther Smith's house in Beattyville. There we met other bereaved parents and learned about their children. It was so heartbreaking to see grown men stand and cry as they told about their children. There is no hurt like losing a child! If I hear about a family losing a child, I just want to be there for them.

All of my energy was taken by the effort to just push on with my life. I lost thirty pounds. Most every thought was of Don V. As a matter of fact, one person said that they couldn't talk to me without my talking about Don V. Imagine! Some of the comments people make are terrible. Naturally I talked about my son. I hope and pray that the people who make such comments never have to go through losing a child. I know they didn't mean to say what they did. Maybe I took it wrong. My world was gone, and I would do what I had to survive. I still go to the cemetery every night. It has been sixty months, but I still go and cry each night.

That first Christmas was almost more than I could bear. I didn't want to face any of the holidays. It would be wonderful if I could sleep from Thanksgiving to New Year. My husband and I spent that Christmas in a hotel room in Louisville. I just could not function that day - I cried all day. The day did pass which is the most I can say for it. On New Years my family normally went to a Holiday Inn in Louisville so the boys could swim and party most of the night. We have not been able to do that since Don V.'s death. What we once did we no longer do anymore.

Many memorials have been created for Don V. at his high school. The 1994 yearbook had a color picture in his memory. Then in 1995, the year he would have graduated, the yearbook had special memorials to four students who would not graduate with the class: one was murdered, one was struck by lightening, and Don V. and another student had died in car accidents. We were unable to attend graduation, but we had roses placed in chairs in memory of them. The graduating class wore white roses in memory of the four who graduated in spirit with them.

I am still working at Peoples Bank in Gravel Switch and after twenty-five years have attained the title of Vice-President, Loan Officer, and Branch Manager. Donnie is semi-retired and enjoys working on his farm and selling cars. The pain from losing our son has not gone away, but we realize that keeping his memory alive is of extreme importance. Don V., until we meet again...we love you.

Chapter Twenty-One
Andrew Gutgsell

ANDREW ROBIN GUTGSELL

By Kathy Jo Gutgsell

"Dr. Gutgsell, we have your son in the emergency room" said the voice on the telephone to my husband. "He collapsed at his work site, and we're trying to resuscitate him. If you have a minister, you'd better call. It doesn't look good."

With these words, we left our three younger children at home and began the slow-motion drive to St. Joseph Hospital in Lexington, Kentucky. We were in an altered, dream-like state of consciousness as we talked about our first-born son's birth, life, and now probable death two months after his 18th birthday. The details of his health, easily submerged over the past twelve years, were now crystal clear. Andrew had been born with a rare congenital heart defect known as tricuspid atresia. His cardiologist had been grim as she told us matter-of-factly: "Take him home and love him. He may live a week. He may live years. We'll have to wait and see."

Despite his dire prognosis, Andrew thrived. He was small and wiry and his color was a bit dusky, but he made up for it in determination. In almost every way Andrew had a normal childhood. He went camping at six weeks of age, played on the Pacific Ocean coastline, went to preschool, rode his bike and had so many friends. He seemed to adapt his play to his heart problem. When he tired, he rested, but never called attention to his condition. When he was six, his cardiologist determined that open heart surgery was necessary. Without it he would die within a year, we were told. Off we went, with his three year old brother, Luke, in tow, to the Mayo Clinic for two months of pure, raw, unrelenting fear. It was not a smooth recovery and it took longer than anyone predicted, but with relief and gratitude and by the grace of God, we brought our boys back home just after Easter of 1982.

For the next six months or so we held our breath and

were afraid to relax. Eventually, it sunk in. Andrew was "cured". Little by little we forgot the strain of the first six years of his life. Andrew went out for football, baseball, and finally, his real love...basketball. For months at a time we were able to forget that Andrew even had a heart problem. All the while, Andrew was living life to the fullest. He was the most sociable boy we have ever known. He was either on the phone to a friend or with a friend virtually every waking minute. His passion was sports. His enthusiasm on the playing field was infectious. I recall a football game in which ten year old, half-pint Andrew begged his coach, "Just let me at them, coach! Let me play. I'll help us catch up." The other players dwarfed him in size but not in enthusiasm. That's how Andrew was: mighty in his spirit and love of life.

The summer Andrew was nine and Luke was six the three of us attended my Robinson family reunion. As I parked the car, I suddenly got cold feet about facing a roomful of relatives I vaguely knew. Seeing my hesitation, Andrew said, "You and Luke wait here, Mom. I'll go in first and meet everybody, then I'll take you in and introduce you." He was Mr. Gregarious, and did exactly what he said he would.

During those twelve years following his childhood surgery, we found it easy to put away fears of an early death. We now recall times that Andrew brought up the question of his mortality. On his last visit to his cardiologist at which he was pronounced healthy, he asked her, "So, based on how I'm doing today, how long do you think I'll live?" Sitting next to him in the exam room, I felt my heart go to my throat, stunned. I had never heard him question his life expectancy. He lived his life as if he had not a care. On the other hand, it seems to those of us who knew and loved him well that Andrew lived so fully, with such gusto, velocity, and volume, that he was trying to pack ninety years of living into eighteen. Even now that he has crossed over to the other side, we often sense his presence, and invariably it is accompanied by a flurry of activity

For many years we had a family of four: Terry, me, Andrew, then Luke, three years younger. From the time Andrew was six, and coinciding with the year of his operation, we have lived on a sixty acre horse farm outside of Lexington, Kentucky. When Andrew was twelve and Luke was nine, God blessed us with a third son, Michael. Seventeen months later, Jessie, our only daughter came along. People liked to comment on our two families. These were whirlwind years when we tried to balance two in diapers with Andrew's involvement in sports and Luke's gymnastics and theater productions. It was a major challenge, and Terry and I often shake our heads in wonder at our life then. He was heavily immersed in his private practice in Internal Medicine. I was managing the horse farm and directing the choir at our church. It seemed as if those busy days would last forever, but our lives changed drastically when Andrew died.

Andrew celebrated his last birthday, his eighteenth, two months before his death. That night Terry noted that Andrew was "out of sorts." He dropped plates, his food, his glass. A picture taken that day shows Luke, Michael, and Jessie leaning over Andrew's cake while he seems suspended behind them. He had on his Atlanta Braves baseball hat with a large white A. Was the "A" for angel; had he already gone on in spirit?

Losing Andrew has been without question my most difficult assignment in life. During the first year after Andrew's death, there were many days when my major triumph was getting out of bed in the morning. Images that come to mind are drowning in an ocean of sorrow, amputation without anesthetics, and teetering at the edge of a cliff. Aside from our individual anguish there was the difficulty of patching up our sense of family. The balance we had so mindfully tried to nurture, especially since the births of Michael and Jessie, was thrown off kilter. We wobbled like a three legged chair. It was so hard to support each other. I know we made some big mistakes in parenting these past three years, but honestly, I sometimes wonder how our family survived at all. It was during this period that the loving care of family, friends and church community was most critical. We all leaned heavily on our rock solid faith in the goodness of God and the certainty of the afterlife.

With our grief came a yearning to know more about what had happened to Andrew when he died. We read everything we could about dying, near death experiences, and the afterlife from many cultural viewpoints. The more we read, the more we were reassured of the ultimate safety of the universe. We found ourselves slowing down. No longer were Terry and I willing to work exhausting long hours that left no time for family and personal pursuits. Adjusting to your son's death is hard work. We found ourselves needing about double the time to accomplish our usual tasks. I was too physically tired to do much strenuous activity that first winter, but I found solace in, of all things, working jigsaw puzzles. Terry found browsing thought the computer to be a relaxing hobby. We gave each other a lot of space and tried to be understanding. Our relationship grew stronger through this difficult time. Luckily, we share a faith in the afterlife. I doubt if our marriage could have survived otherwise.

Before Andrew's death, I had let my spiritual life become secondary to hard work and accomplishing goals in the physical world. Through all my reading and redemption, I came to a new appreciation of our true spiritual nature. The part of us that is timeless, that is, the soul, is of the most value. Our bodies are merely the physical covering for our precious souls. I wanted to grow more lovely on the inside. I sought a discipline, a practice, that would help my soul mature. About a year after Andrew died, I began to meditate in silence once a day. After quieting my busy thoughts, I was better able to pray, to listen to God speak His comfort to me, and to connect to Andrew. Concurrently, Terry and I began to discuss the possibility of career changes. As we came to see death as a mere blip on the screen on the way to life in another form, our values about life on this physical plane shifted. Andrew's death enlarged our vision of the fullness of life, like looking through a wide angle lens. Now, instead of an event to be feared, dreaded, or ignored, death became a transition to a fuller life, and we wanted to be nearby. We decided to do hospice work. In all the twenty-three years of our marriage and even though he is a physician and I am a nurse, we have never worked together professionally. This was a big step for us. Terry left his medical practice of nineteen years, I resigned from the church choir directorship and scaled back my work on the farm. We moved to Cleveland for him to do a fellowship in Palliative Medicine at the Cleveland Clinic.

Our year in Cleveland was wonderfully restorative. Our family was in a warm little cocoon with few outside distractions. We nurtured ourselves with the music and cultural opportunities in Cleveland, and with each other. I bought a folk harp, found a marvelous teacher, and was healed by the beauty of music for hours as I practiced. I volunteered every week at a hospice group home for the indigent. Singing and playing the harp to the residents was a deeply curative experience. I also became interested in learning energy work using gentle therapeutic touch for pain control and relaxation. My dream is to combine my nursing and musical abilities in hospice work.

Terry loved his Palliative Medicine fellowship. He felt throughout the training that he was in the right place at the right time doing the work he loved. We have both sensed Andrew's delight in our new ventures.

Our other three children are, I believe, healing as well. Luke, now eighteen, has graduated from high school and is touring the United States with friends. He seems to be at peace with his brother's death. Luke has always been a deeply spiritual person. I think he will weather this storm successfully. Michael, at nine, and Jessie, at eight, are so naturally tuned in to God and Heaven and angels that they do quite well relating to their brother as a spirit. They take their cues from us as well. We pray for Andrew every night and talk of him through the day. I think they see death as a natural part of the whole life experience. We decided to home-school them to keep them closer to us.

Almost four years from Andrew's death, I stand so much in awe at the profound changes in our lives, from money-centered values to human-centered ones. I can only say thank you to Andrew - our greatest teacher who even now is with us.

Chapter Twenty-Two
John Donan

JOHN DONAN

By Beverly Donan

Our family has always had many pets. Through the years, we had horses, dogs, cats, and even sheep and goats at one time. Katharine, our oldest child, is the cat lover, and John, our youngest child and only son, loved dogs. John had two favorite dogs, Red and Daisy. Red was a part red bone coon hound that loved to play and run free with John. He would meet the school bus every afternoon and he went everywhere with John. Red disappeared and never returned about a year before John's accident. Daisy is a Jack Russell Terrier who is still much loved by our family. I know "Red" continues on with John.

As I sit and struggle to write about my beautiful son, it is also a struggle to put into words all the changes that have taken place in our family since the tragedy of John being killed in a car accident on October 2, 1993, at age 15. Our family, as we once knew it, is no longer intact, never to be the same again. We must continue to walk forward; we are still a family, but different. I think that this is what many people do not understand. They expect you to be the same. We will never be the same.

In October of 1993, my husband and I had gone out of town for a short Thursday through Sunday business meeting. John was staying with his grandmother while we were away. On the Saturday night before we were to return on Sunday, John sneaked out of his grandmother's house with two other boys, one sixteen and the other fifteen like John. The fifteen year old "borrowed" his grandmother's car and all three of them went joy riding and decided to bash mailboxes. One homeowner, angered after realizing his mailbox had been bashed, took off after the boys. Realizing they were being pursued by another car, the boys drove at excessive speeds through a subdivision. The fifteen year old driving the car lost control and crashed. Our son was thrown from the backseat of the car and was killed. It could never be proven that the boys were being chased. Our lives changed completely with the midnight phone call from our minister that John had died.

John was such a promising young man. His innate curiosity and unique personality made him a joy to be around. Even as a young child he loved to dismantle anything that he could then put back together. Scouting and outdoor activities were a big part of John's life. He was an Eagle Scout and had attended the scouting World and National Jamboree twice. Being a well-rounded young man, John was also a member of his high school golf team. He was gifted mechanically and had hoped to pursue engineering in college. John was a young man who would have made a difference in this world.

How am I coping? Early in my grief, I had so many questions. At times, some of these questions still come to the surface. Was it just a bad choice on John's part? Was it just an accident? Were there other reasons why John could not continue on in this life? No one has the answers. I have finally found peace in a statement made to me by a very spiritual woman I met in Arizona. She said, "Beverly, you finally just have to let things be." So, after much seeking and struggle on my part, I have decided to rest in the wisdom and peace of this statement.

I have sought out a mixed bag of healing methods to deal with my grief including counseling, Native American healing, support groups, massage, bodywork, reading, and writing down my feelings. Many of these methods are ones that I had never entertained before. I feel very strongly that many different people and situations were put directly in my path through John's help. I found a women's health specialist that viewed healing in a holistic manner. She has helped me in so many ways to deal with my grief as a whole - working through my mind, body, and spirit.

How are we coping as a family? I asked our daughter Katharine to answer this. She said, "As a family, we are totally separate in our grief." She's right. We all do grieve differently, coping in our own way and at different stages. Things that helped me did not help my husband. We are there for each other, but we can't help each other. After almost five years, I have learned that we never get over the loss of our children. We only learn to deal with the loss, each in our own way. It is important to give each family member time and space to grieve. Counseling should be an option to be explored either individually or as a family.

New paths of spiritual growth have opened for me since John's death. My old religion no longer served my needs. I now live one foot in this world and one foot in the spirit world. To survive I realized I had to let go of the old ways of thinking as I became more free in spirit. I had to learn ways to carry John with me. Letting him go from this world in my own time frame finally set both of us free. My conscious decision to grow from this terrible tragedy prevented me from getting mired in my grief.

The loss of a child takes its toll on a marriage. It is a struggle. Hopefully, somewhere along the line your paths will intersect and you will have a chance to take a new path. In this new path, your lives will have renewed hope that you both can share and grow together. This takes time, an awareness of each others' needs, and a lot of work. My husband encouraged me to pursue my desire to attend a school to become a gemologist several years after John's death. Both Katharine and I completed the course in California and found the experience to be a positive one. My husband realized I had too much time on my hands, and truthfully, he needed the space. We were all open to change which proved beneficial in many ways.

Driving to the funeral home the day after John's death, I saw a large hawk in a tree. Later I learned that the American

Chapter 22

Indians feel that any large bird of prey brings us messages from the Great Spirit. John was sending me a message the day after his death, and he continues to send me messages to this day. Every time I see a hawk, it lifts my spirits and reaffirms that John continues on in spirit.

I had a vivid dream about him that affected me deeply. In this dream, we were hugging, and I was crying because he had to leave. The dream was real but it left me so empty. The dream now gives me hope, and in quiet times, I can still feel myself hugging John. I know this dream was John's way of letting me know that he is always with me.

Chapter Twent-Three
John Foss

JOHN FOSS

By Eleanor Foss

There is no way I would have attempted to write the painful story of John's life except that I would not, could not, ever refuse the request of the woman who is so precious to us. My life, while happy, was mundane. What makes it extraordinary, tragically, is the illness and death of our beloved son John.

Immediately after my husband Artie and I were married, I had emergency surgery to remove one and one-half of my ovaries, producing a dismal prognosis for childbearing. Undaunted and with great surprise, I very soon gave birth to a beautiful, blonde, blue eyed girl- Susan-the perfect, cherished and adored baby girl. With only the certainty and stubbornness of the very young, we never thought we could love another child with the same intensity.

Within two years, God delivered our son John into our lives. Unknown to us, he was a precious gift only on loan to us for twenty-eight years. How glad I was that he was a boy. Long, skinny and not even close to his gorgeous sister in physical beauty, he captured our hearts. My fears of his physical shortcomings when compared to his sister dissipated quickly as John very soon filled out, became physically beautiful, and laughed and conned his way into everyone's heart.

Four years later, we were again blessed with our Carolyn, a little girl much like her brother in nature: fun, good, kind, cooperative, beautiful, wonderful sense of humor, a caregiver, but not quite an extrovert. Our lives continued along the bumpy road that we find as we mature is defined as "life."

As he grew up, there was at times a particular dark cloud that seemed to hover over Johnny. The incidents seemed minor when they happened, but in retrospect, I wonder. John was the boy that lightening always struck. If someone got hurt, it was John. If a bunch of boys were playing with matches lighting firecrackers, only John would be caught or hurt. When John was in college, he and a friend were in a car that was hit by a drunk driver. John suffered a serious head injury and was in a coma for a month. We never left his side. We cheered him through months of hospitalization and a year of cognitive and physical therapy. His recovery was miraculous and unprecedented. He not only returned to college, but he was even admitted to law school.

John started law school in San Francisco in September of 1989. That October, the earthquake hit San Francisco. We saw the news reports and were frantic, especially seeing that little red car so like John's BMW at the top of the broken section of freeway. We called everywhere to no avail. In twenty minutes, John called to say he was fine. He actually had a wonderful evening just exploring the city. Everything was lit by candlelight. He really didn't have any idea of the extent of the damage until later when he was finally able to read about it in the newspaper.

After John's first year in law school, I was lying in bed one night and the phone rang. It was John calling to tell me he had a pain. I tried to be very calm about it, tell him to go see a doctor out there, but I have to say that in my heart I knew that it was very bad news. The doctors out there seemed to think that he had a bladder infection, but he was not getting any better. It was almost Thanksgiving, and we asked John if he would come back here to see our doctor. When he came back, he first went to our general practitioner who was not happy with the results of the urine test and insisted he go to a urologist. He went to the urologist, and they still kept thinking it was a minor problem.

Never, ever, will I forget that morning when I took him to the hospital. They were just going to do a scope to look inside and see what was happening. John was very apprehensive about it, very nervous, and he was still in pain. I was waiting in the waiting room. Within ten minutes' time, the phone rang, and I got on the phone. The doctor said, "Mrs. Foss, I'm sorry. I do not have good news for you." My heart dropped to my toes. I tried to question him further, but he was very evasive and told me that he didn't think it was at all possible because no one John's age had ever had bladder cancer, but it did look like it was a tumor and that it was cancerous. However, he said that it was up to the biopsy. I ran to the public phone. I had no change. I couldn't remember my credit card number. I waited for John to come out of recovery. He said to me, "Well Mom, how am I? They didn't find any tumor or anything, did they?" I said, "John, you're going to be fine. Whatever they found, they're going to be able to take care of." He went back to sleep, and I was frantic. I ran out of the hospital. The only place I could go was home because I didn't even have the ability to make a phone call. I called Artie and told him. I went back to the hospital, and John was awake. The doctor had told him the news. He was okay about it, but to me it was very, very scary. We waited and waited for the prognosis. Christmas came. Two days after Christmas the doctor called us back with the diagnosis and told us that it indeed was a malignancy. The good news was that it was a number two on a scale of one to four, and the bad news was that it had already begun to spread.

We took John up to Sloan Kettering Hospital in Manhattan, a specialized cancer treatment hospital, and began series of so-called minor surgeries. By February, the doctors knew that the cancer was spreading, and the only thing they really could do was to remove his bladder. Removing John's bladder meant that it would end his sexual life. He was still only twenty-five. It would prevent him from having children in the future, so he had to make the decision himself since he was an adult. We went to see an oncologist at Sloan who gave us the name of a friend of his who was the top urologist/oncologist at Johns Hopkins in Baltimore. The friend had created this remarkable surgery where they could remove the bladder and still keep the nerves intact so that he could still function sexually. When we contacted Dr. Brendlar at Johns Hopkins, he did give us a lot of hope. He was a young man. We took John down to Johns Hopkins. The night before the surgery, Dr. Brendlar was very upbeat and wonderful, and it felt like everything was just going to be fine.

The morning of surgery, we were at the hospital first thing, and John was already in surgery. The surgery took thirteen and a half, almost fourteen hours. I sat in the waiting room in a stupor. At times I cried. I sat on the floor. I sat on the couch. I walked. I paced. There was nothing that anyone really could do to reassure me, but the nurses and Dr. Brendlar kept coming out with these wonderful reports that all the parameters were fine, the perimeters were fine, everything around the bladder was fine. There was absolutely no sign that the cancer had spread.

Well, seeing John that night was something that will remain with me for the rest of my life. There wasn't an opening in his body that didn't have tubes in it. I would say there probably were fourteen different places that he was cut open from which tubes were draining. He was receiving blood transfusions which were his own. He was in horrendous pain. He was on a respirator, and he kept pushing the respirator out of his mouth. It was something upsetting beyond comprehension and thinking about it just takes me straight back as if it were yesterday. He was in the hospital for a long, long time. It is just impossible to really describe what it is like to go to that hospital where there were thousands of people so desperately ill: babies, old people, young people, men, women, children. To watch them in wheelchairs just disintegrating, just wasting away. To see your child in a bed in that hospital is something that just defies description. We had to get a limo to take him home from Maryland to New Jersey because he really was not able to be confined in a car. When John came home, he began his chemo. John handled the chemo with the same upbeat attitude he handled everything. He wore his baldness with as much panache as anyone could have worn a full head of hair. He was going to be fine. He was going to kick it he said, but all we could hear was him constantly vomiting and so sick from the chemo. It was something beyond belief.

After the winter time, John decided he was not going back to law school, but that he was going to Florida to live and to set up a business. Our hearts were just torn into pieces. As we looked at our tall, handsome son, we wondered how much time he really had left.

He was in Florida from March to December, when I got a call to come to Florida because my Dad was dying. I flew to Florida and went directly to the hospital. I spoke to John on the phone. I knew he was not feeling well, but he was in total denial, insisting that he just had a slipped disc. Artie came down from New Jersey to go to John. He took John up to Sloan Kettering, and I dealt with my Dad's funeral.

My sister and I had to drive back from Florida because John's car was down there. We had my Mom still down in Florida with my other sister. I came back on New Year's Day, and went directly to Sloan Kettering. Getting off that elevator and walking into that room to see my son lying in bed again was probably one of the hardest trips I ever had to make. Artie had to force me to walk into his room. I could not see him in bed…again. But that's where he was. He wasn't doing well at all. He was losing a lot of weight. It was so unbelievably painful to look at him and to pretend that everything was going to be all right.

John came back to our house after the chemo. He wanted to go back to Florida when he got better, but all we could do was hold the buckets when he vomited and be there for him and hold his hand. Finally, we put him on a plane back to Florida to let him maintain some dignity. There is no way to describe walking through life like a zombie because that's all we did. Three weeks later, he would come up again. After the second round of chemo, it seemed as though some of the tumors, one on his forehead and one on his jaw, seemed to be getting smaller. They decided in Sloan Kettering that they could not keep him on that drug because the drug was causing blindness. They just couldn't add to his problems. They decided to put him back on the other chemo that didn't work in the first place. Again, every three weeks, a week in the hospital, two weeks to heal, then back again in the hospital. John was getting thinner and thinner, weaker and weaker. He would call us from Florida, and he would try to be so strong.

In May, we went down to Florida to see him. They had stopped the chemo because it just wasn't working. They had put him on radiation to shrink the tumors. He was in so much pain. I did nothing but rub his neck with mineral ice. Finally, we had to come back home and shortly thereafter he called me during the night. I had Artie on the other phone calling his doctor in Florida while I was talking to John. I flew down immediately. That was in June sometime, and I never left him. He wouldn't let me leave him, not that I wanted to. He tried to keep his spirits up until finally it came time to take him back home to New Jersey. That was the middle of July. I flew back with him.

Oh God almighty, I will never forget what he looked like! He had this plastic brace on his entire body from under his arms all the way down to his hips. The way the people looked at him on that plane with I guess pain, I guess sympathy, maybe disgust, maybe curiosity, but how I tried to smile for him. I did what I could. They didn't have the wheelchair waiting for him. He had to literally claw his way along the halls until Artie got him a wheelchair. We took him back to Sloan Kettering.

We took John home and oh God how he tried. At first, John stayed in bed, but he was able to get up for meals, to come down into the kitchen. We had meals together. Then gradually he couldn't get up for meals, so we set up a table in his room. We had meals together there. Then, he couldn't get out of bed to have meals at the table anymore, but we still made him everything he wanted. I slept right on the floor next to his bed. I stayed with him, and I washed him. I changed his diapers. I did everything I could for him. All we could do was increase the pain medication. At one point, he said to me, "Mom tell me something. I'll believe it if you tell me. Am I going to get better?" I said, "John, do you want to get better?" He said, "Yes." I then said, "Then you will." I lied to him. I can't forgive myself for that. He said to us, "I have no idea what you guys are going through. I can't imagine how you can live through this." I said, "John, we would do anything for you. We would change places with you in a second. I just don't know why it has to be you." He replied, "Mom, it has to be someone." I told him that if this didn't work out, we would be together again. And he said yes he knew that. I told him, "John, please make sure you find me. Make sure you're there for me because I will be with you again."

On that last Saturday, John started to get panic attacks. Artie had to inject the Ativan right into the I.V. bags. We kept pressing the buttons for him so he'd be out of pain and not in a panic. He told Rose his nurse, "I'm dying." She said, "No you're not John. You're not dying." With that he calmed down. We were with him around the clock; we never slept. You couldn't even touch his pinkie because he was in so much pain. We just stayed with him. Finally, Tuesday morning around five o'clock, we had dozed off and John started to make horrible breathing sounds. By ten to nine, it was over. My Johnny was gone and nothing has ever been the same since. I saw him go. I saw him leave. By the time we came back home from the funeral home, the hospital bed was gone and the bed was made as if nothing had ever happened in that room.

After the death of her brother, our daughter Carolyn had lost her way. She lost her direction, her sense of security, her sense of who she was, and her self-esteem. She was home from college with a new career and all of her friends were off with new jobs and marriages. Susie had a hard time as well and, unbeknownst to us, got involved with drugs. Our family was limping along, though actually Artie and I were probably doing a lot better than the girls.

It has been four and one-half years… Cancer happens to not one member of the family but the entire family. There is no other way to describe it other than the way this grief counselor did at a seminar I went to. The family is like a mobile. When something horrible happens to it like one member of that mobile being yanked out, the rest of the mobile clangs together, bangs together, and smashes against each other until finally, after a long time, it settles down. But it is never balanced again. It is never the same again. Each person in the mobile does assume part of its individuality, but the unit is never balanced again. There is really no other way to put it. That is really the way it is. Artie and I have resumed our relationship. Unfortunately, we are co-dependent on our children being happy which is not really healthy but tell me another way.

Sometimes we know that John is with us. This past Valentine's Day, we took Carolyn and a girlfriend to dinner in a restaurant that we always took John to right here in Rumson. Artie and I arrived first because the girls were still getting dressed. We immediately felt John's presence. The girls came, and we had a wonderful time. When dinner was over, the waitress came over with three yellow roses at which point Carolyn burst into tears. This in itself was a miracle. Her friend put her arm around her and said, "Carolyn, let it out, just cry. I don't know what this is about, but it has to be about John." We related the story of how yellow roses had come to mean so much to John during his illness. It began when a woman sent him a dozen yellow roses after befriending him on one of his hospital stays. From that point on, we always gave him yellow roses because they brought him such pleasure. Carolyn's friend said, "Mrs. Foss, you will not believe this, but we are the only ones in the restaurant that got yellow roses. Everyone else was given a red one, a pink one, or a white one. They had to come from John." John continues to give us gifts. We hope to give the same in return. That's all we can say. I am devastated that he suffered and that he's gone, but I am so grateful to God for having given me the opportunity to nurse John and to have taken care of him.

The following story was written by John's father, Art Foss.

As a young boy aged 12-13, I was interested in Boy Scouts. It became the most important thing in my life. As an avid first year scout, I attended every meeting, went on every hike, and earned badges in a timely fashion. As a result of my participation, I was scheduled to receive an award at the annual Father's Night. As we were about to leave the house, my Father said, "I am not going. I don't feel like it."

I was devastated. I went alone, an older scout substituted for my "Parent." The result of this encounter with extreme hurt and bitterness caused me to make a solemn promise to God, "If ever I am fortunate enough to have a son, I will accompany him anywhere, anytime and for any reason." And I did exactly that for twenty-eight years. I broke that promise on October 5, 1993 at 8:45 in the morning. That's when Johnny passed on to a better state. I cry out his name and no one answers. I await the day when I call, "Johnny, Johnny" and he answers, "Here I am Dad."

Chapter Twenty-Four
Ralph Coomer

RALPH COOMER

By Dana Coomer

The Spring of 1994 had been so special because my only son, Ralph, was graduating from high school. I felt that our lives at this point were better than they had ever been. I never suspected in my wildest dreams that my life would take such a tragic turn.

Like in most families, life moved so fast as our children were growing up. Thinking back now, I wonder where all the years went. I suddenly looked around, and our children were grown. Teresa had married and had started a family of her own. Her first child was a beautiful daughter that we all adored. Her second child was a son who had just had his first birthday in the summer of 1994. When he was born, my husband Ralph wanted Coomer in his name. I thought that this was ridiculous because the baby's name would then be Travis Stephen (after his father) Coomer Mays. I told Ralph that Ralphie would one day have a son to carry on the Coomer name. Ralph said to me, "You don't know. Ralphie may never have kids."

When Ralphie was eighteen, he decided that he wanted to do the things his Dad had done when he was a teenager. One exceptional feat Ralph had performed many years ago was to dive off the Beattyville Bridge. The fathers of Ralphie's friends would tell that tale to him over and over again because it was a legend in our small town because of the height of the bridge. While his Dad (Big Ralph) and I had been to Georgetown, Kentucky, to visit friends, Ralphie did what his father had done twenty-five years earlier: he dived off the Beattyville Bridge. As we drove in to town later that day, we were stopped by several people who told us what Ralphie had just done. Even though he was all right, I was really upset with him.

June 11, 1994, was a Friday. I had worked from 6:00 A.M. until 2:00 P.M. that day. Big Ralph was planning a fishing trip that night while I was planning on visiting friends later that evening. Before I left, I fixed Ralphie a couple of cheeseburgers, a teenager's favorite supper. I gave him a big hug, kissed him right on the corner of his mouth, and told him that I loved him too much. He hugged me back and said, "Mom, you worry too much." I told him that I couldn't live without him. When I said that, he sort of pulled away from me and said, "Mom, don't talk silly." He then looked at me and said, "Mom, nothing is going to happen to me. I'm tough."

Ralphie only finished one cheeseburger that night and left to catch some bait for his Dad to take fishing that night. As I was leaving a couple of hours later about 6:00 P.M., I met him coming home. He said that he was hot and tired and he seemed in a hurry to go in to take a shower. I gave him some money, told him again that I loved him, told him to be careful, and said that I would be home around midnight.

That night, I got home a little late, around 12:30 A.M. Ralphie was not at home so I thought he had gone back to town since I wasn't home yet. I stayed up for a little while, waiting for him to come home, but lay down finally because it was late. It was 2:05 A.M. when I heard him pull in the driveway. Although I knew he had his own door key, I met Ralphie at the door to see if he was all right. I asked him if he was going back out again because he did that sometimes. He said, "No, Mom, I'm home to stay." He went into the kitchen, got a snack and something to drink, and got on the phone. Ralphie would always call the girl he had gone out with on the phone after he got home. Normally this would have been his steady girlfriend, but he and she had just broken up, and he now dating other girls. Ralphie had many friends, many of whom were girls that were just friends. His good looks and his big heart made him very popular with everyone.

As I finally lay down that night, Ralphie was still talking on the phone. Often, he would talk till 3:00 or 4:00 in the morning. I remember hearing him hang up and go into his room. Thinking he was going to bed, I was surprised to hear him go in the bathroom across the hall from my room. I got up, and he was combing his hair. He stepped out of the bathroom and said that he was going back to town. I distinctly remember walking right behind him as he walked through the house. I said, "Honey, remember, it's after 2:00 A.M. It's late! You said that you weren't going anyplace else." He opened the refrigerator door, got out a cool pop, his favorite snack, and headed for the door. I kept saying, "Ralphie, it's late. Don't go anywhere else." He just looked at me and said, "Oh Mom, I'll be all right." Immediately, he was out the door and in his truck. I wanted to stop him, but he was almost twenty years old and had done this before. Maybe he was going to see his old girlfriend and would be able to work out their differences. Having decided that he'd be back in a little while, I went back to bed. It was now about 2:35 A.M.

Around 3:00 A.M. our phone rang. Teresa, our daughter, told me that Ralphie had been in an accident and was in the doctor's office in town. I asked if he was OK. She didn't know but just told me to come to town. Grabbing up anything in reach to wear, I ran to my car and headed toward town.

Somehow, I finally got through the traffic clogging the accident site and within minutes was at our family doctor's office. Having been there so many times, I knew where his emergency room was, so I ran directly there. The terror of seeing my son lying on that table is beyond describing. Someone held me and said, "Let the doctor do what he can. Let him take care of him." The next memory I have is of being in the front seat of an ambulance. How much time had passed since I had arrived at the doctor's office? I had no idea. Dr. Noble and three paramedics were in the back of the ambulance with my son. The fog that night was unbelievable! I kept begging the driver to please hurry but only had to look out at the road to know that he was doing his best. I remember thinking, "How are we going to get to the hospital? How can he even see to drive?" I kept looking back in the ambulance and asking Dr. Noble if Ralphie was all right. He told me over and over that he was "the same". One vivid memory I have is of looking back and seeing them cut the jeans off my son.

Getting my son to the hospital was the most important thing to me that night. Even though I knew in my heart that he was seriously hurt, I was sure that he would be all right if we could just get him to the hospital. The ambulance driver had radioed ahead for a helicopter to be sent from Lexington to Jackson, the small rural town where we were headed. We did reach the hospital that night, and I was taken to a waiting room while the hospital personnel treated my son. My daughter arrived shortly after I did. She had stayed behind to get someone to find her Dad who was out fishing. Other relatives began arriving as word spread through our town. A receptionist that night showed me so much compassion and kindness. She took me in her office and found a place that I could answer all the calls coming in to the hospital for me about Ralphie's condition. I do not remember anyone who called that night or what I said to any of them. Over and over I kept praying that he would be all right. I truly felt that he would be.

Seemingly a long time later, several doctors were standing in front of me. I ran to them and asked about my son. One of them said, "There's not anything we can do." I said, "What about the helicopter? Why isn't it here?" I remember them saying that the helicopter had left Lexington but had to turn around because it was so foggy. I begged Dr. Noble to have the ambulance try to drive him to Lexington to the regional trauma center there at the University of Kentucky. He agreed but told me that this time I could not ride in the ambulance. I would have to follow in another car.

Scott and Annette Arnold, our very close friends, offered to drive me to Lexington directly behind the ambulance.

My last memory is of holding on to Ralphie's stretcher as they loaded him into the ambulance. Our car followed the speeding ambulance to Lexington and about three miles before arriving at the hospital, the ambulance had a flat tire! My heart almost stopped as I wondered how could this happen. Darren Arnold, Scott and Annette's son, told me that there were four tires on the back, and they would keep going except maybe somewhat slower. After what seemed like hours, we all finally reached the emergency room. My husband Ralph and his brother came shortly after we arrived. Ralph's brother had found him where he was fishing and had driven him to Lexington.

I had no idea of how much time had passed (later I would learn that it was about 5 hours) when a doctor came to tell us that our son was brain dead. I begged them to keep him on life support! How could there not be anything that they could do for him? We had managed to get him to the best hospital in the state.

I still don't remember leaving the hospital, although somewhere in my memory I can see the faces of all Ralphie's friends who were there. I couldn't even speak to any of them. I remember looking over at my husband once and saying, "How are we going to live without our baby?"

Our home was filled with family and friends when we arrived. The first thing that I did was to push the redial button on our phone to see who was the last person my son had called that morning. We knew the girl. She told us later that when she had been talking to Ralphie that morning, he had gotten another call, and she didn't know who that caller was. We think that maybe he was going to meet that person but never made it. I guess I will never know who that was. I do not blame anyone for my son's accident because it was just that, an accident. The fog that night was horrible and, if anything, I think that may have had a lot to do with the accident.

So many wonderful people reached out to us in the

early months after our son's death. Not only did I have my family, but Ralph's family and our friends came to support us. Also, people that we hardly knew who had been through the loss of a child came to help us. With all of this support, I still have to say that only God gave me the strength to go on. Even several months after the accident, my appetite had not returned. I had lost twenty-one pounds and only wanted to stay in bed and not get up, but my family and Ralph's family would not settle for this from me. They kept calling me and stopping by. These people would just not let me give in to my grief. They knew I had to work through it and not give in to it.

It has been over four years now since the death of my son. Truly, I never dreamed that I would still be here. I would say that by the grace of God and the love and prayers of many caring people, I am better. Many of Ralphie's friends still visit me every weekend. Never a day goes by that one or two of them won't call me. Their support has gotten me through many times when others have not been around.

Ralph Douglas Coomer, Jr., lived nineteen years and eleven months on this earth, and in that time left a mark that most of us never make in a lifetime. There is no way that I can express my thanks to his friends, my family, Ralph's family, and our friends for reaching out to us after his death. Even with all this support, I still feel so much emptiness. His father and I have done two important things to memorialize our son. First, we erected a cross in his memory at the site of his accident. We are told by his friends and by other people in our town that they always think of Ralphie when they pass his cross. Secondly, we started a Ralph Coomer Memorial Scholarship that has been given for the last two years at our local high school where Ralphie graduated. This award goes to a senior who will be going to college. Both of these memorials have meant so much to us and have helped us work through our grief.

Something that is still very hard for me is to see the

grief surrounding my daughter Teresa. As her mother, I want to relieve her pain but know that I cannot. For awhile, I feel that she thought that not only had she lost her brother, but also her mother too. I was so consumed by my grief that I couldn't reach out to her. I thank God everyday that she has such a caring and supportive husband who has stood by her in those times that I couldn't.

Three weeks after Ralphie's accident I had a special dream about him. Sometimes I call this a vision rather than a dream because it was so real. Ralphie came to my bedside. He was exactly life-size, the 5' 11" handsome boy that I so loved. I can remember turning over in bed, and he was standing right before me. My line of vision started at the floor where I saw that he was barefooted and that his legs were so tan, just like they were the day of his accident. When I finally looked at his face, he was struggling to get in the room. The small space between my bed and the closet wasn't big enough for his wings! I looked up at him and said, "How did you get in here with those big wings?" These wings were larger than he was and had snow white feathers. To this day, I can still see those feathers and how white they were. Ralphie never answered my question, and my next recollection is of hearing a brushing noise. He was gone, but this brushing sounded like Ralphie going down our narrow hallway with his wings brushing up against the side of the walls. I woke up my husband Ralph and said, "Ralph, Ralph, he was here! He was an angel. He had the biggest white wings I have ever seen." I remember my husband saying, "Be quiet for a minute." We listened and heard all three of our dogs barking wildly. These were Ralphie's dogs, and they were howling at the top of their lungs. Suddenly, all three stopped at once. Needless to say, I did not go to sleep that night. In my mind, I kept seeing my Ralphie over and over as an angel in heaven with the biggest white wings I had ever seen. To this day, I thank God for that dream, or was it a vision that he allowed me to have of my son? I think the dogs knew he was there too, the same was they know when a storm is coming.

After reading *Lamentations*, Dinah Taylor's monthly bereavement newsletter, I decided to write to some of the parents who had managed to survive a year or so after losing their child. I needed to see how they were doing and what to expect. One contact was Kathy Kegley whose only child, Kevin, had died a year before Ralphie. We developed a close friendship with our few phone calls and more numerous letters. Even though I had asked her repeatedly, Kathy had never sent me a picture of her son. One night, I had a vivid dream in which Ralphie and two boys were in a big warehouse obviously getting ready for a parade. All three boys were up on the back of a convertible, dressed, oddly enough, in what looked like firemen suits. Ralphie looked tan as usual and seemed like he was having fun. I didn't recognize either of the other boys but the one with glasses made an impression on me. Two days after this dream, I hurriedly opened a large manila envelope from Kathy Kegley right at the mailbox - out came a newspaper clipping and Kevin's picture. Kevin was the boy with glasses from my dream two nights earlier! Crying, I ran to call his mother to tell her about my dream. Our sons were as connected in heaven as we were here. Kathy cleared up my confusion as to why the boys were wearing firemen suits. Kevin had been a volunteer fireman.

These and other dreams have comforted me so much. Ralphie will never be forgotten. I will see my son again. I will see him in Heaven.

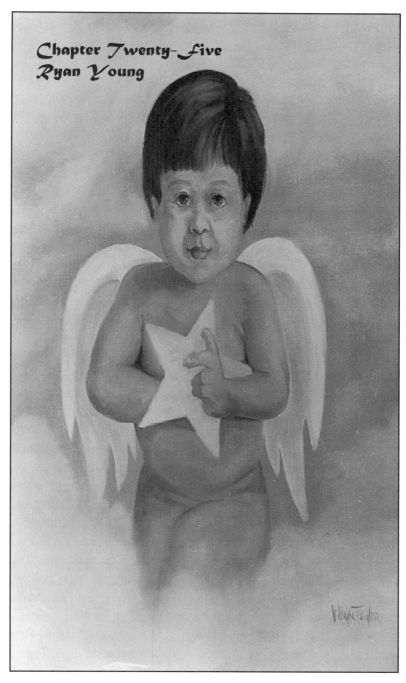

Chapter Twenty-Five
Ryan Young

RYAN GARRETT YOUNG

By Gene Carole Nochta

    Something very different was happening. There are no words or feelings that could adequately describe this change….everything was just becoming different. Was it all pre-death visions or was it a spiritual energy force guiding and preparing all of us for the unimaginable? You know the kind of things that happen to other people, but certainly not to our family. All I know as I look back on events leading to the day of July 4th, 1994, and beyond, all our lives have been transformed. What on the exterior appears to us to be a series of unconnected events may well have been a higher level of design by forces dwelling in eternity.

    One month before July 4th, 1994, I suddenly, without any obvious warning, decided to change jobs. My reason for changing jobs was a mystery to all who knew me and even to me. I was accepting a job for less money and simply for the reason it just felt like the right thing to do. The right thing to do? It was a crazy step by all worldly types of thinking. I can remember my current employer saying… "let this job give you a life." What a strange thing to say but how true it later became. At the same time my best friend and her husband of sixteen years were on the verge of a divorce. Somehow I thought maybe our family could help them refocus their marriage. We invited them to celebrate the 4th of July at our house with a little swimming in our backyard pool. There would be hot dogs for the kids and hopefully great weather for all of us. Even with these plans for the future big changes were occurring. A very different feeling entered my life. I guess the words to describe the feeling was a sense of confusion and sadness but why not? I was changing my job "just because", and I was watching my friend experience turmoil in her marriage. There were some other thoughts and feelings I was experiencing, too. These thoughts and feelings were my secret because if they ever got out, I was smart enough to know that other people would think I needed serious counseling. I <u>now</u> know these inner experiences that are so difficult to explain were God's pillows that would later soften the event that occurred on July 4th,1994.

I never had dreams that I could remember as an adult, but suddenly during the immediate time frame before July 4th, I began to dream or have visions of my son Ryan. I would see Ryan's face up close in a deep sleep, in a sleep very different from the one I was used to seeing. I would wake up with a very rapid heart rate and very scared.

Ryan was born with physical and mental handicaps, but his pure and honest spirit and gentle heart earned him many friends and admirers. He presented a challenge to our family, and we found ways to meet the challenge. Ryan said "Hi" and "Bye" to everyone, even to the neighbors most uncomfortable around an individual with handicaps. Ryan's determined spirit was not discouraged when people looked away and pretended not to hear him. Ryan would just project his little voice and repeat his friendly message, "Hi...Bye...Bye...Bye." I can remember on July 3rd as I pushed him in his wheelchair around our neighborhood having a gut piercing thought that Ryan was going to die. He was saying good-bye on that day like he knew it too. I started crying and pushed him faster and faster around the cul-de-sac in our neighborhood. Actually, our entire family really thought of this neighborhood as Ryan's, for it was because of the big swimming pool in our back yard that we bought this house. This house was for Ryan: there were no stairs, all the living space was on one floor, and of course the main attraction was the swimming pool.

Ryan loved to swim. He could move his body in the water in a way that was impossible to do when the forces of gravity on land worked against him. He would laugh in the water. He could dive in the water. He could play ball in the water. He could share his brother's friends in the water; even those friends who were afraid or uncomfortable with a handicapped child were willing to play and interact with Ryan if it meant swimming in a big private pool.

It was the morning of July 4th. I was getting ready for our guests. The house was perfectly clean and the weather was sunny and warm. I can remember feeling that strange sense of sadness I've tried to describe so many times as I talk about these events to anyone willing to listen. Somehow when I start to use earthly words to describe the feeling, it seemed to minimize it. I looked around the house, and I was proud of all the things we as a family had acquired; nice furniture, antiques, an entertainment center, and many decorative accessories. I was to start a new job the next day that was supposed to change my life and give me more time to be with my family and spend less time at work. So why was I sad in such an inexplicable and mystical way? Most people thought I had everything to make anyone happy; in fact, I was happy until this strange sadness entered my life. At the time all this was going on, I never thought of the sadness as a premonition of what was about to happen, but in retrospect I know it was a little taste of the sadness I was about to experience. Somehow a higher force gave me a taste of sadness to cushion the pain that was about to happen. I truly believe God knew I couldn't handle the pain of the future all in one blow…God knew I needed one of His pillows.

My friend and her family arrived. There were enough hot dogs and chips at my house to feed the neighborhood. All the kids wanted to swim in the pool. The grill was by the pool and so the party began. My husband, my girlfriend, and all the children were in the pool. I was about ten feet away watching everyone in the pool.

I was listening to my girlfriend's husband talk about how much he wanted his marriage to work. I had a sympathetic ear, and I thought I had a watchful eye on the children in the pool too. My husband was about three feet away from Ryan as he played in the water with the other children. I can remember him jumping in the pool, throwing balls and toys around in the water. I remember him saying "Mama" and jumping up and down in the water as he usually does. I can remember thinking Ryan was looking for one of the toys that had sunk to the bottom of the pool. Then I started screaming. I remember my husband standing up and looking at me startled. The next thing I can remember is realizing my son was not breathing, and I could not feel a carotid pulse. I am a nurse, and I have done CPR on other people, but never on someone I knew personally. Now what was I doing? I was doing CPR on a lifeless body that I loved more than life itself. For twelve minutes, I was breathing for him and pumping his little heart. Looking back, I don't know how I did this but somehow I did. The EMS driver later told me that I did a good job; in fact he told me I knew exactly what size endotracheal tube to place in my son's oral airway. To this day, I am not sure how I knew that - just that I did it instinctively. My son's heart rate was now in a normal rhythm. It was beating, and he was no longer turning blue. However, the EMS driver told me that he was still sleeping or not responsive. What hospital did I want to go to? I decided that the large Medical Center would be the best.

As I entered the front seat of the ambulance, I noticed there were many cars and people all around my house and surrounding the ambulance. Some people had video cameras, and they were aiming them at me and my son. I then noticed that every news channel in town was at my house video taping the worst possible tragedy I could imagine. I became enraged at their insensitivity. This story could be material for the television show 911. This tragic day would be a great story for dinner news. I sat in the front seat feeling as lifeless as Ryan did a little while ago.

The feeling of sadness intensified and penetrated deeper

into my heart. I could feel a dull thick film surround my physical body...that film later became a brick wall which protected and prevented any feelings from entering or leaving my body. Time was surreal; hours would pass and I could not remember any of the details. I could only remember walking into the intensive care unit and seeing Ryan on a ventilator in a very deep sleep just like he appeared in my dreams. I would try to block that familiar picture out of my brain, but it was there, and it wasn't going anywhere else. I can remember when one of the nurses caring for Ryan brought in the musical cassette tape from the Lion King. As I listened to it for the first time, there was one song that confirmed to me that Ryan was going to die. Later on when I saw the Disney film the "Lion King," I realized the song I remember as Ryan was dying was the same song played as the Lion King was dying. Again I shook my head to try to get rid of those negative and unthinkable thoughts, but I couldn't. One week had passed, and Ryan's condition was not responding to medical science.

All of Ryan's life we had overcome obstacles. We were going to overcome this somehow, even if I had to quit my new job and take care of him on a ventilator at home. As I shared my latest thoughts with medical staff and family, I pretended I didn't notice their eyes look away with sadness and disbelief. Ryan and his mom were a team; we did everything together, and there was never a day I regretted.

Every day with Ryan was full of love and happiness. That may be hard for some to believe for I know there are not many parents who could honestly say that. Being the parent of a child with handicaps is a very different experience than being a parent of a normal child. I know, I was both. Ryan was my special child, and Tina and Pete were my "normal" children. I can say there were days when I had to discipline my normal children; there were words said that have caused some momentary regrets, but that was not so with Ryan. He was pure unconditional love, never a moment of regret except

264

for that one day in the pool on the 4th of July. I had failed my son. I was not there when he needed me most, and so the guilt process began, and to this day I'm not sure if it will ever end.

My daughter Tina said in one of our family "what are we going to do discussions," that we have always tried to create a life where Ryan could be given choices. Imagine that a child with handicaps be given choices. Sounds easy, sounds logical, but somehow it just wasn't that simple in real life. The "system" was set up in the world where people with handicaps are viewed by experts as needing this and needing that, but no one ever seemed to take the time to see what the handicapped person might want. After all, people with handicaps were somehow different, therefore, they were treated differently. So something as obvious as choices in daily life occurrences were not a common thing in most of the lives of people with handicaps. Instead, the norm was a set of professionals working hard to design a daily plan of what they felt was right for Ryan. It was a constant struggle for me to encourage those professional folks to take the time and energy to find out what Ryan might really want. Easier said than done because Ryan did not talk except for saying "Hi, bye, and mama." However, Ryan could communicate in ways that were nonverbal and best understood by his mom and family.

So, there we all were…Tina, my husband, my son Pete, and I trying to decide what to do for Ryan. We all felt helpless. Ryan was still in a deep sleep and he couldn't communicate to us in his nonverbal ways like he used to do. The attending physician was starting to hint at stopping life support measures. Of course that was not an option I was ready for, so I thought he'd better keep his sterile medical thoughts to himself. I can remember getting really defensive about his medical plan…It was his plan. It wasn't our plan, and it certainly can't be Ryan's plan. Ryan needs his mom and that is all there is to it. I believe this thought process went on for maybe days or maybe it was just minutes. Who knows, since time gets so distorted when you are living a nightmare. Then my daughter's wise words penetrated the brick wall surrounding my heart and brain. She said, "It seems like everyone is trying to decide for Ryan whether or not and how he should live the rest of his earth-bound life. We are doing to Ryan what we have criticized others for doing. We are trying to make a decision for Ryan that maybe we should leave to Ryan. We need to give Ryan a choice even though it may be his last choice on earth." He had been on the ventilator for a week, and his brain activity had diminished significantly. He couldn't communicate with us in the ways we were used to or could he? Tina then said the unthinkable, maybe we should let Ryan make the decision on whether or not he should live. There was silence for I don't know how long. There were certainly lots of tears. I know that is when I submerged deeper into the surreal. I couldn't believe that Tina had the fortitude to say that…she was right, but I didn't want her to be. Her thoughts needed to be considered.

I went back into the ICU and looked at all the monitors and equipment keeping my son alive. What did Ryan have to say about all of this? The answer to the future was no longer in our hands; it was in Ryan's hands, and it was in God's hands. To simply state it, I was losing control of the situation. I started getting morbid thoughts; thoughts that terrified me and inflicted panic attacks. Those thoughts were visions of Ryan in a grave…visions I could not handle. The next thing I knew, we were actually orchestrating how we were going to remove Ryan's life support. Ryan's biological dad is a physician, and he was there to assist. My only request was that I could be holding Ryan when the ventilator was removed. I got in the bed with Ryan and held him close to my breaking heart. My ex-husband, the physician, placed an adult size face mask on his little face so as to muffle his last breaths. I had my eyes closed tight, and then suddenly I felt the most powerful and foreign energy force. The energy propelled itself from the center of my son's body. It was a "whoosh" shooting up into heaven. I had no doubt that Ryan had gone to heaven, and I felt a sense of peace and a sense of numbness that I had never experienced in my life. My daughter was on the other side of Ryan holding him as I was. Later, I found out that she felt it too. That experience relieved my fear of Ryan being in a grave for then I knew, not just believed, that he went to heaven. Finally, I <u>knew</u> there was a heaven. I felt the transition of Ryan's soul from his body to eternity and the afterlife. No longer did I fear the grave for the grave site was just the house for Ryan's body, not his soul and spirit. It soared like a powerful magnet up to heaven. It was a comforting pillow or gift from God, selected just for me, to help me cope with the death of my son.

In fact, I can remember thinking that the role of the attending MD pronouncing my son's death as insignificant. What I experienced was at such a high spiritual level. The doctor's words seemed so mortal; they were like an afterthought. It was an earthly ritual that seemed almost silly in comparison to the higher level of communication with my son I had just experienced.

The funeral I simply do not remember, but the days after it presented more challenges to our family. The days were centered around just coping with loss: the loss of Ryan, loss of appetite, the loss of the will to go on ourselves. Just when you thought you might get through a day okay, someone else in your family was having a bad day. The pain then became pain on top of pain. Their pain on top of your pain, your pain on top of theirs compounding unbearably. At that point I knew I needed help. I was wearing down mentally and physically.

I went to a psychiatrist. I made a late appointment. In fact, I knew the doctor stayed <u>late</u> to see me at 7 PM. When I arrived, there was only one other person in the waiting room. I had come straight from work and was wearing my lab jacket. The man waiting in the doctor's office asked me if I was a doctor. I told him I was a nurse. He looked down and softly said, "I've never been to a place like this." I told him that sometimes things happen that force you to get help. I further explained that I was here because my son just died, and I couldn't sleep, eat or seem to function. He looked at me for a while and said, "I'm here because my son died six months ago, and I still can't sleep or eat." As we shared stories about our sons, we learned that they were both fourteen years old. What are the chances of two different psychiatrists in practice together scheduling special sessions with two strangers who shared such a sorrowful bond? To be honest, the talk I had with the stranger in the waiting room I will always cherish for I knew his pain and I felt the love he had for his son who suddenly died after complaining of a headache which was later discovered to be a brain aneurysm. His son's last words were—"I love you Dad." I never saw this man again but our meeting made a lasting impression.

One night my husband decided we all needed to go to a local Catholic church's Oktoberfest just to get out. My son Pete ventured over to the prize raffle booth. There must have been thirty prizes being raffled off. Together, Pete and I rounded the booth placing a dollar here and a dollar there, entering his name in the pot of wishful winners. I can remember writing Ryan's name on one of the tickets just because I missed writing his name. I missed talking about him. It seems not only do you lose your child but you lose your right to talk about him because it makes other people uncomfortable. People in general don't know what to say, so they really end up saying nothing.

Hours passed, and it was getting late, so we decided it was time to go home. I looked over at the raffle booth, and all the prizes were gone except one. It was the one my son Pete had said he wished he could have. It was a fancy black racing bike with white balloons tied onto the handlebars. I can remember Pete saying, "I wish I could win that bike." I can then remember wishing and begging God to please give me a sign that Ryan was okay. As we were leaving the Oktoberfest, I said to my husband, "I am going to see who won that bike." As I approached the bike, I got this strange feeling. I felt Ryan's presence, and then I was shocked to see Ryan's name on the bike. Ryan had won the bike for his brother Pete, and it literally was that "black and white" sign I had been begging God to give me to let me know Ryan was okay.

Once the bike episode occurred, I began to wonder what other signs might come to our family from Ryan. I soon found out that my daughter was suffering because she felt she didn't have the opportunity to say good-bye to her brother. That thought would haunt her at night. She would cry alone and keep her private pain to herself. One day Tina shared with me a dream that to her was real. Ryan visited her and let her hold him for a second or two, and then they each said bye. She knew from that experience that he was okay. She also told me that using earthly words to describe the experience could not adequately convey the reality of the occurrence. All I know is that whatever it was, it worked. A layer of pain and guilt was removed from my daughter's soul and hence from my own.

My husband probably suffered internally more than anyone could imagine. After all, he was an ex-football player, six foot four inches tall, and showing emotions didn't come easily. He handled his stress in physical ways. I know he painted our house after the funeral. I don't know how many times he painted it; all I remember was that he was often on a ladder somewhere outside painting. I think he put a new roof on the house too. I know he jogged seven or eight miles a night starting at 10 P.M. When was his sign from Ryan going to come? Then I remembered that the night before Ryan died my husband had told me that everything was going to be all right. He shared with me a dream he had. He said the dream was real. I thought he was crazy, but I didn't say anything. He explained in the dream he saw his dad who had died about ten years ago, and his dad told him that he would take care of Ryan. My husband even described what his dad was wearing. The next day at 6 P.M. my son Ryan had died and was meeting his grandpa for the first time. To this day, my husband feels this dream was a real life encounter with his dad, and in retrospect, I feel it was sent from God.

It has now been almost four years since that fateful day in July. Many layers of pain have been chipped away. The pain hasn't gone away; it just seems to take on new forms. I have since met many people who have lost children. They are ordinary people that have had extraordinary experiences that are hard to explain but very real. Real in ways that the average person may have trouble believing. Tragedy perhaps can close the door of rational thinking in order for a higher level of communication to occur. Tragedy may strip a person of all worldly defenses that prevent encounters with the afterlife. All I know is that every parent I've met who has lost a child has had at least one extraordinary and mystical experience.

Chapter Twenty-Six
Heather Perdue

HEATHER PERDUE

By Rissa Perdue

When Heather Renee Perdue was born on March 25, 1977, a dream came true for my husband, Charlie, and me. We became the proud parents of a beautiful baby girl. Never had we been so happy and content. Then without warning on June 18, 1995, we lost Heather in an automobile accident. Our lives were shattered. Blond hair and blue-eyed, Heather was as sweet as she was pretty. Not to say she didn't do sneaky and mischievous things, she did, but her sunny disposition made her a pleasure to be around. Although I wanted Heather to dress and act like a little lady, in reality she was a tomboy. She did what she loved to do...climbed trees, waded creeks, rode bikes, and pretended to be Daisy Duke, going in and out of car windows.

Heather wanted a baby brother to help care for, and when she was four and a half years old, we gave her Heath. When someone would ask her baby's name, she would always say without a pause, "Heath Banford - I hate that name", but she was very proud of her baby brother and loved him unselfishly.

A very special bond formed between Heather and her Granny (my mother) on the day she was born. Through the next few years, seldom did a day go by that they were not together talking, taking walks, and just enjoying each other's company. No other person influenced Heather more than my mother did. Even though her granny died when Heather was only five years old, her presence remained and instilled in Heather courage, determination, and the need to care for others less fortunate than she. The full impact of this influence was clear to me only after Heather's death. Reading through Heather's autobiography written during her senior year in high school, I found these words, "The thing I remember most in my life was my granny, my mom's mom. She died when I was five years old. I can remember everything about her and even what her house was like. I could write a book about her, but whenever I think about her I get upset. I love her as much as I do my parents. She was a very special woman." Throughout Heather's life it was evident in her eyes that she missed and longed to see her granny again. I believe that longing has been fulfilled.

Strong family relationships don't just happen; they are cultivated with a lot of love, determination, and dedication. There are few parents fortunate enough to have a close relationship with their teenager. When Heather reached her teens, I was prepared for rebellion and lack of communication. I was not prepared for her to remain my friend and it disarmed me. Heather was not ashamed of her father and me; instead she trusted our judgment enough to seek our advice when she or a friend needed guidance. As a family we were comfortable and easy with each other. We allowed ourselves the freedom of just being who we were and enjoyed each other's differences. The greatest gift shared between a mother and a daughter is that of friendship. As with my mother and me, Heather and I could confide in each other and enjoy all types of conversation. Of course, sometimes Heather only told me what she wanted me to know. More than anything else, I miss those conversations and the laughter we shared.

On Saturday, June 17, 1995, just two weeks after Heather's high school graduation, we received the phone call that every parent fears. The State Police informed us that our daughter had been involved in an automobile accident. Heather and two of her close friends (sisters), the older one driving, were on their way home from a neighboring county when the car they were in left the road and hit a tree. We were told that our daughter was being transported to a nearby hospital in Jackson, and we needed to get there as quickly as possible. As we drove to the hospital that night, we feared that Heather might be seriously hurt, but I don't think we ever really believed she would die.

The EMTs met us in the emergency waiting room and tried to prepare us for the seriousness of the situation because they had already lost her twice. The doctor came out and explained to us that Heather had suffered severe head and internal injuries. He told us they were trying to stabilize her so they could fly her to the University of Kentucky hospital where the best team of neurosurgeons was standing by to do surgery. We knew at this point that her situation was critical. We just got a glimpse of her as they rolled her out to the ambulance waiting to take her to the helicopter. We were on our way home to pick up a few things we would need when a police car pulled us over. They told us there was no need to go to the hospital. Heather had died. This was about three and a half hours from the time we got the call that changed our lives forever. It was as though someone had crushed my heart. How we got through the next few days, I don't know, but there were arrangements and decisions that had to be made. There was no time to curl up and try to die myself because Charlie and Heath needed me, and we had to give Heather her final farewell. Personally, I had to make sure that everything was perfect because I knew this was the last thing I would ever get to do for my daughter. Had just one small detail been out of place, I might have collapsed.

It seemed the line that formed for her viewing went on forever and so many people waited hours in line just to see her one last time. The funeral itself was unusual in that the minister took the opportunity to admonish those attending to put their lives in order because the hour of death, as in Heather's case, is uncertain. We are thankful that almost a year before her death, she made the decision to become a Christian and was baptized into Christ. Trusting that she is in the hands of a merciful God makes losing her easier to bear. We laid Heather's body to rest in the most perfect place - on top of a mountain overlooking her home. The tombstone we selected reflects our undying love for her and how special she is to us. It is rose-colored and heart shaped, and her senior portrait is embedded in it. The words inscribed on her stone, 'Forever To Bloom In the Master's Bouquet', were chosen because we feel God picked her just as she was starting to bloom to be in his garden, never to fade.

For the longest time, the very idea of shopping, whether at the mall or a grocery store, filled me with panic. Realizing the longer I waited the harder it would be to tackle these everyday challenges, I eventually decided to face them. Somewhat easier now - about three years have passed - I still turn my head while going down certain aisles at the grocery so I won't see what were once her favorite foods. Trying to visit certain shops in the mall, especially Heather's favorite, is useless. When I look around, all I can think about is how much I miss buying clothes for her and how beautiful she would look in them. Wiping away the tears, I turn and walk through the door, carrying with me urges that will never again be satisfied.

Needing to fill the long winter hours that lay ahead doing something constructive, Charlie, Heath, Bryan (Heather's boyfriend), and I decided to build a little cabin in the woods up behind our house. For several years our family had talked of doing this, and now the time seemed appropriate since we were having such a difficult time getting involved in living again. Wanting Heather to somehow be a part of the project, we used the money from her life insurance policy to buy the materials needed for the cabin. We did all the work ourselves, after nearly five months we were able to spend the night there. Several of Heather's toys are in the upstairs room for children to play with when they visit, and a picture of her sits on the mantle above the fireplace. For me, especially, this has become a place of refuge and peace. Sometimes when I walk over and just sit on the porch or lie on the bed, I feel a closeness to Heather, as if she knows how much of her presence is here. This story was written in our little cabin by kerosene lamp over a period of several weeks, and though my thoughts were difficult to put into words, they seemed to flow freer there than any other place.

Having three years of holidays and special occasions without Heather behind us now, we know that if we could survive them then, we can again. After all, we do not have a choice. For us, the key to surviving the traditional get-togethers was to do something totally different than when Heather was with us. It doesn't make us miss her any less; it's just easier than reliving past memories. Since Heather's accident, though my faith has been tested like never before, I feel God's comforting love more than ever. Sometimes I still want to ask "Why?", but I am confident that someday I will know the answer to that question. From an early age, I have known that death is merely a passing on into a different realm. So, instead of dwelling on living the rest of my life without Heather, I remind myself that I have no idea how long the rest of my life will be.

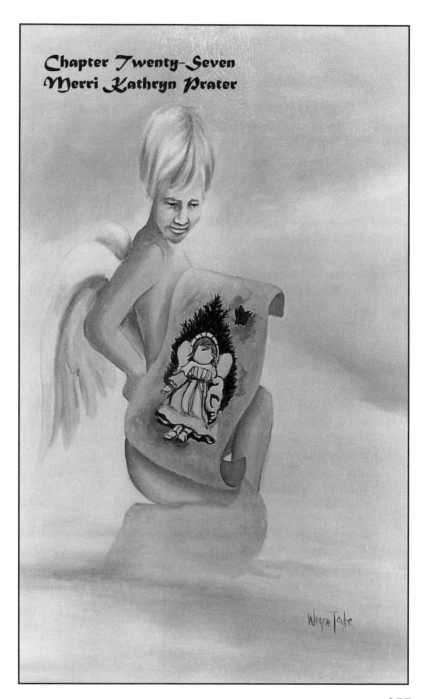

Chapter Twenty-Seven
Merri Kathryn Prater

MERRI KATHRYN PRATER

By Ella Prater

There seemed to be no hope of a second child for us. We prayed and prayed. Friends prayed and waited in anticipation. Babies everywhere—was there not one for me? Then it happened. I was pregnant. Our six year old daughter, Tammy, was ecstatic. Her hands caressed the growing bulge of my tummy, and her ears pressed in close "to hear" her baby brother or sister. She smiled in glee when she felt the soft thrust of tiny hands and feet.

She was born beautifully and wonderfully made. She was our Merri Kathryn. After a mere two hours of labor, at 10:27 A.M. on a Sunday morning, June 4, 1978, she came into this world. She was perfectly wonderful—even the doctor said so!

What wonderful years those were. Merri Kathryn was my shadow. "I love you Daddy, but I stay with my mommy," she said in her small voice when invited to go places with her Dad. There was so much for us to share: picnics on the porch, throwing gravel into the creek to watch the ripples, slow companionable walks, story times. Oh, how I cherished our time together. She was such a sweet baby and such a pleasant child. Little Miss Meticulous—her hair was whiter than white, and her skin so fair it was transparent. So tiny, so dainty—Merri Kathryn, I love you. She grew—but not much—and time beckoned that it was time for kindergarten. Home and family were never again the all consuming focus of her life. She reached out to form friendships. Those friendships revolved around gymnastics, (Imagine a three year old posed with pointed toes in stance for a cartwheel!), dance recitals, piano recitals, cheerleading, speech competitions, the endless birthday parties, Girl Scouts, and church.

Like Tammy's desire for Merri Kathryn, Merri Kathryn

pleaded for a baby brother or sister. Please??? The entire family wanted another baby, but did I? Well,—if everyone must have another baby in the house—okay, I'll be an agreeable party to that family decision. How thankful I am for that decision and God's blessing upon us in the form of a son whom the family named Christopher. Because of Merri Kathryn's incessant pleadings and God's master plan, our home is not empty. Merri Kathryn deserves the accolades for a loving, special son whom I can now hold when I miss her so intensely.

How quickly time passes. It was time for Christopher to enter kindergarten, and I decided to return to the classroom. Life was so full. Tammy, my oldest, graduated from high school and went off to Centre College. I had one fledgling leaving the nest, and Merri Kathryn would soon be entering high school. I had been back in the classroom only one year before Tammy graduated, but I would share the same high school with Merri Kathryn every day. How would she react? How would her friends react?

At first I didn't exist. "Don't tell anyone you are my mom"—as if anyone would not make the connection. Prater was not a common name to our community! However, very quickly she realized it wasn't so bad to have your mom teach at your school—even if she did foolish things at pep rallies and on school spirit days. I think the most remarkable insight for her was the newfound perception of me as more than her mom. I was a teacher. I was a person. More and more, she would come to my classroom for money, food, paper, pen/pencil, help, or just to stop by with a friend. How I long to hear her soft knock at my classroom door and see her sitting on my stool at the lectern, legs dangling and the smell of Big Red chewing gum on her breath. The halls and classrooms of Knott County Central High will never be the same for me. I hear a knock or see a small blonde wisp of a girl walking down the hallway, and I hold my breath in painful awareness that it is not my Merri Kathryn.

The days of our lives slip by, one by one, and we too often take them for granted—not taking the time to savor the moments of sacred joy, love, and laughter life gives to us through our children. Time passes. Our lives change with the passage of time. On April 1, 1995, my husband suffered a heart attack, and our family learned how very fragile life is. Willie survived the heart attack and subsequent angioplasty, but our lives were changed. Merri Kathryn wrote in her senior memory book that the three happiest moments of her life were her sister's wedding, the day her Dad came home from the hospital, and the day she got her car.

During the months following his heart attack, my husband's health prevented him from being able to work as he had before. Financial security for the future was a real concern. We still had two children to provide for and educate. What if there were other health problems? What if I were left to care for Merri Kathryn and Christopher by myself? I cried that I wanted things to be the way they had been. I was determined to give her the same opportunity given to her sister. I would not, could not, deny her that same jubilance of driving her very own car for the first time. It was July 28, 1995— eight months to the day until an accident with that new car would ultimately claim her life.

Merri Kathryn's grandfather, Merri Kathryn, Christopher, and I went shopping for her "wheels". What a wonderful day! Etched in my memory and heart is the pure joy on her face and in her voice when she was given the keys to her 1995 hunter green gold package Camry, complete with spoiler, power sunroof and stereo system. What a pleasure to see such joy happen for your child! She and I drove away from the car dealership followed by her grandfather and Christopher. Ray-Bans on, sunroof rolled back, sun shining at its zenith, and stereo playing—she drove us toward a local shopping mall saying nothing—but singing at the top of her lung capacity with a song on the radio.

A few days before Christmas 1995, Merri Kathryn received her letter of acceptance from the University of Kentucky. In February of 1996 her cheerleading squad won the regional cheerleading competition. A few days later the top ten seniors in the class were announced. Merri Kathryn was number nine. She was very active on her school yearbook staff. She participated on a very successful mock-trial team. She was one of her senior class officers. I can see so many astounding elements of closure that occurred during those last days of Merri Kathryn's life. She had attained most of her goals.

On one of those last days, Merri Kathryn bounded downstairs announcing she wanted to call Judy Nygard, a former next door neighbor of ours who was very special to Merri Kathryn but who had returned to her home in the upper peninsula of Michigan years ago. It had been some time since their last conversation, but Merri Kathryn did call her, and they talked and caught up on the details of their respective lives. So strange, but a bit of closure that must be very special to Judy.

Five days before Merri Kathryn's accident I shopped at a nearby dress boutique—really just wanting a pleasant Saturday afternoon diversion. A dress made of the softest ivory linen overlaid with billowy embroidered chiffon kept calling Merri Kathryn's name to me. I looked. I touched. It was so beautiful. I rationalized that it was a dress she could wear on any end of school special occasion or college function the following year. It was her dress! It might be perfect for the spring portraits to be done on Monday! I bought the dress and brought it home.

Closing my eyes, I can see her as she twirled in that dress in the upstairs hallway outside her room. The soft ivory melted against her fair skin and pale blonde hair. It was a picture of youth and beauty.

She chose not to wear the dress on Monday for the

portraits because she learned the photographer was using a white background. She feared the lighting might not sufficiently contrast the different shadings. I have no picture of her in that dress to cling to, to pore over, but I have a clear vision of her being carried by God's angels into His presence wearing such a flowing gown. It is a beautiful image. It was a beautiful dress. I did not realize I was purchasing my Merri Kathryn's burial dress.

I have had a poster hanging in my classroom for some time that reads, "There is nothing to writing—Just open a vein and let it begin". As I address the day of Merri Kathryn's accident, I feel such a pressure in my chest. It is a congealed mass of anguish and remembrance… I open the vein…

It was an uneventful day of school for me. It was Thursday, and I stayed after school to tutor some students in English, give make-up exams, and do some paper work. Merri Kathryn unexpectedly came back to school to see me, something she had never done before. She sat with me for a few minutes and said she and a friend might go to the baseball game if it didn't rain. I told her I would see her at home later. When I arrived home, Merri Kathryn was watching a program on television. She and her friend Meredith kept missing one another on the phone, so they hadn't gone to the game. It was some time later that she left home on an errand, telling me she would be back in just a little while.

I was ironing when the phone rang. The voice of a lady whom I knew asked me if I had been called. Perplexed, I said, "No." I heard words saying I should get there quickly. A terrible accident had happened, and it was said to be Merri Kathryn. I did not believe it! I asked Christopher if anyone had called. No. My husband was still at his office next door. I called him, and we rushed away. We met an ambulance— lights flashing, sirens screeching. It couldn't be our daughter. I would know. Using the cellular phone, I called Christopher to see if a call had come. A sigh of relief—no. We drove on until the site of the accident could be seen. We parked and ran towards the scene, still not believing it could be our Merri Kathryn. Our local sheriff and one of his deputies, who also served as a deacon in our church with my husband, stopped us. Yes, it was Merri Kathryn! Oh, God! The sheriff put us into his car saying he would drive us to the hospital. Anthony said he would take care of our car and see to arrangements for Christopher. We were on our way, racing towards the hospital.

My dad arrived, and my heart lurched. He had always had such a fear and dread of his grandchildren being killed in an accident. Not Merri Kathryn—God? Our nephew Jeff, Dr. Prater, came out to tell us it truly was very bad. The trauma team was trying to stabilize her for transport. Arrangements were in process to air lift her to Lexington and the University of Kentucky head trauma center. We waited. If I could only see her! Jeff came back to tell us the air ambulance could not come from Lexington because of weather conditions. It was raining, and cloud cover gave very poor visibility. Knoxville was contacted, but it was the same scenario. The mother of one of Merri Kathryn's friends made a call to a friend of hers in Knoxville who had a private transport company. He would come—but by that time the doctors were wheeling Merri Kathryn out of the emergency room towards the waiting ambulance. She couldn't wait for air lift. To see my daughter unconscious and on life support systems crushed my spirit. I thought I was going to be ill. My baby—so pale, so lifeless. "Merri Kathryn, Mommy's here. I love you baby." I was crying, but only inside. I hurt so badly I was shaking. Daddy pushed hundred dollar bills into our hands saying, "You may need this." The sheriff said, "I will drive you folks and Brother Mike (our pastor) to the hospital. I can get you there more quickly, and you are in no condition to drive." We were so loved and cared for. Merri Kathryn's cousin, Dr. Prater, had made the decision to accompany her in the ambulance. She was in the care of family, and we were being cared for by our sheriff and our pastor.

The following hours and days were mixtures of horror, anguish, thanksgiving, and awe at what was to transpire. The sheriff and our pastor had left during the early morning hours after learning that her vital signs were stable and it would be a matter of just waiting to hear the prognosis. Jeff had spent the night, leaving only for a few hours to go to a local motel to get some much needed rest. When he returned, he was able to share with us what he had learned after a conference with the other doctors and assured us that Merri Kathryn truly was in the finest center for head trauma that medicine had to offer. He was such a comforting reassurance for us. We began to wait.

It was some time before we were allowed to see Merri Kathryn. She was so still. The only sounds were of the respirator and monitors. In the silence I looked beyond the tubes and equipment to see the real Merri Kathryn. I talked to her. I sang to her. I cuddled her in my heart because I could not hold her in my arms. I kissed her toes, her fingers, her freckles—every accessible inch of her. I love you—I love you—I love you. My time was unlimited with her. The staff felt it could not hurt her, and it might be of help.

By the time two days had passed since the accident, we were utterly emotionally drained. The upheaval of all the crises Merri Kathryn was going through was taking its toll on her young healthy body, but we kept the belief in her ultimate victory foremost in our thoughts and words. We all gathered; family, friends, and students from her school, in a huge circle in the downstairs lobby, hands and hearts clasped together. Brother Anthony with his majestic voice led us in singing "Amazing Grace". Hundreds of people came to the hospital that day. Words cannot begin to express the humbling gratitude for the love given to us and Merri Kathryn. The hospital staff were overwhelmed, but they were so kind, so good, so caring towards us, the young people, and most importantly—Merri Kathryn. She survived obstacles that medicine could not explain—but the swelling of her brain continued to increase the cranial pressure.

Early Wednesday morning after having slept a few hours in the waiting room, I went into Merri Kathryn's room. It was so peaceful. The monitor showed marked decrease in the cranial pressure! Excitedly, I called for the nurse. It was not good, but she was not at liberty to explain. I must wait for the doctors to talk with us. It was not a long wait. She had lost the battle. Two tests were yet to be done to confirm conclusively that my beautiful Merri Kathyrn was clinically brain dead.

We went home—a home with a bedroom marked with a sign on the door—Merri Kathryn's Room—but now there was no Merri Kathryn to fill that room's purpose. The rain had begun to fall again. The elements cried with me. It was not a night of desolation and despair, but it was a night of blackness and emptiness and loneliness and the disbelief that I had really lost my daughter. The next day would be Easter Sunday—Resurrection Day, with its symbolic and comforting promise.

I don't really have words to explain it, but life does move forward. Two weeks after the funeral, I decided to return to my classroom. It was compulsive behavior. I am a teacher, and my students become my children. My situation was complicated by the fact that my students were Merri Kathryn's senior classmates. I taught five classes of senior English. If I did not return, those young people had lost not only a friend and classmate but also a teacher in whom they had learned to trust. I returned to school for them. I returned for Merri Kathryn. I would finish the school year for her.

I had seen the television and newspaper coverage of Merri Kathryn's accident and death, but I was unprepared for the tumultuous emotions I would experience when I drove onto the campus for the first time. I cringed, yet I was glad when I saw all the green ribbons. My heart raced when I saw her parking space set apart. Is this real? I walked the halls, looking for her, seeing her everywhere I looked. I went to her classrooms and touched the desks that were hers. Her locker…I can't do this! But for our children we will do anything. I tried to reassure my students that there was nothing they could do or say that would make the pain worse. They did not have to walk as though "on egg shells". We laughed together. We cried together. They welcomed me with open arms. Each hug was a little bit like a hug from her.

Each day presented a new challenge. My face clearly showed the ravage of unceasing pain, tears, and lack of sleep. I forged ahead. I was on a mission for my daughter. On those days that would bring a pounding pain I stayed home: the day the seniors received their caps and gowns, the day of the senior picnic, and senior "skip" day. My being throbbed in awareness that she would have been a joyful part of those activities.

The special days are difficult; every day is difficult. Friends and family do help. They cannot fully understand the fullness of grief we hold, but they do help us in a loving way to carry the burden. As I record these thoughts and events during the anniversary of Merri Kathryn's death, I, too, find a bit of closure. I have learned much from my daughter. Because of her I have no fear of death. Through Merri Kathryn I have learned that individual grieving is as unique as the person lost. There are no given rules. Each of us must do what we must in order to survive the pain that envelops our lives. We cannot hide from the pain. The depth of our pain is a manifestation of our love. I am learning not to look to all of the days ahead and question my very survival; I deal with today and meet whatever pangs of sorrow I encounter with resolve. I have lost a child—my beloved Merri Kathryn, but our family will share eternity together.

Chapter Twenty-Eight
Buzzy, Stephen, Todd and Kami Greer

287

THE FAMILY OF GAM AND BECKY GREER

By Becky Greer

Warren G. Greer, Jr.	December 15, 1951 -
Rebecca Bottoms Greer	December 2, 1951 -
John Michael Greer	January 14, 1972 - January 17, 1995
Warren Stephen Greer	March 27, 1977 - November 17, 1979
Robert Todd Greer	November 29, 1980 - January 16, 1995
Kamela Lynne Greer	August 7, 1984 - January 16, 1995

What is wrong with this picture? It is, of course, obvious. My husband Gam and I are alone. We do not like being alone. We do not want to be alone. We are not used to being alone. What we are used to is running to basketball practice, soccer practice, ballet and tap lessons, guitar lessons, piano lessons, karate, gymnastics, choir practice, baseball practice, Boy Scouts, softball practice, skating parties, birthday parties, swimming parties, hand bell practice and ball games. We are used to loud music in the house and in the car. We are used to a house full of kids running and playing and laughing and doing all the fun things that kids love to do. We are used to muddy feet and fingerprints all through the house. We are used to dirty clothes and wet towels and toys lying on the floor. We are used to brothers and sisters arguing over who gets to go first or who broke what. We are used to rushing around in the mornings to get everybody off to school or to church. We are used to working on school projects and helping with homework. We are used to bedtime stories and heart to heart talks. We are not used to being alone! We do not like being alone! The family of Gam and Becky Greer appears today to be a family of two, not six. Children are not supposed to die before their parents. That is not the natural order of things. It is not fair. What are we to do? What are any of us to do? Where can we go to find answers? We can't find answers. When people ask, "How are you doing?" I feel like saying, "How am I supposed to be doing?" We just go on as best we can because that is all we can do. What choice do we have but to go on? There is another choice, and that is the choice not to go on. It is one that I'm sure many other bereaved parents have also considered during the many hours of suffering the loss of our children. I am talking about the choice of ending the pain because the pain is unbearable…but the other choice is not the answer either. The other choice would not honor our children or God. I believe the answer is love. I have found that when I reach out to others my pain becomes more "bearable". Why don't I reach out more often? Why do I hold back? Why do we hold back? We are all called to reach out to one another in love. It is through the love and caring and the reaching out of fellow strugglers that I am still here and able to tell my story. I share my story in the hope that others can come to know my children. I share my story because I do not want my children to be forgotten. I share my story in the hope that it will in some way help someone else who is suffering, someone else who is struggling and wondering how to go on after losing someone as precious as their own child. I am reaching out…I am bearing and sharing my pain, because that's the only way I can stand it.

On November 17, 1979, our two and one-half year old son, Stephen, died of leukemia at the University of Kentucky Medical Center. It was a day that changed our lives forever. Our loss was so great we were sure we would never again have to suffer such pain. We were so wrong. The truth is that none of us can ever be sure of anything. On January 16, 1995, our eldest son, Buzzy, received a phone call from his girl-friend as our family was having dinner. After he hung up the phone, he stood up and with a trembling hand began shooting a gun that he had hidden in his pocket. We did not know Buzzy had a gun. In fact, there had never been a gun in our home - ever. We did know that Buzzy had been struggling with drug problems and was, once again, trying to get his life back in order. We didn't know at the time, but have since learned, that the drug Buzzy was addicted to (methamphetamine) was known to cause extreme violent tendencies. When the gun was finally empty, our son Todd, who was fourteen years old, our daughter Kami, who was ten years old, and our son Buzzy, who had just turned twenty three, were all dead. My husband, Gam, had been shot three times and was seriously injured. Miraculously, no bullet struck me. January 16, 1995, a day which started out as an ordinary day, became a day that would change our lives forever.

Gam and I have never been a family of two. Our family started out as a family of three. When Gam proposed marriage back in 1975, he knew he was getting a "package deal". Along with his bride, he was also getting a beautiful little three year old boy named John Michael who was my son from a previous marriage. Even though John Michael is a beautiful name, and he was a beautiful baby, he was nicknamed "Buzzy" soon after his birth. Shortly after we married, Gam legally adopted Buzzy. We moved to London, Kentucky, and began our life together as a family of three. So you see, Gam and I have never been alone...until now.

When I speak to kids about what can happen when you mess with drugs, I try to get them to see that Buzzy was a regular kid, just like them. He was not a bad kid or a problem kid...just a regular kid like them until he started using drugs. Drugs change everything.

Buzzy was a very sweet child and so kindhearted. He loved to make people laugh and was always telling jokes or saying funny things. Always. He was voted "Funniest" in his senior class. Many people often told him he would make a great stand up comic. I think so too. Buzzy was smart, witty, good-looking and talented...but he didn't think so.

Buzzy loved to do all the things kids love to do. When he was little, he loved playing G.I. Joe, Star Wars, He Man,

Spiderman, Batman, and Superman. He loved to go to Kings Island and ride all the roller coasters. He loved playing Nintendo, watching TV and listening to rock music. He played T-ball and baseball a few years but didn't really enjoy it. However, he loved the uniforms! Buzzy was very active in Boy Scouts for several years and came very close to becoming an Eagle Scout. Sadly, we learned years later when he was in drug rehabilitation that it was in Boy Scouts when he first experimented with drugs.

Buzzy had a very sensitive and loving heart. He loved his family. He loved his brothers and sister and no one, no one, who ever knew him could ever imagine that he could do what he did. Drugs change everything. When you are dealing with someone who uses drugs, you are not on a fair playing field. Buzzy was a very caring person with a pure heart who made some terrible choices and ended up destroying himself and his entire family.

Buzzy was a very intelligent boy who just did not have much success at school. He would see how easily school came for his friends, and it frustrated him. He didn't understand. Neither did I. Through the years, he was tested to try to find out why such an intelligent boy struggled so with school. Nothing changed until his freshman year when we found out that Buzzy had Attention Deficit Disorder. He transferred to a smaller school with smaller classes where he was given more personal attention and then did quite well with his school work. Some success at last, but the years of not understanding why he was different had taken their toll. Buzzy had extremely low self-esteem. During the testing that was done to determine the ADD, we discovered that, in fact, only 2% of kids Buzzy's age felt worse about themselves than he did. It broke my heart. It still breaks my heart.

I do think Buzzy enjoyed his high school years. During his first semester of college, he became very depressed. One weekend I noticed that he had a huge knot on his neck.

Upon having it tested, we discovered a defective thyroid which had to be removed. He would have to take medication for the rest of his life to regulate the hormones that the thyroid naturally controls. At the time of our tragedy, Buzzy had not taken this thyroid medicine for almost three months. I believe this contributed to his emotional behavior.

Buzzy was in college when we first found out he was using drugs and had been using drugs for some time. We truly had no idea. Gam and I used to comment on how proud we were that Buzzy didn't run around with a wild bunch. He was mostly home on weekends and weeknights. He spent many, many hours watching TV, listening to his numerous cassette tapes and playing his guitar. He loved all the old reruns of "Gilligan's Island", "Brady Bunch", "I Love Lucy", "Leave It To Beaver", and "Andy Griffith" - all the old shows. He would watch them over and over and over. I know that many times I would hear parents say they had no idea that their kids were using drugs, and I would say, "Yeah, right." Now I know that it is very possible for parents not to know. Even though Buzzy was at home most of the time, he still found ways to use drugs. People who use drugs are very sneaky and can very easily fool a lot of people, even people close to them. Those of you who have experienced this know exactly what I mean. Others will continue to say, as I did, "Yeah, right." We live and we learn.

Buzzy was truly a special person. He was very sensitive (perhaps to a fault) and a loving and lovable young man. I miss you Buzz…I wish you peace.

Buzzy and Gam and I remained a family of three until March 27, 1977. That is when our son, and Buzzy's little brother, Stephen, was born. How happy we all were to have him join our family. Oh, how Buzzy loved his baby brother! He would talk to him, sing to him, feed him, and play with him. He was the big brother, and he would watch over and protect his baby brother. He was never jealous of Stephen even though he had to share the attention of his mom and dad. He truly loved and welcomed his new little brother.

Stephen looked just like his daddy. And, of course, his daddy was in awe of him and in awe of the birth experience. Getting to be in the delivery room and being a part of the birth process made a tremendous impact on my husband. Gam was never the same after experiencing Stephen's birth. One of Gam's favorite memories of his "little buddy" is how Stephen would always make a little contented sigh whenever Gam would hold him or sit Stephen in his lap. Gam was so proud to be his father. He was filled with a love he had never known before.

Stephen's favorite food was an apple. He ate lots and lots of apples in his short lifetime. They didn't keep the doctor away, though. On a rainy Wednesday afternoon in October, Gam and I took Stephen to the doctor for a routine checkup. It was a day like any other - until the doctors told us that he had leukemia. How could that be? There must be some kind of mistake! He had not been sick or shown any signs of a physical problem whatsoever! We were just there for a checkup! When his routine blood work came back, there it was - leukemia. From that day on, October 17, 1979, an ordinary day that started out like any other, our lives would never be the same.

Stephen was immediately placed in the hospital and chemotherapy treatments began that very afternoon. Because we did not know how long he would be there, Buzzy went home with my parents to Perryville, Kentucky, and enrolled in school there. Buzzy was seven years old and in the second grade. How frightened and confused he must have been. As any mother, I felt torn. How could I "be there" for both of them? They both needed me.

A couple of days after Stephen had checked into the hospital, we found out that he had a very rare form of leukemia which did not respond as well to treatment as the more common forms. We had not adjusted to the fact that he had leukemia, let alone a rare type. The prognosis was not good.

The first two weeks Stephen seemed to be himself. He was a very good patient and did not complain at all the poking and jabbing with needles that went on around the clock. The treatments did not appear to be bothering him too much. Two weeks after entering the hospital, as Stephen was receiving one of his many platelet transfusions, he began to have a terrible physical reaction. The room was immediately filled with many doctors, interns, and nurses, as they worked to stop his seizures. After that experience, Stephen's health deteriorated very rapidly.

Two weeks after the platelet reaction, exactly one month after we found out that our son had leukemia, Stephen died in my arms with his daddy by my side. I lost my precious baby boy, Gam lost his "little buddy," and Buzzy lost his beloved brother. This is not supposed to happen.

I was twenty-eight years old and felt that I had learned a very important lesson in experiencing the loss of Stephen. I now knew what was "really important" in life and wanted to live my life accordingly. I wanted everyone to know how important and special their children should be to them because none of us knows what each new day will hold for us. None of us knows if today might be the last day we have with someone we love. Sadly, this is a lesson that many people don't learn until it is too late.

A little more than a year later, our family was blessed with another beautiful son, Robert Todd Greer. He was named Robert, after his grandfather, and Buzzy chose the name Todd. God had given me another son to love and enjoy. Life would go on. Life was good again. Once again I had two sons to love and from whom to receive love.

Todd was an independent little guy. From a very early age it seemed that he knew what he wanted, and he would not give up until he was successful. He knew from before the time he went to kindergarten that he wanted to be a basketball player for the University of Kentucky Wildcats. In fact, he told his kindergarten teacher more than once that someday he would be a Wildcat. She believed him. Years later, Todd would say that even if he was offered full scholarships to other schools, and Kentucky wasn't looking at him, he would still like to go to Kentucky as a walk-on. Todd was an excellent three-point shooter. He often practiced at least two hundred three-point shots a day and had his sister keep track of his shooting percentage. He was dedicated to improving his skills and wanted to be the "go to" guy on the team when the pressure was on.

Todd was also a very good student. He had excellent study habits and wanted to do his best in everything he tried. The reason he always tried to do his best was not to please his mom or dad, or his coach or his teacher. The reason he always wanted to do his best was for <u>Todd</u>. At the end of Todd's first grade year of school, his teacher wrote a note on his report card saying that she knew that Todd would always be successful at whatever he did because he competed with himself and always wanted to be better. She knew him well. He did not give up until he met his own goals. This was not something we taught Todd to do, this was just Todd. He knew himself and had a very healthy self esteem. He was indeed his own person. This is what I want people to know about Todd, and I think, this is what Todd wants people to know about him. That was my Toddy Boy…I miss him so…

When Todd was four years old and Buzzy was twelve years old, they were joined by a beautiful little sister named Kami. No longer would the house be full of basketballs, footballs, soccer balls, baseballs, G.I. Joes, matchbox cars, Star War figures, He Man figures, Lincoln Logs, fire trucks, race cars, and all kinds of boy toys. The boys had to make room for lots and lots of stuffed animals, books, magic markers, crayons, baby dolls, Barbie dolls, horses, ballet slippers, hair curlers, lots of kittens, and a little white dog. After three boys, Kami made a BIG change in the Greer family….a wonderful,

wonderful change.

Kami was truly the apple of her daddy's eye. It is true that with the birth of each of our children, Gam was awed, amazed and changed. After three little boys, we finally brought home a precious little girl. Gam has <u>truly</u> never been the same. He even began to treat me differently after her birth because he could now see me as "my daddy's little girl", and he certainly wanted whoever Kami married to remember that she was her daddy's little girl. I guess because she was the only girl after three boys, we often called her "Girl." We could be in the middle of a huge crowd, and if we called for "Girl", she would know we were calling for her.

Kami was always the first one to wake up in the mornings at our house, and she always woke up with a smile on her face. It never ceased to amaze us how she woke up smiling. It was just her way. She loved all kinds of animals, and her most recent favorite animal was a horse. "Go For Gin" won the Kentucky Derby the year Kami turned ten, and she named a stuffed horse she got for her birthday, "Go For Ten." Kami wore horse earrings, horse necklaces, horse pajamas, and horse vests. You name it, she was horse crazy. She was working real hard on talking her dad into getting her a horse, and he was weakening. He wanted her to have a horse, but he did not want her to get hurt, so he kept putting it off. Now, of course, we wish she could have had the joy of riding and taking care of her own horse. She had a dream of someday having a horse farm which she had already named "Hopeful Farm." That is also the name she gave her toy horse farm, which she spent hours and hours playing with.

Not only was Kami beautiful with her long blond hair and sparkling blue-green eyes, she was very athletic. She was active in gymnastics, ballet and tap. She absolutely loved to play softball and was a strong and intense player. She played first base and could hit the ball to the fence. Kami could also hold her own with her brothers. They could not push her around, and she liked that. Even though she was a strong athlete, and could hold her own, she was also a little lady. Her daddy always told her that he would buy her a prom dress, but she couldn't go to the prom! (Her mom was going to help her out with that problem). She played in the hand bell choir at church and was learning to play piano.

If anybody in the family ever lost anything, it seemed that Kami always knew where to find it. She loved to hide things from her brothers. Kami was a beautiful, talented, precious little girl. I was looking forward to watching her blossom into a strong, confident, beautiful woman. I miss you Girl....

A friend of Kami's, whose name is James, wrote the following about his friend:

A GIRL NAMED KAMI

In my second grade year at Sunday School, I was in a class with a girl named Kami Greer. From then on, we were friends. After that second year, we were always in the same Sunday School Class.

Last year, when I began fifth grade at London Elementary, Kami was in my class. We had lots of fun, and she was my friend. I can remember our sock hop in October because she dressed as Dracula, and she made a very scary Dracula.

In December, we later found that her brother, Buzzy, had just come home and he had a very bad drug problem. On January 16, 1995, we were out of school that day. That evening she was killed by her brother. It was a very sad time for all of her classmates. We had to attend a funeral for her on the following Saturday.

As soon as it was over, our class figured out that we could teach kids that drugs are not cool. Kami was killed two weeks before we started our D.A.R.E. program. We were all very sad. This was when our class thought, "Hey, we could go from school to school telling kids about D.A.R.E. and drugs."

We felt a little better because we figured out we could

help a lot of people that have the chance to be asked about drugs. We told them to hang around with the right people and to always say no to drugs. After all of that, we had a D.A.R.E. graduation. My friend went up and received Kami's D.A.R.E. bear in her honor.

January 16, 1995. What began as another ordinary day became a day that changed our lives, again, forever.

Before we left the hospital in London, I was told that all three of my children were dead. I did not find out until the next day that Buzzy had been taken to the University of Kentucky Medical Center and died there. Gam was flown by helicopter to the University of Tennessee Medical Center, where emergency surgery was performed to repair his wounds. I was in total shock.

The world was swirling around me. People were going about their lives. Didn't they know the world had stopped? I was reminded that time had not stopped the following morning in the hospital waiting room when Gam's wristwatch (which had been given to me by the nurses) started beeping at 7:40 A.M. This is the time Kami had set her daddy's watch to remind him that she did not want to be late to school. Oh, how I wished we were still on our regular schedule getting ready for school. How can it be that my family is gone? Kami had her own watch set to beep when it was time for school to be over. It still beeps at 2:50 P.M. everyday, just as Gam's watch still goes off at 7:40 A.M. every morning.

I had to leave Gam on Thursday to come home and make the funeral arrangements. Of course, it was a very, very hard thing to do. Gam was unable to help me. His only request was that the music be beautiful. We again included the hymn, "It Is Well" in the funeral service as we had in Stephen's service. Buzzy, Todd, and Kami had all been very aware that "It Is Well" had been my favorite hymn all through the years since Stephen's death. They were aware of the meaning it held for me. I did not find out until very recently that this hymn had been written in the 1800's by a father who had lost his four daughters in a shipwreck on the Atlantic Ocean. I can now see that it is no small wonder that his words have moved my heart for so many years after experiencing the loss of Stephen.

We were not able to come back to our home after the funeral. We just were not able to face the harsh reality of the memories of our last dinner together. Luckily, we had good friends, Ken and JoAnn James, who provided us with a beautiful furnished apartment where we would try to start healing both physically and emotionally. We gradually began to try to make our way back home. At first, we would just drive by the house. Another day, we might pull in the driveway for a few minutes. Another day, we might walk around in the yard. When we were finally able to go inside the house, it would be for a few minutes, then an hour, and so on until we were able to spend a whole day. Finally, we were able to spend the night, and after about four months, we were able to move back into the house. I will say that it was and has been much easier for Gam to be back in our home than it has been for me. I think it is because I was a "stay at home" mom. There are just so many, many memories for me in every nook and cranny of the house. It can be an awful lot to deal with.

We have learned through experience and through counseling that no two people grieve alike. For example, on the first anniversary date of our tragedy, I knew I did not want to be in our house, or even in our town. Gam, however, felt he needed to be in the house. I went for a visit with our counselor, and he stayed home. I believe it was a lot less stressful for both of us. It has helped us to recognize that we all grieve differently. Even though we both lost all our children, Gam did not lose what I, as a mother lost, and I did not lose what he as a father lost. Understanding our grieving differences has played a big role in our healing process.

As time went on, I began to sink deeper and deeper into my grief. Nothing, or no one, could help me feel better. I had so many questions, and I knew no one had answers for me.

I began to question God. How could you let this happen? God, You know what is in my heart. You know I love You and have tried to live my life for You. What about all the evil people in the world? They don't love you! What about the drug dealers? They don't even give you a second thought! They are evil, and they still have their children! How can this be? How could you let this happen to our family?

These are the thoughts and questions that came to me in what I call "my dark time". I could find no reason or purpose for living. My children had been my purpose for living, and they had been tragically taken from me. I did not want to continue to live in such a dark place. During this dark time, I did not want to see or talk with anyone. I knew no one had answers to my questions, and I also did not want people to know that I was having such questions. Just because I had lost God, I did not want other people to lose their hope. Even though I felt they were just kidding themselves, they were better off than I who had no hope.

I eventually began to share my thoughts and feelings with Gam, our counselor, and a close friend. I have come to realize that when I began to "share" my feelings (talk about it and get it out), that was when I started down the road toward healing. I believe that what we least want to talk about is what we need to talk about the most.

Through the love and persistence of fellow strugglers and friends, I was finally able to see a tiny "pinhole" of light in my dark place. I was able to find this pinhole of light through the reaching out and persistence of Rosemary Smith. I did not know Rosemary, and, in fact, had never even heard of her when I started receiving phone calls from her. Who was this stranger? Why was she calling, and why did she care about me? During my dark time, I did not answer the phone, but she would always leave a message. I did not return her messages.

She shared with me how she had lost her two precious sons, Drew and Jeremiah, in a terrible car accident. She wanted me to know that she was thinking of me and wanted to help us in any way. Each time Rosemary left a message, she would tell me a little more about herself. I said to Gam, "Who is this woman, and when is she going to give up and stop calling?" We were leaving town for the holidays and I told Gam, "Surely she will give up by the time we get home again!" WRONG! When we got home, there were still more messages, and she continued to call. On a very snowy day, actually blizzard like conditions all over the state, the phone rang again. She knew, of course, that no one could be out of the house on a day like that! Gam answered the phone and handed it to me. I had no choice. I finally had to talk to this woman who would not give up. I am so thankful I did. Truly, Rosemary's reaching out and her persistence in doing so, saved my life. I found out from Rosemary later that she had been "assigned" to me by another fellow struggler who had lost a child, Dinah Taylor. Dinah had been trying for almost a year to reach me through her newsletter, through gifts, through homemade bread, cards, and through a mutual friend, Sharon Kidd, who also reached out to me, but to no avail. I could not be reached. Dinah knew whom to "assign" this impossible case. Thank you Dinah, Sharon, and Rosemary for not giving up on me.

As time goes on, my "pinhole" of light continues to get bigger and bigger. I began to see hope again. You see, the light that I was beginning to see was God's light. I was able to see God's light through His people reaching out to me. God never gave up on me. God never left me. Even though I know this to be true, I still have many days when my pain is so consuming that I am unable to reach out, but it is comforting to know that there are fellow strugglers who understand my pain and are there ready to reach out to me when I need them

In the eyes of the world my husband, Gam, and I are a family of two. The IRS sees us as a family of two, the insurance company sees us as a family of two, the census bureau sees us as a family of two, someone seeing us walk down the street sees us as a family of two. I have found that the eyes of the world rarely see things as they really are. The family of Gam and Becky Greer is, in truth and reality, a family of six. Our children will forever be a part of each and every person who knew them.

To say that Gam and I are a family of two is to say that four beautiful children never existed. Buzzy, Stephen, Todd, and Kami Greer did exist, and their lives did make a difference. They walked and talked with us. They played with us. They loved us. We can never be the same after having known them. I am grateful for the time I was able have with each of them. We must all remember that it is the love we share that lives on.

****

THE CHILDREN OF THE DOME

THE CHILDREN

DREW SMITH

JEREMIAH SMITH

JIM TAYLOR

MYRA STAMPER

THE CHILDREN

PEGGY O'CONNOR

DENIS O'CONNOR

BRIAN PENKALSKI

ROGER HERNDON

306

THE CHILDREN

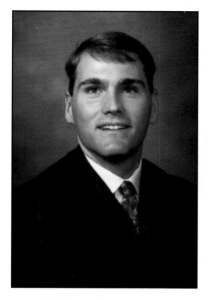

SCOTT SHANNON

GRETCHEN GEIER

KELLIE CARPENTER

SHELBY WARNER

THE CHILDREN

MICHAEL PRICE

FRANNIE SMITH

KRISTIE KAUFFMANN

MITCH WARREN

308

THE CHILDREN

GEORGE DIEBOLD

ANNABETH BURNETT

BRANDON HOLBROOK

DON V. DRYE

THE CHILDREN

ANDREW GUTGSELL

JOHN DONAN

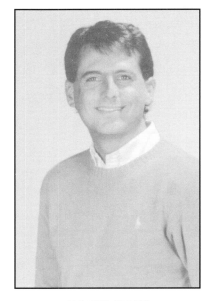

JOHN FOSS

RALPH COOMER

THE CHILDREN

RYAN YOUNG

HEATHER PERDUE

MERRI KATHRYN PRATER

CHRISTOPHER FREUNDORFER

THE CHILDREN

STEPHEN GREER

TODD GREER

BUZZY GREER

KAMI GREER

THE CHILDREN

TAIANN WILSON

NOTES

NOTES